ARTORIUS

Reconstruction of the Large Artorius Inscription (Alessandro Faggiani). 'To the Spirits of the Departed: Lucius Artorius Castus, for himself, Centurion of the Leg. III Gallica, also Centurion of the Leg. VI Ferrata, also Centurion of the Leg. II Adiutrix, also Centurion of the Leg. V Macedonica, also *primus pilus* of the same, *praepositus* of the Classis Misenensis, twice *praefect* of the Leg. VI Victrix, *dux* of the three British legions against armed men, *procurator centenarius* of the Province of Liburniae with *ius gladi* six times, he himself while alive built this for himself and his family.'

In memory of two remarkable men:
C. Scott Littleton (1933-2010)
and
Helmut Nickel (1923-2019)

'You've got to think second century'
Rory McGrath and Jimmy Mulville,
Chelmsford 123

CONTENTS

Contents

ACKNOWLEDGEMENTS

First, we would like to acknowledge the significant contributions C. Scott Littleton made to this manuscript prior to his death in 2010 and those of the late Helmut Nickel, without whose work this book would not exist. Special thanks to Caitlín Matthews for her work on the translation of 'The Sovereign's Chair' and for reading the manuscript several times. Thanks to Professor John Colarusso for his insightful Foreword. Also, our deepest gratitude to Antonio Trinchese and Alessandro Faggiani for allowing us to make extensive use of the paper they co-authored with Linda A. Malcor, 'Missing Pieces'. Antonio Trinchese as Consul of Italy in Dortmund, Germany and later as Consul of Italy in Dakar, Senegal, helped organise research trips for Linda A. Malcor with financial and other assistance from Francesco Rippa (association FENALCA), the late Amato Lamberti, Gennaro Pianura, Giuseppe Donadio (association COOPERAFRICA), and Lamine Gueve (association AMSAFRIT). To Wil Kinghan, for his sterling work on the maps and his paintings of the shields and banners of the legions, as well as the redrawn images throughout. To Nenad Stanić for the photograph of the original inscription of Lucius Artorius Castus on the cover and interior of the book. Thanks to David Elkington for reading and correcting errors, Kresimir Vukovic for his knowledgeable comments on various chapters, and to Kenneth J. Atchity for his keen eye and helpful suggestions. The authors also wish to thank Nenad Cambi, Christopher Gidlow, Miroslav

Acknowledgements

Glavičić, Charles Graham, Anamarija Kurilić, Kresimir Vukovic, Victor Mair, Joseph V. Malcor, Mario de Matteis, Željko Miletić, Elmira Gutieva, Giuseppe Nicolini, Sabato Scala, Zoran Jurišić and the Artorius Society, for their contributions to and support of our research.

In addition, we would like to thank the following people who contributed to our GoFundMe campaign to raise money for the artwork and illustrations in the book: Alessandro Faggiani, Elisia Sierakowski, Julie Lawrence, Elyn Aviva, Janene McNeil, Kathy Gower, Rosemary Philpott, April M. Love, Ann Mason, Philomena Temple, Alyzande Renard, Daniela Brunner, Margaret Sumner-Wichmann, Elmdea Adams, Jane May, Karen Lewis, Christopher Pickles, and Theresa Jory. We offer our sincere apologies to anyone we have inadvertently omitted. Finally, we wish to emphasise that the ideas and interpretations that are presented in this work are strictly our own, and we take full responsibility for them.

Linda A. Malcor (Laguna Woods, Ca)
John Matthews (Oxford, UK)

LIST OF PLATES AND MAPS

Front of jacket: The Artorius Inscription (photo Nenad Stanić)
Frontispiece: Reconstruction of the Large Artorius Inscription (Alessandro Faggiani)

Maps

Figures

FOREWORD BY PROFESSOR JOHN COLARUSSO

Few bodies of lore are more fun to read than those of the Celts, the Irish and the Welsh (Freeman 2017; MacKillop 1998). Both, but especially the Irish, have a sense of exaggeration underlying much of them that at times borders on the humorous. The Welsh has a more 'elegant' sense about it, with gods, goddesses, heroes, and maidens, and a tendency to more courtly settings. The Irish, more extensive, has the same sort of inventory, but also adds components that are distinctive: a 'book' of invasions, a sort of ethnic history of Ireland; a division of the country into five regions with the west, Connacht, and the north, Ulster, having the richest material. There were gods. Dagda (dag- 'good', da 'god') was one of the oldest gods, 'good' at all skills. Dian Cécht is another, a healing god. He had a cauldron that resurrected slain warriors when they were dunked therein. A god of the sea was prominent, Mannanán mac Lir in Irish and Manawydan fab Llyr in Welsh. There are heroes, Lug and then from a later generation Cú Chulainn, the Hound of Culann, with Lug persisting as his spirit father. Cú Chulainn also exhibits the unique set of battle 'tremors', *ríastrad*, distortions of his body that seize him when he slides into battle rage. (Our bloated, green Hulk is a Hollywood appropriation of one of these tremors.)

All the heroes are under personal prohibitions, or *geis* (plural *gessa*), which are often their undoing. The rivalry among the Ulster heroes (Cú Chulainn, Leoghaire, and Conall Cernach) plays out dramatically in several tales. At feasts the rivalry, regardless of the heroes involved, canters upon the 'Champion's Portion', the best cut of meat. There is Finn (White) mac Cumhail who has healing magic and who leads a warband, the Fenians. Strong women also play crucial roles, such as Medb (Honey) whose envy triggers the great war retold in the Táin Bó Cuailgne, the Cattle Raid of Cooley, where Cú Chulainn plays a central role. This hero in turn has acquired much of his martial skills under the tutelage of an amazon-like figure, Scáthach, who had a sister Aife and a daughter Uathach. Aife bore Cú Chulainn a son, Connla, whom he will later mistakenly kill in a duel.

Then there is Cormac mac Airt of Tara, an early king, who had a cup of truth. This vessel fell apart if a lie were spoken but came together again when the truth was told. Another prominent king was Conchobar mac Nessa, the lord over Cú Chulainn. His amorous efforts ended in tragedy, as with Eithne and with Deirdre of the Sorrows. Lurking in the background in many tales and surfacing to launch wars are the evil Fomoire of Tory Island. Apparently, all of this was recorded by Christian monks in the twelfth century when it was apparent that the narratives were in danger of disappearing.

Then there is a rupture.

Also allocated to the Celtic inventory of lore is the medieval set of tales centering upon a new figure, King Arthur, one of the great cycles of medieval literature, and one that in some fashion is still alive today in that it can inspire modern 'products', such as the musical *Camelot*. Gone are the old gods. Gone are the Fomoire. Gone are the heroes. Gone are their gessa. Gone is their rivalry at the feast. Instead, the new heroes sit around a round table of egalitarian significance. Gone are the women save for three, Guinevere, Morgan le Fey, and the Lady of the Lake. There is no magic from Dian Cécht or any other god, but rather a wizard, Merlin. The only elements that survive are the cup of truth of Cormac, perhaps Christianized in the form of the Holy Grail, the hero's battle with his son, Arthur against Mordred, and the beheading game. The division of the realm into five parts has been replaced with a persistent theme of saving Britain (or a civilized portion thereof) from barbarian assault.

No one with an open mind can look at these corpora without wondering where Arthur and his knights came from. As the book itself says in a new translation of *The Sovereign's Chair*, Appendix 1, line 51, 'Nothing comes from nothing.' Obviously some strong and dramatic elements have entered into fashioning a new body of lore, one where even the name of the central figure, Arthur, is a puzzle. In Old Irish *art* is 'bear, hero, warrior', in Welsh *arth* is 'bear', (as with Latin ursus, Greek *arktos*, Sanskrit *rksa*). Such a link is tempting, but it is crucially incomplete: the *-ur* is stranded. The name itself, therefore, does not seem to be Celtic, although the fricative < th > suggests assimilation to Celtic fashions of pronunciation. In addition, the emergence of the Arthurian Romance, as it has come to be called, in the early medieval period coincides with the decline and slide toward oblivion of the original Celtic material, with its survival as a frozen, written heritage. This timing alone, the decline of one body of lore and the rise of another, points strongly to the introduction of a new set of elements.

What the authors have done in this volume is to lay out in extraordinary detail the case for King Arthur being based upon the historical figure of a Roman *dux*, or battle leader, of Britain, one Lucius Artorius Castus. They give a remarkable overview of the organization of the Roman military. The Roman Empire was a product not only of the ferocity of its legions, but of its penchant for structure and bureaucracy. It made the warriors of a band into the soldiers of an army. This Roman soldier left behind a long memorial stone inscribed with the details of his career. As an Equestrian (the Roman equivalent of a knight) of the late second century CE he fought in several wars on the frontier of the empire, becoming familiar with the Iranian-speaking Sarmatians, a dominant cavalry force of the era. As a senior military commander he escorted a Sarmatian contingent to Britain, a province suffering turmoil, both internally and from invaders from beyond Hadrian's Wall in the north. Thus Artorius brought peace for four years, before he went to Liburnia as procurator. He may have had a strong rapport with his Sarmatians. His cognomen Castus means 'pious', while his Sarmatians were of the Iazyges tribe, whose name is based on the Iranian root yaz-, meaning 'to sacrifice'. This root appears as well in the name of the sole Zoroastrian city in Iran, Yazd, or the name of the Yezidis. He would come out of retirement to head a Sarmatian contingent in Gaul (also Iazyges) in the civil war between Albinus and the emperor Septimius Severus. This Roman appears to have been the nucleus around which the Arthurian Romance was built.

The details of his life that have echoes with that of Arthur are numerous, but this is not all. Other features can be found in the medieval lore that emerges in the near millennium after his life. Parallels extend even through the next millennium where the Nart tales (Colarusso 2002, Colarusso, Salbiev 2016) seem to have preserved many features of what must have been Sarmatian lore.

There is fighting on the wall together with the kings of Britain, where his troops have a strange accent. Iranian would have sounded quite odd in the Celtic and Latin world. The Narts ('heroes') are ultimately of Steppe Iranian origin. They have a magical drinking horn, much like the Cup of Truth of Cormac and the Holy Grail of Arthurian Romance. The Narts also have a round table. They have a kind of chivalric combat code, offering reprieves to opponents. Like Arthur pulling a sword from a stone, a Nart hero pulls his weapon from the earth's nine layers to prove his heroic nature; another pulls his from an anvil and then embeds that anvil in the earth's nine layers. At death the sword of the hero Batradz is cast into a lake (see Mair 1998 for a Uyghur parallel), as with Arthur's Excalibur, although the Narts do not have a Lady of the Lake. Nevertheless, Linda Malcor and John Matthews have found a likely real source for Avalon, where Arthur is taken to be healed by the ministrations of nine women. Likewise, in the Nart material it is the women who know the means of healing. There is an implied resurrection in that both Lancelot and Batradz (Pataraz) are raised in the Otherworld, to emerge therefrom to embark upon their heroic journeys. There is also a beheading game, one of the few parallels with the Celtic lore. There are two women who offer parallels. Lady Satana (Satanaya) is brought to the Nart land (actually abducted) from afar, as with Guinevere. Both suffer abductions.

While Artorius' earthly life spanned the middle of the second century to the beginning of the third, his legendary life was timeless. His name, like that of Caesar, may have been applied to any Roman, and after the departure of the legions from Britain in 410 CE, to any hero who fought for the survival of civilization in Britain. He was like the sun, exerting a gravitational attraction to deeds and themes that circulated among the bards of the early medieval era and bringing these into orbit about himself. His name evoked a dim recollection of a better time, when a high culture had brought peace, even if only for a few years, to a land locked in violence and warfare. Malcor and Matthews have given us not only a source for the central figure of Arthur, but also sources for a web of elements that constitute the Arthurian Romance in many of its parts. They have given to us a solid view of how three disparate cultures, the Celtic, the Roman, and the Steppe Iranian, have fused together to produce one of the great monuments of world lore.

Colarusso, John. 2002. *Nart Sagas: Ancient Myths and Legends of the Circassians and Abkhazians.* Princeton and Oxford, Princeton University Press.

Colarusso, John, and Tamirlan Salbiev. 2016. *Tales of the Narts: Ancient Myths and Legends of the Ossetians.* Walter May, trans. Princeton and Oxford: Princeton University Press.

Freeman, Philip. 2017. *Celtic Mythology.* Oxford.

MacKillup, James. 1998. *Dictionary of Celtic Mythology.* Oxford.

Mair, Victor. 1998. 'Review of C. Scott Littleton and Linda Malcor, 'From Scythia to Camelot'. *Religion* 28, 294-300.

Introduction

THE SEARCH FOR THE REAL KING ARTHUR

King Arthur. Everyone has an idea of who he was. It's a familiar story. A boy who pulled a sword from a stone, became king, married the beautiful Guinevere, commanded a Round Table fellowship of knights, sent his knights on a search for the Holy Grail, saw his best friend betray him with his wife, fought a Civil War and died after seeing his dream destroyed by his bastard son, Mordred. His knights wore shining armour, carried swords and lances, were identified by images painted on shields, and flew a dragon banner. His world is a fairyland that includes figures like Morgan Le Fey, the Lady of the Lake, Merlin, and even giants and dragons. He and his knights fought to unify Britain and were based in a mystical city named Camelot.

This vision is from a collection of legendary tales and romances from Continental Europe, mostly written over a three-hundred-year period between the thirteenth and fifteenth centuries. But there is another Arthur – perhaps more than one. He and his knights, who looked something like the ones from the romances, and fought to protect Britain from invaders, were real. This Arthur ruled from Caerleon in South Wales and a place called 'The City of the legions', probably identified with Chester in North Wales or York in modern-day Yorkshire. His tales come from a branch of the Arthurian tradition described as chronicles, represented primarily by the twelfth-century writer Geoffrey of Monmouth and those who followed in his footsteps. The fanciful elements, such as the Sword in the Stone or the Quest for the Grail, don't appear anywhere in these stories, but what is left reads as something akin to the modern-day idea of history.

This is where the trouble begins. Many people now believe there was a historical King Arthur, and several have spent their lives looking for him. The most common hunting grounds are the fifth and sixth centuries AD for a variety of reasons, the most common of which is that a cleric named Gildas, who does not mention Arthur, says the Battle of Badon, in which tradition says Arthur lead the British forces, was fought in that time. Unfortunately, this is a period ruled by a man named Ambrosius Aurelianus, who is remembered as 'the last of the Romans' in Britain. Somehow stories of the historical Arthur became scrambled with those of Ambrosius, and the result is that Arthur's legend became firmly fixed in this time frame.

And there it wants to stick. Suggest moving it to another time, and amateurs and scholars alike rush to attack you. The same thing happens, to a lesser degree, if you neglect to have Arthur draw a Sword from a Stone, try to take Guinevere and Lancelot out of the story, forget about the Round Table, omit the knights and their quests, remove the wizard Merlin and the sorceress Morgan Le Fey and any number of things associated with Arthur's legend. With these features from the romances, you have a little more wiggle room, but all deities, known and forgotten, help you if you try to have Arthur fight the Picts – as Geoffrey of Monmouth had him do – instead of Saxons, or mess with any of the other pieces of the standard tale as it is known to audiences through movies such as John Boorman's *Excalibur (1980)* or Guy Ritchie's *King Arthur: Legend of the Sword* (2018).

But there's a problem with all of this: the historical Arthur's story didn't start in the fifth or sixth century. It began long before that, in Roman times, under the reign of the Emperor Marcus Aurelius in the second century AD. The discovery was made almost by accident.

In the early part of 1924, an American medievalist named Kemp Malone (1889-1971) was researching the origins of the Arthur legend. Following a reference from an eminent German philologist,

Heinrich Zimmer,[1] and a further mention in the first full-length exploration of the Arthurian literature by James Douglas Bruce in his *Evolution of the Arthurian Romance* (1923), Malone became increasingly convinced that the true origin of Arthur was not a fifth- or sixth-century warlord, but a much earlier soldier, a veteran of the Roman legions named Lucius Artorius Castus, whose dates placed him in Britain in the late second century AD, and whose name was very like that of Arthur.

The Quest for Arthur's Name

As a philologist, Malone shared Bruce's opinion that the name Arthur does not derive from a native British source but rather from the Latin family name Artorius, which pointed to a Roman – or at least a Roman-influenced – point of origin. Bruce had been clear about his intention: he wanted to demonstrate, despite the many scholars who saw both the name of Arthur and the figure himself as deriving from Celtic sources, that the name, together with its most famous bearer, were in fact Roman.

Malone decided to follow this line of reasoning by searching for any appearances of the name Artorius in early British history, and quickly found, to his surprise, that it was extremely rare. Until recently only one person was recorded in the historical record covering the time between the Roman occupation of Britannia in 43 BC and the period generally ascribed to an historical Arthur in the sixth century – a Roman officer named Lucius Artorius Castus. The recent discovery of a ring bearing the name Artorius suggests either a second person with that name, or an artefact actually belonging to him.

Malone then found a reference in the work of historian Charles Oman, *England Before the Norman Conquest*,[2] which suggested that this same man 'may have left numerous relatives or freedmen in Britain'. Malone later noted that 'Arthurian scholars seem quite unaware of his existence.' Malone at once set out to discover more about this mysterious personage, turning to the comprehensive collection of Latin inscriptions begun by Theodor Mommsen as the *Corpus Inscriptionum Latinarum* (CIL) in 1853, which currently runs to seventeen volumes with a further thirteen supplements covering more than 180,000 inscriptions from across the Roman Empire.

Malone discovered only two references out of this vast collection that exactly matched the name Lucius Artorius Castus. They referred to two inscriptions, both damaged, which had been uncovered close to the road running along the Dalmatian coast between Spalato (modern Split) and Almissa in present-day Croatia. The larger inscription, which we will examine in a moment, outlined the life and achievements of Lucius Artorius Castus in sufficient detail to allow Malone to offer a brief and tentative biography, outlining the deeds of a career officer in the legions who was also a member of the Equestrian order, the 'knights' of the Roman Empire.[3] He was also able to confirm that Lucius Artorius Castus (hereafter referred to as Artorius) was stationed in Britannia in the second century, holding a high-ranking post in legion VI Victrix.

Malone prepared a paper, which was published in the learned journal *Modern Philology* for May 1925. Titled simply 'Artorius',[4] it laid out Malone's findings and asked the question: 'Was L. Artorius Castus the historical prototype of Arthur?' Malone went on to say that it was 'impossible to be sure' but that the 'the two men certainly have things in common.' These he listed as follows:

1. Their names may be equated without phonological difficulty.
2. Both were defenders of Britain against barbarian invaders.
3. Both lead a British army overseas to conquests in Gaul.

This last statement has since required qualification, as we shall see, but it demonstrated that for Malone at least, he had found the first historically provable source for the figure of Arthur – one which placed him some three hundred years earlier than the time still widely accepted as accurate.

Malone's paper was immediately seen to be controversial, and it was largely ignored by the community of scholars interested in the historicity of Arthur. It was not until Helmut Nickel, then curator of Arms and Armor at the New York Metropolitan Museum, came across Malone's article, and saw within it much more than the older scholar had found, that the idea developed dramatically. Nickel's essay: '*Wer waren König Artus' Ritter? Über die geschichtliche Grundlage der Artussagen*' ('Who were King Arthur's knights? About the Historical Foundations of Arthurian Lore') published in 1975,[5] fleshed out Malone's findings with information of a startling kind. He stated his belief that there was a further level of similarity between the two men – the Roman officer and the semi-mythical king of British legend – and that this lay in his association with a group of peoples whose origin was in the Caucasus. These people, the Sarmatians, belonged to a group that includes the Ossetes, the Alans and the Scythians. Within their mythology, preserved in the sagas of their descendants, Nickel demonstrated extraordinary parallels with the later Arthurian legends, as we shall see.

At almost the same time, anthropologist and Indo-Europeanist C. Scott Littleton began to explore an identical set of ideas and sources. He and Nickel were in contact and discussed the material at length. Littleton went on to publish several articles on the subject, indicating further parallels between the stories of the Grail, the Arthurian legends, and the myths of the Sarmatians.[6] In time this led to the book which Littleton wrote, *From Scythia to Camelot*, teaming up with Arthurian specialist and Indo-European Comparative Mythologist Linda A. Malcor, which outlined many areas of similarity among the Scythians, Alano-Sarmatians and the Arthurian legends.[7]

The Celtic origin for Arthur has been taken as something of a given in popular scholarship since the American scholar Roger Sherman Loomis and his supporters began advocating the idea in 1927;[8] the notion that there was a real Roman officer whose biography eventually became scrambled with folklore and mythology has been around at least since a writer named William Skene proposed the idea in 1868.[9] Another Celticist, Sir John Rhŷs, in his 1891 book *Studies in the Arthurian Legend,* found the Celtic-origin model appealing, but argued for the existence of a Romano-British Arthur as well.

Much work has been carried out on this material in the last ten years by a number of scholars, greatly extending it from Malone and Nickel's original ideas. Many now believe that Lucius

Artorius Castus was indeed the original figure whose name, decked out in all the panoply of medieval romance, is the source for its subsequent development. That he is, in short, the real King Arthur.

This book sets out to prove this once and for all – giving us a source for the romantic legends we all know so well.

I

THE ARTORIUS MYSTERY

The Artorius Inscriptions

Much that we know directly about the life of Lucius Artorius Castus comes from two inscriptions dating from the late second century of the Roman Empire. Little though this may seem, much can be inferred from these, and for several decades, scholars have been debating what they can tell us. The first inscription is short and unambiguous, the type of label that would have marked a sarcophagus or a niche holding an urn of ashes:

L Artorius
Castus P P
Leg V Mac Pr
aefectus. Leg
VI Victric

When the abbreviations used in the inscription are expanded, and additional expansions made using the second inscription, this reads: 'Lucius Artorius Castus, *Primus Pilus* of the legion V Macedonica, *Praefectus* of the legion VI Victrix' (see Plates 1 and 2).

Found in the area of Epetium (Podstrana in modern-day Croatia) where Artorius built his family villa and where he was laid to rest around AD 197, it's clearly a memorial to a notable soldier. We should also note, for reasons that will become clear later on, that the border of the inscription is decorated with stylized roses.

Plate 1. Fragment of the Small Inscription. (Photo N. Cambi)

The main inscription, which tells us much about Artorius' military career, comes from near ground once occupied by the coastal villa owned by him just south of Liburnia. It survived because, when his tomb was destroyed, the pieces were used to

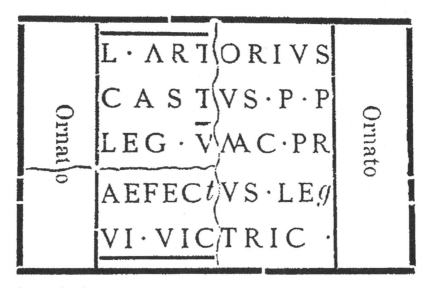

Plate 2. The Short Inscription Reconstituted by Theodor Mommsen.

build the wall of the graveyard of a chapel dedicated to another significant figure from Roman history – Saint Martin of Tours.

Ironically, in order to follow Artorius' biography from the beginning of his career, we need to look at the message he left for us at the end of it. But before we can begin to explore his remarkable life, we need to understand what the longer inscription says (see Plate 3).

Artorius clearly wanted to tell the full story of his military accomplishments, but this meant that the inscription had to be abbreviated to fit what was undoubtedly a block of pre-cut stone, intended to face outwards on the wall of his tomb in Epetium. The result is a series of letters, some hidden and others missing, that make the reader feel as if the text should be handed over to the likes of Alan Turing to break the code. Adding to the problem is the fact that the lines decrease in height, probably because it was mounted at a certain elevation, forcing the stonecutter to create an optical illusion that all the lines were of the same height by shortening the letters toward the bottom. This means that a small gap at the bottom could result in the loss of several letters.

There are other problems with the large inscription. Controversy has revolved for some time around a break in the stone and the loss

Plate 3. The Main Lucius Artorius Castus Inscription. (Photo Nenad Stanić)

of the pieces that once filled it. Most of the disputes have resorted to an argument that says, simply: 'the stonecutter made a mistake.' This is largely because some words refuse to fit the preconceived notions of those who have studied them and their determination of what the inscription *should* have been.

Since the main inscription concerning Artorius was discovered near ground that had at one time been the actual site of his home and was a rather expensive memorial, the idea that the stonecutter would have been unable to carry out his task seems an unlikely assumption. Instead, the point of view from which this inscription should be read is that the stonecutter made *no* mistakes. In other words, when the translation of the inscription appears to make no sense, it's really because we are failing to understand something which would have been perfectly obvious to those who read it at the time it was carved into the limestone.

Recent re-examination of the so-called 'missing pieces' of the inscription will be discussed later, when we examine the way in which the inscription can be broken down and argue its exact meaning. For the moment let us look at the way it has been interpreted previously, and at what it appears to say:

```
D ............................................M
L ARTORI [...............] STVS 7 LEG
III GALLICAE ITEM [......] G VI FERRA
TAE ITEM 7 LEG II ADI [.......] TEM 7 LEG V MA
C ITEM P P EIVSDEM [............] PRAEPOSITO
CLASSIS MISENATIVM [............] AEFF LEG VI
VICTRICIS DVCI LEGG [.............]M BRITANICI
MIARVM ADVERSVS ARM [....] S PROC CENTE
NARIO PROVINCIAE LI [..................] GLADI VI
VVS IPSE SIBI ET SVIS [....................] T
```

Allowing for the breaks in the text, and the numerous abbreviations, Theodor Mommsen reconstructed this to read:

DIS MANIBUS L. ARTORIUS CASTUS. CENTURIONI LEGIONIS III GALLICAE. ITEM *CENTURIONI* LEGIONIS VI

FERRA TAE. ITEM 7 LEG. II ADIUTRICIS. ITEM 7 LEG V MA
CEDONICAE. ITEM PRIMO PILO EIUSDEM PRAEPOSITO
CLASSIS MISENATIUM PRAEFECTO LEGIONIS VI VICTRICIS.
DUCI LEG COHORTIUM ALARUM BRITANICI MIARUM
ADVERSUS ARMORICANOS. PROCURATORI CENTENARIO
PROVINCIAE LIBURNIAE IURE GLADI. VI VUS IPSE SIBI ET
SUIS ST

This was previously translated as:

> To the Spirits of the Departed: Lucius Artorius Castus,
> centurion of the legion III Gallica, also centurion of the legion
> VI Ferrata, also centurion of the legion II Adiutrix, also
> centurion of the legion V Macedonica, also *primus pilus* of
> the same, *praepositus* of the *classis* Misenatium, *praefectus* of
> the legion VI Victrix, *dux* of the legions of cohorts of cavalry
> from Britain against the Armoricans; *procurator centenarius*
> of the province of Liburnia, with the power to issue death
> sentences. In his lifetime he had this made for himself and his
> family.

Much of this remains unchanged, though there are some parts
of the translation that need to be reconsidered. For the moment,
if we begin by looking at Artorius' name as it is presented here,
we find that his *praenomen* (first name) was Lucius, quite clearly
indicated by the large 'L' in the first row. We have enough letters
of the next word to know for sure that his *gens* (family name)
was Artorius. Then there is his *cognomen* (middle or nickname).
While the '-tus' is still visible, you have to look quite closely to
see the curves that formed the 's' before the 't'. This leaves us
searching for a cognomen with the ending '-stus.' Mommsen
originally guessed that the missing letters were 'Iu-', rendering
the name 'Iustus' ('Justus'– the Latin alphabet did not include
the letter 'J'). The smaller plaque, completely intact, gives his
cognomen as 'Castus.' When we put these together, we know that
his full name was Lucius Artorius Castus – as confirmed by the
shorter inscription.

The next mark is something that looks like the number 7. This is an abbreviation for the rank of centurion. 'LEG' stands for 'legion', then the number and name tell us which one. The Latin word 'item' means 'also'. Artorius is listing, in rapid succession, a series of legions in which he held the rank of centurion: the III Gallica, the VI Ferrata, the II Adiutrix, and the V Macedonica, all legions commanded by the co-emperors Lucius Verus and Marcus Aurelius.

The list is impressive, as are the successive promotions attached to each succeeding posting, which show him rising through the ranks; he was clearly a more than competent soldier. From this we can trace his military career, and by examining the whereabouts and activity of the various legions listed, we begin to get an increasingly detailed picture of his life.

The Ring of Artorius

The recent discovery of a ring (see Plate 4) bearing the inscription ARTOR FORTUNA (BM number 1917.0501.597) by independent researcher Giuseppe Nicolini in 2020, has added a footnote to the evidence placing Lucius Artorius Castus in Britannia in the Second century AD. The ring, originally discovered in Great Chesterford, Essex, in the mid-1800s, tells us two important things:

1. A member of the *gens* Artorii (the family of Artorius) was in Britannia during the second century AD.

Plate 4. The Artorius Ring. (© Trustees of the British Museum)

2. The dedication of the ring to Fortuna – the goddess Fortunata, who not only ensured good luck to the ring's wearer, but also protected sailors and others involved in shipping – which, as we shall demonstrate, was a large part of the Artorii interests, and especially that of Artorius himself during his period overseeing the Misenum fleet. (see Chapter 5) A reference to Fortuna in a poem by the Roman satirist Juvenal, criticising the Artorii, suggests a further connection with the family.

The type of ring – Anulus Aureus – was worn specifically by important members of the Equestrian order, which of course includes Lucius Artorius Castus, and in particular by military officers of a high rank. When these factors are brought together, we have a very real possibility that the owner of the ring was a) Lucius Artorius Castus himself, or b) a member of his family, whose name could have been Artorius Fortunatus.

In addition, we have the suggestion that the inscription (which appears to be a very personal one since the owner's *cognomen* would normally be used in such a setting) could be interpreted as meaning: *Artorius to the Goddess Fortuna*. This interpretation, by independent epigraphist Alessandro Faggiani,[1] suggests a personal dedication by a man who was both a soldier and a sailor and who, by this token, dedicated himself to the care and protection of the goddess.

The use of his personal name suggests either that he was well known, or more likely, that this was a highly personal adornment. Given the highly likely connection of the Artorii and Artorius himself with the goddess Flora, as indicated by the roses carved around his mausoleum (see chapter 2) this would be in keeping with its owner being Artorius himself.

The location of the ring, in Essex, though it places its owner some distance from the primary theatre of Lucius Artorius Castus, can be explained by the existence of a Roman fort at Great Chesterford. Did the ring slip from his finger during a visit to the area? We cannot be sure, but given the evidence it is certainly a very real possibility. At the outside it confirms the presence of a member of the Artorii family in Britannia during the second to third centuries AD, when Lucius Artorius Castus was in the country, commanding the detachment of Sarmatian calvary.

We can date Artorius' probable birth by counting backward from his attainment of the rank of *dux* (leader) listed on the inscription, apparently as a result of actions that took place between AD 187 and AD 191. If Artorius had served five tours of duty by this time, as the inscription shows, each lasting approximately four years, this takes us back to a likely date of 157 for joining the army. Since it was usual for men destined for a military career to enlist at the age of 18, this gives us a birth date for Artorius of c. AD 140, at the beginning of the reign of the Emperor Antoninus Pius (AD 138-161).

The Empire

If we look now at the world into which Artorius was born, we find it set firmly within the Roman Empire, which at this time stretched from the Euphrates in Syria to Hadrian's Wall in Britannia, and from the Nile Valley to the Rhine. It completely encircled the Mediterranean, known to its citizens as *Mare Nostrum* or 'our sea', and covered in total an area of some five million square kilometres – policed by its formidable armies and run by a well-oiled civil service. It was the most powerful Empire in the known world, rivalling those of Persia and China, with an estimated population of around 60 million people. It boasted a rich and varied literature and a love of sport seldom seen until more recent times. Its wealth was vast, and its hold on the countries it had overcome was as ruthless as anything ever seen, before or since. The city of Rome was the centre of 'civilization'– at least as seen by the Romans themselves.

The rise and expansion of this great power took place over a long period, between the eighth century BC to the end of the fifth century AD, when it finally fell apart from within. The first two centuries of the new millennium began with a period of comparative stability (though no shortage of conflict and warfare) that was known as the *Pax Romana*, or Roman Peace.

Beginning as a monarchy that evolved into a republic and then into an empire, Rome was ruled by successive emperors (many of whom were mad) and ostensibly governed by the Senate. Internecine strife dominated their history as power bloc after power bloc ranged back and forth. Most of the early emperors fought their way to the top and then held their own by murdering and plotting against each other. The imperial families played with various patterns of succession between the time of the Emperor Augustus (31 BC–AD 14) and the end of the first century. Below are the Roman Emperors from Augustus to Septimius Severus.

Dates of Reign	Emperor
31 BC–AD 14	Augustus (Octavian) (Julio-Claudian)
14–27	Tiberius (Julio-Claudian)
37–41	Gaius (Caligula) (Julio-Claudian)
41–54	Claudius (Julio-Claudian)
54–68	Nero (Julio-Claudian)
68–69	Galba (Year of Four Emperors)
69	Otho (Year of Four Emperors)
69	Vitellius (Year of Four Emperors)
69–79	Vespasian (Year of Four Emperors; Flavian)
79–81	Titus (Flavian)
81–96	Domitian (Flavian)
96–8	Nerva (Adoptive Emperors)

Dates of Reign	Emperor
98–117	Trajan (Adoptive Emperors)
117–138	Hadrian (Adoptive Emperors)
138–161	Antoninus Pius (Adoptive Emperors)
161–169	Lucius Verus (Adoptive Emperors)
161–180	Marcus Aurelius (Adoptive Emperors; Joint with Verus; Joint with Commodus)
177–192	Commodus (Adoptive Emperors; Joint with Marcus Aurelius)
193	Pertinax (Lasted 3 Months)
193	Didius Julianus (Bought Emperorship at Auction; Lasted 3 Months)
193–211	Septimius Severus (Founded Severan Dynasty)

Rome actually did rather well under the Adoptive Emperors, as they were called, who chose their heirs according to their abilities rather than their familial relationship. This contrasted sharply with Augustus, who went through several heirs before naming Tiberius as patriarch of the dynasty. Tiberius, unfortunately, then made the not-so-wonderful choice of Caligula. Thanks to the Praetorian Guard, who took matters into their own hands to rid the world of this madman, Claudius became Caligula's successor. But he in turn made a bad choice when he transferred the office to his stepson Nero. When Nero was murdered, four generals spent much of AD 69 battling for supremacy, until Vespasian emerged as the victor and established the Flavian dynasty. He was succeeded by his son Titus who was followed by his rather nightmarish brother Domitian. When Nerva took over from Domitian he realized that keeping matters in the family wasn't the best way to go about things and established the practice of adopting the man best qualified to succeed him.

This is how Trajan, Hadrian and Antoninus Pius ascended to the Purple, earning the right to wear this colour alone among the ruling class. When Antoninus Pius couldn't make up his mind, he named both Marcus Aurelius *and* Lucius Verus as his heirs. Lucius Verus died, probably of smallpox, soon after, and Marcus Aurelius decided to name his own son as his heir, a mistake the legendary King Arthur would also make by naming his son Mordred as his successor. Almost 100 years of peace then ended, and the Empire wound up with Commodus, who apart from several other serious mental issues, thought he was the reincarnation of Hercules. He plunged the Empire into chaos.

The Empire was constantly expanding, almost from the time of its inception. One territory stood out: Britannia. Julius Caesar had his eye on this prize, deeming it a rich and plentiful land, as did Augustus after him; but it wasn't until Claudius that the Romans established a foothold there in AD 47. The general Agricola is credited with the final conquest of Britannia, which took him from AD 77 to AD 84. The emperor Hadrian built his Wall across the north, which remains as the southern border of Scotland in AD 122. By 142, shortly after Artorius was born, Antoninus Pius had established the Antonine Wall, though it was abandoned twenty years later, with the Romans giving over the defence of the area between the two Walls to client tribes, just as King Arthur gave over the defence of this area to King Lot and his sons Gawain, Agravain, Gaheris, and Gareth.

This set the borders of Britannia in Artorius' lifetime. The northern European border of the empire was marked by the Rhine River, which was defended by several legions across the provinces of Germania Inferior and Germania Superior. King Arthur would later be said to fight against Saxons hailing from the same lands. From there the border shifted to the Danube, a boundary that was constantly at war and that remained fluid through the end of the Marcomannic Wars in AD 182. The Black Sea prevented invasion from the east, while the province of Cappadocia on its southern shore, which was adjacent to the client kingdom of Armenia, blocked attacks from there. Because of the Sahara Desert in the South, there was little warfare on that front.

Then there was Syria. Although Augustus cautioned against expansion in the region, Lucius Verus invaded the kingdom of Parthia to the east in AD 161, shortly after Artorius had transferred from his first posting with the III Galicia to the VI Ferrata in Judea, signalling a further outbreak of hostilities on the eastern limits of the Empire.

Artorius began his career under the *Pax Romana* of the Adoptive Emperors, and from there, possibly because he was related to Marcus Aurelius, he managed to survive the frequently chaotic times that followed, during which Verus made the mistake of attacking the Parthians while Marcus Aurelius was fighting for the Empire's life against the Germanic Marcomanni and Quadi tribes and their allies, the Sarmatian Iazyges.

Against this background of expansionism and almost constant warfare, Artorius' career continued to bring him fame and fortune, as he rose through the ranks from centurion to *primus pilus* to *praepositus, praefectus, dux* and finally *procurator centenarius*. At the end of his life, he would be interred in a magnificent mausoleum with an inscription listing his military career and the legions he served with. This inscription – a limestone slab catching the sun glinting off the Adriatic – would almost be destroyed over time by the erosion of wind and rain. But it survived, in pieces now, retaining the story of the life and deeds of this remarkable man. Without question it would have been recalled and honoured by his family and descendants. To discover the origins of the man we need to look first at this family– the Artorii.

2

THE ARTORII

Lucius Artorius Castus wasn't the first member of his family to stand out and be noticed. Indeed, the whole family blazed like a comet through the history of the Roman Empire. Over the years, a number of scholars have referred to Artorius as a 'Dalmatian' because the fragments of his tomb are located in what used to be the Roman province of Dalmatia. But this is rather like referring to an American soldier who was buried in Vietnam as Vietnamese. There is no evidence that any of the Artorii lived in Dalmatia prior to Artorius' lifetime. This was just the place to which he chose to retire.

Romans from particular areas were traditionally assigned to specific legions according to where they enlisted – mostly local to their place of origin – and since Artorius' first posting was to the legion III Gallica, this indicates that his family probably came from somewhere in Campania, a lush, water-filled land south of Rome that was famed for its horses and produce. Whether or not the Artorii started out there, by Artorius' time they were all over Campania, and all signs point to the fact that as early as the reign of the Emperor Augustus, from 27 BC until his death in AD 14, they belonged to the Equestrian class: the Knights of Rome.

Further Inscriptions
The Artoria *gens* (family) left a number of inscriptions, indicating the family's keen involvement with trade, medicine, and farming, particularly of wine, olive oil, and horses. Most of these inscriptions

tend to be clustered near the estates of each family group, though some regions that *don't* boast Artorii inscriptions are mentioned as places where an Artorius, at one time or another, performed military service for the Empire. We find an inscription for one Marcus Artorius Rufus Zophyrus near Capua, so this is probably the region where at least one of the Artorii's major villas was located. If this is the case, since Capua was prime horse country, it tells us that the family may have been horse-breeders – something which ties them at an early stage to a group of premier mounted warriors with whom they were to become closely associated: the Sarmatians.

Before we can discuss the family history, and their configuration when Lucius Artorius Castus lived, we need to take a closer look at the inscriptions mentioned in Chapter One and see what they can tell us about the family as a whole.

The name Artorius begins to appear in Magna Graecia, near the colony of Dicaearchia (City of Justice), which became Puteoli in 194 BC, shortly after the Second Punic War (218-201 BC). Throughout the clan's history, several prominent individuals maintained strong ties with Greek communities such as Ephesus (for example Artorius' descendant, Lucius Artorius Pius Maximus).[1] This explains why some of the earliest inscriptions are in Greek rather than Latin.[2] They are found scattered in Naples, Pompeii, Delos, Athens, and Smyrna. Naples and Pompeii are in the Roman regions of Campania (see Map 1), which included part of Magna Graecia, while trade routes from east to west, particularly that of the slave trade, passed through the island of Delos in the Aegean Sea where a certain Marcus Artorius Geminus once served as governor. Athens was in Greece, and Smyrna, famous for its school of physicians, was in Greek Ionia.

From Puteoli (modern Pozzuoli) and Naples, the family spread out around the area of the Bay of Naples to port cities from Pompeii, and up along the western coast of Italy to what would eventually become Ostia. They helped handle the massive grain trade between Rome and Egypt that passed from Alexandria to the Eternal City itself – places where the Artorii are known to have lived and worked, given the inscriptions found at Alexandria,

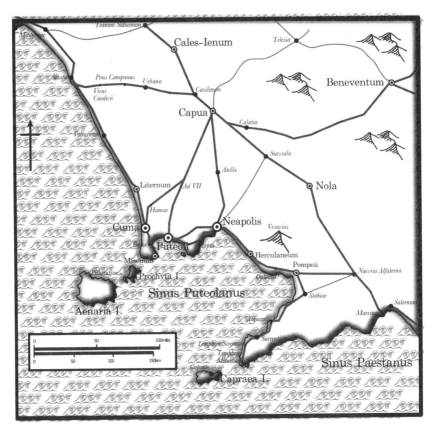

Map 1. Campania.

Puteoli and Ostia. Some were bankers, others clerks, while the branch in Alexandria boasted sailors in its ranks. Indeed, when the grain trade switched to the port at Ostia, some of the Artorii followed it. From Puteoli and Pompeii the family settled areas across the mountains, through Nola and Abelinum (modern Avellino) to Barium (modern Bari, capital of Apulia, Italy).

Once settled in the Adriatic, they went about establishing a family branch in the northeast as well (see Map 1). Before Puteoli, they were in Capua, already established there by the time of the Second Punic war in 218 to 201 BC. According to the great historian Livy,[3] an Artorius fought a battle against the renowned Campanian cavalry commander, Cerrinus Vibellius Taurus, and later founded the businesses that would earn them Equestrian rank under the Emperor Augustus.

The great poet and satirist Juvenal confirmed that the original wealth of the Artorii came from gladiators and building contracts, when he wrote:

Let Arturius, let Catulus live in Rome.
Let the men who turn black into white remain,
Who find it easy to garner contracts for temples, and rivers,
Harbours, draining sewers, and carrying corpses to the pyre,
Who offer themselves for sale according to auctioneers' rules.
Those erstwhile players of horns, those perpetual friends
Of public arenas, noted through all the towns for their
Rounded cheeks, now must show themselves, and kill
To please when the mob demand it with down-turned thumbs;
Then it's back to deals for urinals, why not the whole works?
Since they're the ones Fortune raises up to the highest sphere.[4]

Certainly, by AD 70, the Artorii owned an elite villa on the Bay of Naples at Puteoli. They also owned gladiators, whom they kept at Capua, where Spartacus fought, Rome, Pompeii and Puteoli. They engaged in building, politics, religion, banking and other unsavoury, at least according to Juvenal, occupations as well. In other words, they were Equestrians through and through.

Names

Although we cannot be certain where the Artorii originally came from, the odds are fairly good that it was somewhere controlled by Greece. The name Artorius itself isn't a lot of help. Most commentators argue for a Celtic origin, but that does not work etymologically. Going from Latin Artorius to a name in a Celtic language will render Arthur,[5] but that argument tends to become immediately scrambled with Arcturus, a star in Ursa Minor, because of the association of the name Arthur with a bear (*Ursus*). Some scholars have proposed that 'Artorius' means 'ploughman',[6] but this is a rather strange name for a military *gens*, and this has led others to go so far as to suggest that because of the non-military meaning of the name, an 'Artorius' could not be the source for the warlike Arthur of Britain.

Looking at the Artorii inscriptions, another origin for the name comes to mind. If the Artorii were Greeks from somewhere in or near Achaea, which is where the settlers of Magna Graecia started out, they may have come from around the area of a town known as Arta, due north of Achaea. This fits very well with what we see in the Artorii inscriptions near Rome itself, and it leads us to suspect that the proper interpretation of 'Artorius' was not 'ploughman' at all, but simply 'Man from Arta'.

The Romans in general were rather predictable when it came to giving their offspring names, especially in the first and second centuries AD. Among the Artorii, the most prominent male *praenomen* (first name) was Marcus, derived from Mars, a name shared by King Mark in the Arthurian legends. Although this was the third most popular *praenomen* among Romans in general, the family appears to have bestowed it upon the son who was expected to become the *pater familias* (male head of the family) for each generation. Once in a while there were twins who bore the same *praenomen*. For instance, there were two Artorii named Marcus during the Emperor Augustus' lifetime (63 BC to AD 14): Marcus Artorius Asclepiades and Marcus Artorius Geminus.

The second most prevalent *praenomen* in the Roman Empire was Gaius or Caius, and for the Artorii it was by far the most common name they gave to their sons. This makes it very likely that Artorius had an older brother by this name. The *praenomen* may have been granted to the boy in honour of Gaius Julius Caesar, given the patronage they received from the Emperor Augustus and the location of Marcus Artorius Geminus' tomb on the grounds of a villa where Caesar and Cleopatra raised their son Caesarion. *Gaius* and *Caius* are the same name with different spellings, and the name is akin to the Old Iranian Kai, which meant 'warrior'. Indeed, Caius may be the source of the name Sir Kay (Cai) in the Arthurian tradition.

The name Lucius, from *lux* (light), was an even more popular *praenomen* in ancient Rome, and the Artorii were using it as far back as when election graffiti plastered all over the walls of Pompeii were still being written in Greek. Given the importance of the name Marcus and the frequency of the name Caius in the inscriptions, it is unlikely that Artorius was either the first or second-born son in his immediate family. If he were a third-born son, he would have been very precious to his mother, who would have been called Artoria after the practice of the time. Any Roman woman who had three children survive into adulthood acquired rights that women did not see again until the twentieth century, since bearing this many sons was a rarity due to the high rate of infant mortality and was seen as benefiting the Empire. Artoria would have been fiercely protective of all her sons, making sure they had everything possible to ensure their survival – at least until she was granted her rights.

The earliest generations of Artorii tended to have Greek cognomens (nicknames), the prevalence of which can be dated back to the time of the Roman Republic, for example, Asclepiades, Geminus, Antiochus, Zethus, and Stephanus. The men were often named after famous Greek scholars, while the women were usually named after important Greek women or cities, when they had a cognomen at all.

The family was certainly pious, as we shall see, though they also had a sense of humour. The choice of Artorius' cognomen was almost certainly a deliberate pun on the meaning of the word: which could mean 'chaste' or 'pious' (possibly 'devoted [to the state]'). The name could be construed as: The 'Light' (Artorius), 'the chaste', 'pure' or 'pious'. The definition repeats with the name of his descendant, Lucius Artorius Pius Maximus.

The Artorii families seem to have become bored with naming their children after the first four or so sons and started numbering them instead. This gives us Quintus, Sextus, and Decimus among the *praenomens* used.[7] Others include Cnaeus (possibly because of Nero's father Cnaeus Domitius Ahenobarbus, and the family's association with his mother, Agrippina the Younger), Titus (perhaps because of the intermarriage of the Artorii with the Flavian dynasty), Publius (maybe in honour of Hadrian), and Spurius ('extra' or, perhaps, 'bastard') where this was appropriate.

When they were not punning, the Artorii tended to give their children the names of Greek or historical figures (Cleopatra and Monime) or descriptions of their occupations (Asclepiades, for those who followed the occupation of physician), or deities to whom they had a specific devotion (Flora and Zophyrus/Zephyrus). Their slaves, who took the same names as the owners, were less imaginatively named and generally stuck to numbers: Primus, Secundus, Tertius, and so forth.

Occupations and Preoccupations

The Artorii were, almost from the start, extremely wealthy – well-heeled enough to become Senators, though few of them did so. Most of the family kept a lower profile, serving as Equestrians, the class below Senators. Being an Equestrian was certainly a cheaper option, with a mean required income of 25,000 sesterces or about £29,000/$38,000 in today's currency, as opposed to the Senatorial income of some 62,500 sesterces or £75,600/ $98,000 counted in property, which clearly appealed to the bankers in the family. It may also explain how they managed to survive the reigns of psychopathic emperors such as Caligula, Nero, and, in the time of Artorius, Commodus, since they were less likely to attract attention than those of the Senatorial class.

Yet even as members of the Equestrian order, they tended to hobnob with – and sometimes marry into – the imperial families. Because of this, Artorius was actually a cousin to the Emperor Marcus Aurelius and, by extension, Commodus, the Emperor's son – something that may have helped him survive the reign of this notorious Caesar.

Another notable member of the family in Augustus' reign was Artorius Asclepiades, who was the twin of Geminus. Anyone who became a physician at this time was known as an Asclepiades, a son of Asclepius, the god of medicine. This particular Artorius served as private physician to Emperor Augustus and became governor of Asia, based on an inscription found at Smyrna. Here, there was a renowned asklepion, a healing temple sacred to the god Asclepius, where physicians were trained, and Artorius Asclepiades would have overseen this.[8]

Clients brought their dreams to the asklepion to have them interpreted by the priests. According to Plutarch, Augustus acted on a dream described to him by Marcus Artorius Asclepiades before the Battle of Philippi in Macedonia, which took place in 42 BC. In the dream, Augustus was carried out of his camp on a litter. Augustus copied the dream, having an empty litter carried instead. The litter was attacked, and the enemy believed that Augustus was dead. This deception gave Augustus the advantage, and he eventually won the battle.[9]

Asclepiades died in a shipwreck shortly after the battle of Actium, and Augustus erected several monuments to him, possibly even choosing the site for his new city of Nicopolis Actia in 31 BC to honour the former physician who had saved his life – positioning the city at the site of one of the Artorii's ancestral homes.

In the first century AD the Senate chose Marcus Artorius Geminus to be one of Augustus Caesar's twelve *praetors* (magistrates) at some time before his appointment as governor of Delos, which is why we find him, in an inscription referring to him, described as 'legatus Caesaris Augusti'. He was one of the first of two *praefecti aerarium militare*, the officers in charge of Augustus' military treasury, which was established in AD 6 (Geminus died AD 10). Because the position essentially involved banking, it is almost certain that he was part of the Equestrian order founded by Augustus during his reign.

Meanwhile, in Pompeii, another Marcus Artorius was making a name for himself. Some scholars have proposed that this was either Asclepiades or Geminus, but both seem to have had careers that kept them far too busy elsewhere for either of them to have been the Marcus Artorius who ran for the office of *duumvir* (a magistrate holding an office jointly with someone else) in Pompeii during Augustus' reign. This Marcus Artorius was probably the son of one of the famous twins. Since he is not buried in Geminus' family tomb, it's more likely that he was the son of Asclepiades, which would make him the patriarch of that branch of the family. The last Marcus Artorius domiciled at Pompeii probably died in the eruption of Vesuvius in AD 79, since this branch of the family vanishes from the historical record at this time. Curiously, King Arthur also had associations with a volcano in the region since, according to Caesarius of Heisterbach and others, he is said to have retired beneath Mount Etna following the final battle at

Camlan, there to be nursed back to health by his half-sister and sometime adversary Morgan le Fey.[10]

In the first century AD, around the time Marcus Artorius Geminus was serving as *procurator*, Puteoli replaced Delos as the main trade link between the East and Rome, but early on the Artorii's interests lay in the connections between Naples and Pompeii. The bankers of Puteoli had powerful ties with the city that is now better known for being buried during one of the eruptions of Mount Vesuvius than for anything else.[11] The Artorii were there, as either bankers or politicians, or both, running for high offices as attested in the election graffiti preserved for millennia by the volcanic ash.

This Marcus Artorius shared responsibility for the upkeep of the theatre at Pompeii with a rival family, the Holconii, one of whom was the other *duumvir* while Marcus held office. While the Holconii brothers paid for the remodelling of the seats and the area beneath them, Marcus Artorius provided the architect and the funds to rebuild the stage. Upon completion of the project, he freed his architecturally inclined slave, who took the name Marcus Artorius Primus and went on to undertake other building assignments at Pompeii and Herculaneum.

A few years later, under Nero, the Artorii turn up in Pompeii again, this time in connection with gladiators. In one contest, which may have taken place when the arena reopened after its temporary closure due to riots, a certain Marcus Artorius faced an opponent named Crysanthus. Since it is very unlikely that the son of a *duumvir* and the great-grandfather of *a flamen divi Augusti* would take a turn as a gladiator, this Marcus Artorius was probably a slave billed under the name of the person who owned him. The name of his opponent, Crysanthus, meant 'golden flowered', which may indicate that he had blond hair. Crysanthus has an almost identical name to that of Chrysanthus, the slave freed by Marcus' younger brother, Lucius. This would be consistent with Marcus Artorius apparently being defeated, probably even killed, by the slave Crysanthus in the fight. It seems likely that the two brothers, Marcus Artorius and Lucius Artorius, pitted their gladiators against each other at some point in the final years of Pompeii, and that the younger brother freed his gladiator after the man won.

The eruption of Vesuvius put an end to Pompeii, but the Artorii had other properties. They owned a maritime villa at Puteoli on the Bay of Naples, the sort of property at which high-ranking individuals entertained the emperor. It wasn't the sort of place that children were raised, nor were such villas generally self-sufficient. They tended to have a sister property somewhere inland, which supplied produce for the maritime villa. As of this time, the inland villa of the Artorii has not been found, though it may be somewhere near their ancestral holdings in Capua. The children, judging by the inscriptions on their family tombs, were almost all buried in Rome. This suggests that they were, for the most part, educated in the city itself.

The Artorii tended to keep some odd company. The inscription honouring one Artorius Valens at Misenum on the Bay of Naples was paid for by Julia Agrippina (Nero's mother, Agrippina the Younger). She was the wife of the Emperor Claudius, who adopted Nero as his heir, and she had a severe falling out with her son after he ascended to the purple. He tried to kill her several times, including the use of poison, having a boat sink under her and a ship from the Misenum fleet ram her galley when she was on the way to Baia. Finally, Nero ordered a sailor from the fleet to stab her, making her death look like suicide. The cave that is supposed to contain Agrippina's tomb is at Baia, between Puteoli and Misenum.[12] That the murderer could get close enough to her to wield a sword resulted from her habit of entertaining sailors from the fleet, notably freedmen. One such freedman was an Artorius, and he clearly made an impression on her.

This Artorius served on a trireme, a ship with a triple bank of oars, named 'Virtute', which had Alexandria as its home port. He died at the age of 26, having served in the military for just six years. He appears to have been in regular service rather than functioning as an officer and to have enlisted at the age of twenty, probably after realizing that other career options were not going to be available to him. He may have been one of Agrippina's lovers. He would certainly have had easy access to her from the naval base, and, as we propose, just as Cicero's villa may have belonged to the Artorii, her villa would have been a stone's throw away. Whatever the case, this Artorius died in service, and Nero's mother, rather than his own family or fellow servicemen, paid for the burial, indicating his closeness to the imperial family.

Meanwhile, yet another Marcus Artorius – or perhaps a son of the one from Pompeii – was making a somewhat questionable name for himself in the Jewish Wars, which dragged on from AD 66 to AD 73. The Roman-Jewish historian Flavius Josephus reported that this officer, when trapped by flames atop a tower during the destruction of the Second Temple in Jerusalem, proved as wily as Augustus with his empty litter trick. He declared his intention of jumping down and promised to name any man who caught him as his heir. One soldier volunteered to try, and Artorius made sure he jumped in such a way that he fell upon the man, killing him outright, so that he would not have to make good on his promise. This may have been the same Marcus Artorius who owned the gladiator at Pompeii, and he could have been the father or grandfather of the next Marcus Artorius, who lived in Puteoli on the Bay of Naples.[13]

In any case, this Artorius was probably in Jerusalem because he'd started his career with the legions by posting to the III Gallica and then transferred to the legion in charge of that city: the VI Ferrata. This was the same pattern that Lucius Artorius Castus would follow several generations later.

Residences

The villa at Puteoli served as the primary residence for an Artorii of the early second century with the significantly impressive name of Marcus Artorius Marci Filius Palatina Priscillus Vicasius Sabidianus. He lived in the late first and early second century.[14] He was a member of the Palatina voting tribe, who possessed extra privileges when it came to casting their votes, and he would have lived on the Palatine Hill while he belonged to the *flamen divi Augusti*, the priesthood responsible for the worship of the emperors as deities. We can be certain of this simply because of the offices that Geminus held and because the priests were required to live in that location (see Map 2). Juvenal's poem, cited above, also gives evidence that the family had a residence on the Palatine Hill in Rome.

Sabidianus was possibly our Artorius' grandfather. His father was probably the Marcus Artorius satirised by Juvenal as being from an upstart family of outsiders who came from a low and/ or questionable background and source of income and yet had attained great power and imperial favour through their marriages.

This Roman branch of the family seems to have specialized in fighting a particular type of military opponent, in much the same way that gladiators specialized in specific types of weaponry. Given Artorius' later associations with the Sarmatians, it's interesting to note that after initially posting to the III Gallica, as

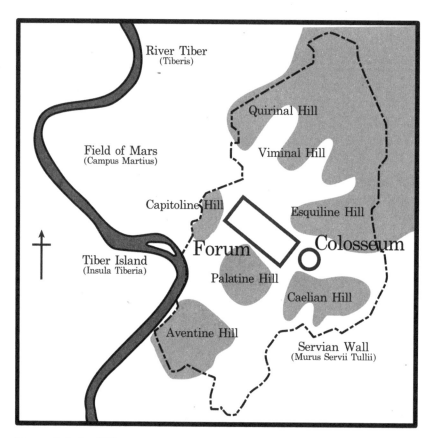

Map 2. Palatine Hill.

all recruits from the Campania region were required to do, several of the Artorii ended up serving in legions that were fighting heavy cavalry. At least one also named Artorius – Marcus Artorius Rufus Zophyrus – may have taken the name from one of Alexander the Great's generals, Zophyrus/Zopyrion, who fell in battle against the Caucasians. This would be significant later on, when Lucius Artorius Castus became the officer commanding a large number of mounted Sarmatian warriors. The aforementioned Sabidianus also led a troop of Pannonians, who could have been of Sarmatian stock.

According to a map by the historian Pomponius Mela (fl. AD 43) the Sarmatians (particularly the tribe known as the Iazyges) had moved to the region immediately east of the Germanic tribes by AD 44. Another Roman historian, Tacitus (d. AD 117) in Book 12 of his *Annals*, relates that in AD 48-54 Drusus Caesar, Tiberius' heir, brokered a deal with Vannius, king of the Iazyges, which ensured that his heavy cavalry would fight for the Romans in exchange for the Iazyges' king becoming overlord of the Germanic tribe of the Suebi.[15] Although the Iazyges in fact lost the battle and fled the field, Vannius remained loyal to Rome, setting up a sort of love/hate relationship that the two peoples would share over the next few centuries.

In Book 3 of the *Annals*, Tacitus records that a group of Sarmatians enrolled in the Roman army in AD 69 in Moesia, and it is possible that members of the Artorii family were trained to fight alongside these allies.

The Iazyges continued to ally themselves with Rome, fighting in the Dacian wars alongside Trajan's forces in AD 85-88 and AD 101. But they proved fickle allies and raided into Moesia in AD 92, where the Emperor Domitian defeated them, resulting in a large influx of Iazygean slaves into the Roman economy. Also, when Trajan fought two wars (AD 101-102 and AD 105-106) and conquered the Dacian king Decebalus in AD 105, there were Iazyges fighting alongside the Dacians, as evidenced by the reliefs on Trajan's Column (see Plate 5).

After this, a sizeable quantity of Sarmatian slaves would have come on the market in the Roman Empire, perhaps being processed

Plate 5. Sarmatians on Trajan's Column.

through Puteoli, where the Artorii would have had first pick, maybe with an eye toward teaching their sons the Sarmatian language, horse-handling techniques and fighting tactics. It's equally possible that some of the Sarmatians became gladiators, offering another opportunity for the Artorii to come to know these great warriors of the steppes. In any case, it meant that the family began to establish connections with the Sarmatian people, which would prove hugely important later on.

Hadrian was the next emperor to knock heads with the Iazyges. In AD 117-119, they battled over control of Dacia. A treaty was signed, which resulted in Iazygean *kontari* (heavy armoured cavalry, who fought with long lances), joining the Roman army as *numeri*, foreign troops, who supported the legions but who did not have citizenship, a pattern that would be repeated several times over the next century. The peace that Hadrian made with the Iazyges lasted for fifty years, which is essentially where matters stood when Lucius Artorius Castus was born, probably near Nola, in c. AD 140.

The Goddess of the Rose

A particularly noticeable aspect of Artorius' mausoleum is the presence of floral rosettes that decorate the edges of the inscription. Though easily overlooked, they bring into focus a further aspect of his life and the story of his family that is not without significance.

During Artorius' childhood and his military career, he would have visited the tomb of his ancestor Marcus Artorius Geminus in Rome. Several festivals required family members to offer libations and even picnic at the burial places of their ancestors, and this was the most prominent tomb for the Artorii in the area. (The other burials tended to be the graves of children.) Here, Artorius would have passed the statue of his ancestor, and at the same time would have been aware of something else, something which was to be much clearer on his own tomb than on Geminus' – the site served as a place to honour the goddess Flora.

Flora was, as her name implies, a goddess of flowers and springtime, whose importance to the Romans was considerable. She has long been considered a Sabine goddess, since Romulus' co-ruler, Titus Tatius, introduced her cult to Rome when he raised altars to the deities closest to his heart near the Circus Maximus.[16] Flora's temple was still in use when Artorius served in Rome in the second century AD, and there is every reason to believe he visited it.[17]

Flora's functions included overseeing early spring buds, cereals, fruit trees, vines, and flowers.[18] Said to have originally inhabited the Elysian Fields in the Underworld, she is something of a reverse Persephone. Instead of being stolen from the world of mortals by Hades and taken to the Underworld, she was stolen from the Elysian Fields by Zephyrus (the West Wind) and taken to the world of men.[19] Flora and Zephyrus shared a cave in Thrace and, along with many other children, produced the horses of the hero Achilles.[20]

Flora was also credited with the creation of the rose. When one of her nymphs died, Flora asked the gods to help change the girl into a beautiful flower. Apollo gave the nymph life; Bacchus gave her nectar; Vertumnus a fragrant scent; Pomona a fruit; and Flora a crown of petals.[21] Roman myth also claimed that Flora impregnated Juno by giving a rose to the Heavenly Queen – the result being the birth of Mars.[22] This connection between Flora and Mars in part explains the goddess' appeal among members of the military and the positioning of her temple beside the Field of Mars in the city.[23]

The ancient rose was not at all what we think of today. Depictions show four heart-shaped petals around the pollen-covered centre, perfect for assigning directions to the various winds, which later gave us the Compass Rose used by navigators.[24] The rose was also the Flower of Death, which may explain its popularity among gladiators, whose bodies were frequently covered in roses flung by the crowds into the arena.

Flora was one of the few deities who had more than one festival dedicated to her during the course of the Roman calendar year, and this was almost certainly because she was a combination of at least two other goddesses. The Romans knew that Flora had combined with the Greek goddess Khloris. As Ovid wrote: 'I was Khloris, who am now called Flora.'[25]

The first festival, called the Floralia, was officially established in 238 BC by the Sibyline oracle at Cumae, near Puteoli.[26] The priests known as *flamen Florialis* presided over the celebration,[27] which took place around 28 April to 3 May.[28] It is possible that members of the Artorii family served in this role, making their link with Flora even stronger.

The Floralia was a moveable celebration, much like our modern Easter. The festivities honoured spring and the goddess' connection with fertility. The celebration was characterized by flowers, including white roses, bacchanalian revels, lewd plays, games, and chariot races that were sponsored by the *aediles* (officers responsible for keeping public order), and held in the Circus Maximus.[29]

The second festival contrasted sharply with the first. This celebration took place on 13 August.[30] It celebrated Flora's connection with the Underworld and was particularly associated with the rose because of the myth about Flora's nymph and with the colour red because of its association with death.[31] Flora's connection with the cycle of life *and* death, combined with the fact that 'Flora' was the secret name of Rome used by the legions in their communications with each other and with the emperor, brought her a further connection with the military.[32]

Interestingly, Herodotus identified Flora with Tabiti, the Scythian Queen of the gods, who retreated to a cave with a monstrous god to create mythic monsters, much as Flora did with Zephyrus. Also, like Flora, Tabiti created a war god, but unlike Mars, the Scythian deity is not given a name by Herodotus. He merely refers to him as the 'Scythian Ares', and with good reason: He is one of the most vicious war gods known to any mythology.

A further strand of connection between Flora, the Artorii, and the Arthurian legends is a growing association and confusion between Flora and the Virgin Mary. The ninth-century monk Nennius' account of Arthur reports that he carried an image of the Blessed Virgin on his shoulder, perhaps as a brooch, and Gawain is known for his affinity with Mary. There is a possibility that our Artorius became a Christian, perhaps seeing the parallel between the Virgin and his beloved Flora. Although the Floralia was celebrated throughout the fourth century AD,[33] the distinction between the worship of the Virgin Mary and that of Flora merged so much by the late second century that it is virtually impossible to tell them apart outside the context of the Floralia.[34] Several early Christian ecclesiastics, most notably Augustine and Lactantius Firmianus, despised Flora, primarily because of the sexual excesses that took place during the Floralia.[35] These same church fathers also discouraged the worship of Mary because the Holy Virgin was perceived by them to be nothing more than Flora in disguise.

When Mary took over Flora's worship, she also took over the symbolism of Flora's rose. She became represented by a rose in the East,[36] while a lily represented her in the West,[37] though the use of the rose as Mary's emblem eventually spread to the West as well. Italians still celebrate May with the display of roses, a practice that most people think stems from Mary, but which actually traces back to the celebration of the Floralia.[38]

At the Feast of the Assumption in August, just two days after the date of the Floralia, a bower of white roses is still used to signify Mary.[39] This is in part because, according to folklore and in a joining of Eastern and Western traditions, lilies and roses filled Mary's tomb in place of her body.[40] This feast, which dates back to at least the seventh century AD and probably earlier, was originally held on 13 August. Because the date does not match that of the Roman celebration in honour of the virginal goddess Diana, some experts have rejected the argument that the Christian feast could have grown out of the Roman celebration.[41] But 13 August does correspond to the Roman festival that honoured Flora in her capacity as a goddess of death.[42] Such pieces of evidence, in conjunction with the protestations of early church fathers that Mary was Flora, argue strongly for the development of the cult of Mary in part from the worship of Flora.

In second-century Dalmatia, the rosette became a sign that the occupant of the grave was a Christian.[43] Elsewhere in the empire, tombs of the Artorii also bear what appear to be Christian symbols in spite of the high-ranking imperial posts they held. The whole *gens* may have converted from the worship of Flora to that of Mary at the same time that Mary absorbed Flora's cult. It is possible, then, that the roses Artorius commissioned to decorate his tomb no longer represented Flora but rather indicated a conversion to a devotion to Mary.

We should also note that a Roman *dux* wore a golden four-petalled rosette as the symbol of his rank in the form of a brooch that fastened his *lacerna* (the mantel worn over a toga or armour).[44] Artorius would certainly have worn this symbol on his shoulders at the time he held this rank, just as Arthur, during the battle of Mount Badon, according to the monkish chronicler Gildas in his *Historia Britonum,* carried the image of the Virgin Mary 'on his shoulders'.

Whether or not Artorius' iconography was originally intended to be Christian, by the time of Diocletian it would have been perceived as such. This choice of iconography may have led to the destruction of the very tomb it was supposed to protect.[45] Given the persecution of the Christians under Diocletian, the demolition of Artorius' tomb may have occurred at this time.

Coming of Age

While none of the Artorii ever became emperors, they intermarried with several of the imperial families. Trajan's mother, Marcia, was from the Artorii bloodline, as was Marcus Aurelius. Artorius himself was born during the reign of Antoninus Pius (r.138-161), politically a time of relatively little upheaval. The family wasn't dealing with one of the various unbalanced emperors that ruled Rome, and life would have been, for the most part, quite good for the young Artorius.[46]

As we saw, the *villa rustica* (inland farmstead) owned by the family probably lay in Campania, so that goods did not have to be transported too far. These farming lands would supply the luxury homes with produce. They were also the most likely place for the families to raise their children, since no one wanted to have toddlers chasing each other round the portico if the emperor stopped by unexpectedly. Older children were likely sent to Rome to continue their education under the watchful eyes of the Artorii on the Palatine Hill. In addition to Capua, a rustic villa may also have been located in Nola, near the town of Abelinum, also known by a variety of spellings as Abellola, Abellula Avellino, Avellula, and Avellana, names which inevitably remind us of Avalon, where the wounded Arthur of the later myths was supposedly transferred to be healed by nine otherworldly women.

Situated amidst the area of Capua, Pompeii, and Puteoli, the location would have made sense to a trading family. The women of Abelinum (Avelinum) were known for their healing arts and their association with water.[47] The healing connection would have attracted the likes of Asclepiades, and the magical women were tailor-made for the Artorii *gens* and their beloved goddess Flora. The villa Augustus was visiting when he died in Nola may well have been one owned by the Artorii. This is because Augustus probably granted the villas at Puteoli and Nola to the Artorii when he raised the family to Equestrian rank at the same time that he created the order, around 35 BC It is possible to see how stories of a group of women dedicated to healing, living in a place with a name similar to Avalon, could have migrated to later tales of the nine otherworldly healers mentioned by Geoffrey of Monmouth in his *Vita Merlini* (Life of Merlin) written more than 500 years later.

A male Equestrian needed to maintain a net wealth of 400,000 sesterces (c. £617,000/ $800,000), and such a grant would have enabled the family of priests, politicians, and physicians to meet that requirement, at least for a few generations. Given the time when the grant for the inland villa was given, the residence would have been of the defensive type described by Pliny the Elder (23-79 BC). It would have had strong walls, its own water supply, and ample fields for produce and livestock.

Career options for sons of the Artorii family were rather limited. They could follow one of the ancient paths, becoming flamens (priests) of either Flora or the divine Augustus, or choose to train as a physician, politician, or bureaucrat. Or they could become soldiers. In a few cases they became priests as well as warriors, but the vast majority of the Artorii wound up in the military.

Artorius' training as a soldier would have begun when he was very young – as soon as he could walk. Later, it's likely that he showed no promise as a physician or clerk and had little interest, at least as a young man, in becoming a priest or politician. This would have destined him for the military. Despite this he would have received as complete a formal education as possible. Given that he was already probably expected to follow a military career followed by a civil post, his education would have included geography, grammar, history, mathematics, philosophy, rhetoric, and science. Since they lived somewhere outside Capua and Nola instead of in an urban setting such as Rome, Artorius would have had a private tutor, probably a Greek, whom he would have shared with his brothers. Beyond these intellectual pursuits, he would have been schooled in the raising of horses, in riding, and in fighting techniques. He may also have learned something of the Sarmatian language and customs from slaves held at his home villa.

In these early years Artorius would have learned the value of being a contributing member of society. His mother would have taught him how a household was run – how to keep the books, how to oversee the staff, how to do every job that needed doing in case no one else was around to do it. His father would have taught him reading and writing, sports such as wrestling and boxing, horseback riding, and, above all, familiarity with various forms of armour and weapons.

Probably bilingual in Greek and Latin, physically fit, with a practical grip on everyday life, a good grounding in poetry such as the *Odyssey* and the *Aeneid*, trained to ride and probably even to swim, Artorius would have been sent to Rome at the ripe old age of ten for the next level of his education. Rome, for the Artorii, meant something different than it did for the Senatorial families who also thronged there. They would have had a residence inside the walls instead of a villa outside so that they were available to handle the administrative duties that fell to Equestrians.

Rome did not allow bodies to be buried inside the Forum, so where a family's graves are located is a good indicator as to where in the city they lived. Marcus Artorius Geminus' tomb was on property owned by Caesar Augustus across the Tiber from the Forum, and many Artorii, tragically most of them children, were laid to rest between there and the Palatine Gate.

As we have seen, the family lived on the Palatine Hill itself, which makes sense as they were directly serving the emperor. This was a dream location for a family of their faith and with their love of Greek philosophers. Flora's temple, representing her aspect as the rose, was located on one side, next to the Circus Maximus, and the Forum with its numerous opportunities for studying under Greek teachers, at a substantial discount to the cost of private tutors, would have suited the family very well. Horses were there to be worked within the Circus Maximus, and just down the street was the Flavian amphitheatre, which may have had included military instructors if the family were still plying their trade with gladiators. There were baths for sports and hygiene of course, along with a three-storey outdoor mall provided by Trajan to socialize and run errands in.

Artorius would have had everything a boy of his social class could dream of, right at his feet. All he had to do was apply himself to refining his writing skills, learning oratory, attending lectures, practising literary criticism and dramatic readings in both Latin and Greek. Since texts from Homer and Virgil were used to teach Greek and Latin, Artorius would have had a working knowledge of the classical myths behind the religions of his day as well.[48]

Aged about fifteen, Artorius would have begun his studies with a *rhetor*, who would teach him rhetoric. Being an Equestrian, he could have become a politician, so public speaking would have been in his lesson plans too, though according to Tacitus, it would have taken the form of storytelling by the time Artorius lived. On the practical side, he would have covered geography and geometry, most likely with an eye to how they could be used in the military.

In his family there would have been absolutely no way to escape philosophy. Literature would have turned to topics useful to someone heading for a military career. He would also have received a thorough grounding in the various religions that existed throughout the Empire, since the Romans were in the habit of letting people keep their own deities as long as they respected the gods of Rome and the Imperial cult. Artorius would also have had to study music, whether or not he could play an instrument, so that he could interact easily with others in the social world of the upper classes.

So, between the ages of sixteen and eighteen, Artorius had to decide what he was going to do with his life – whether he would become a priest, a physician, a bureaucrat, a politician, or a soldier. We cannot be sure what his eldest brother, Marcus, chose. He does not seem to have been one of the family physicians, so perhaps family fortunes were such at the time that he was able to embark directly upon a career as the magistrate of a small town, or in some civil office.

A political career did not suit all Equestrians, so there was a second way to become a high-ranking Equestrian. A soldier could enter the army as a centurion and advance in rank until he became *primus pilus*. This path was risky, because to become a centurion, the Equestrian needed to resign his social status. Only if he survived to earn the rank of *primus pilus* would he recover his social standing upon leaving his legion. In exchange for this resignation, the former-Equestrian received a commission as a *decimus hastus posterior,* the lowest ranking centurion of a legion. This appears to be the path chosen by Artorius' brother, Caius, and it was certainly the path chosen by Lucius Artorius Castus himself.

Since he opted for a military career, we know he did not complete the highest form of the Roman education, which entailed travelling to Greece to study philosophy. What we have, then, is a young man from a socially privileged background, well-educated, and well-trained in the arts of war and oratory, very possibly with detailed knowledge of the Sarmatians, who took the lowest rank, *decimus hastus posterior,* in the III Legion Gallica, which specialized in fighting heavy Parthian cavalry. Once he'd mastered all that Rome had to teach a man of his tender years, he would have enlisted in the army. This meant that, aged 18, he would have found himself in the hell-on-earth that was the Middle East.

3

THE CENTURION

Artorius began his military career as a centurion c. AD 159 at the age of 18 – another indication of his family's social standing and wealth. Several inscriptions relating to the Artorii show members of the *gens* holding ranks that could only be held by Equestrians, and only officers of Equestrian status or higher could enter the army directly as a centurion, as Artorius did.[1]

The lowly legionary made the paltry sum of 900 sesterces (about £1,500, $1,800) per year between the time of the Emperors Domitian and Septimius Severus, while a centurion pulled down 13,500 sesterces (roughly £19,000, $24,000) annually. Food and housing aside, the soldiers had to purchase and maintain their own arms and armour. They were not allowed to marry, so they had no family or lands to worry about. They had to carry everything with them, so to avoid a heavier pack most had little besides coin and spare clothing. The coin tended to go for drink, an occasional better meal, and prostitutes. Among the infantry, especially in colder climes such as Germania or Britannia, their most prized possessions were socks to protect their feet and trousers to keep the lower parts of their bodies warm. Cavalry had horses to purchase and maintain as well.

When the army moved, a baggage train travelled with them, carrying their tents, cooking pots, and other necessities for temporary camps. When the army was in residence at a fort, the supplies were stored inside, but the people who followed them stayed in a *vicus* (town) outside the fort's walls. An entire legion was rarely in residence at its headquarters. More soldiers would be billeted there than elsewhere, but others would be scattered at smaller forts throughout the region or on patrol. The humble legionaries were divided into units of eight, who shared rooms inside the barracks in the fort and tents in the field. They also formed the rows of the century, which usually, despite its name, consisted of about eighty men.

Centurions had their own quarters: one room for themselves and another for guests, such as the entourage that accompanied officials and ambassadors visiting the commander of the fort. The higher the rank of the centurion, the more important the guests he was expected to entertain. The higher pay of the centurion was in part because he had such duties as well as more expensive equipment. Despite their loftier status, the centurions marched on foot with their men, moving roughly ten miles per day. This may have been slow, but it was also relentless – and when the legions clashed with their adversaries, they were an absolutely implacable force that few could resist.

It was into this culture that Artorius stepped when he entered the III Gallica c. AD 159 during the reign of Antoninus Pius.

The III Gallica

Raised by Julius Caesar in Gaul, the legion's emblem was the bull, which appeared on its standard (see Plate 6). Unlike King Arthur's medieval knights, who bore their own devices on their shields, members of a legion carried a shield with the same device (see Plate 7). At the time Artorius enlisted, the III Gallica was stationed at Raphanaea, between Damascus and Antioch, in Syria.[2] The legion's primary duty was to keep the peace, with special attention paid to Jewish and Christian movements within the province.[3] They did this by posting centurions to various villages, a command structure that would later be employed with the Sarmatians at the *vicus* adjacent to the fort of Bremetennacum and in the patrol of that region in Britannia.[4] Artorius' time with the III Gallica gave him his initial training, which would influence his command decisions throughout his career.

Plate 6. III Gallica Banner.   Plate 7. III Gallica Shield.

One of the main enemies the soldiers in Syria were trained to confront were the Parthians, an early Iranian dynasty which lasted for over 200 years. Artorius, as a newly appointed officer, would have come to know them very quickly. The Parthian army included a type of heavy cavalry called cataphracts, from the Greek word for 'completely enclosed'. The horses had a coat of scales draped over them for armour. Ideally, the rider had a shirt to protect his upper body and greaves to cover his legs below the knee. These would have been made of chain mail or overlapping scales sewn onto leather. On their heads they wore a solid metal cap. If the rider were wealthy, only his eyes would be visible between his helmet and shirt. His legs would be exposed only between where his shirt ended and his knees. His horse would be entirely encased, except for the area where the armour fastened across its chest and the lower part of its legs. The less wealthy the warrior, the less armour he and his horse wore. The rider carried no shield because he needed both hands to wield his *kontus* – a long spear used to stab an opponent from the saddle, which did most of the work to keep him in place, since he did not have stirrups.

This heavy cavalry was designed to break through the front lines of infantry – and to inspire fear. Their counterparts, the Sarmatians, wore a different style of armour that addressed some of the problems encountered by the Parthian 'heavies'. The Parthian horses could in fact only carry so much weight for long periods. They were slow on the attack as well as in retreat. They were too cumbersome to do much when it came to hand-to-hand combat, and there were only a limited number of targets they could hit when they charged the Roman front lines.

The primary defence against these horsemen that Artorius would have learned was the cavalry square called the *testudo* (tortoise) first used by Alexander the Great.[5] The foremost soldiers were the ones Artorius himself would have commanded, since the more senior the soldiers, the farther back they were placed, and at this point he was a very junior officer. It was essential that he and his men learn this tactic and learn it well. The first line of men would interlock their shields in front of them. Each rank behind this layered their shields above their heads like scales on a lizard. Soldiers on either side placed their shields to prevent attack from the flanks. Only the back of the unit remained exposed. As a rider charged into them, they would stab at him and his horse with their *pili* (spears). When the horse's forward motion came to a stop, the soldiers would drop their shields and try to wrench the *kontos* from the rider's hands. Working together, they wrestled the rider to the ground and killed him. As for the horses and riders who wore less armour, Roman archers could often hit them, stopping their charge long before they reached the front line. A problem arose if the horse and rider managed to either plough through or ride over the testudo and turn to attack the back. Hopefully, the next century in the rank could pull the rider from the horse on the turn, otherwise the exposed soldiers did not fare well.

During his four-year stint with the III Galicia, Artorius would have had to master all the basics of legionary tactics. He survived his last two years as a centurion of the III Gallica, preparing for war with the Parthians under the command of Lucius Verus and transferred c. AD 163 to the VI Ferrata.

The VI Ferrata

Known as the Ironclad Legion,[6] the emblem of the VI Ferrata was once again a bull, which it bore on its shield (see Plate 9). It also boasted an oddity: a second emblem for its banner, the she-wolf who raised Romulus and Remus, the semi-mythical founders of Rome (see Plate 8). This emphasized its importance among the other legions.

In the year AD 138, the legion transferred to Megiddo in the Jezreel Valley, Syria – the place prophesied as the site of Armageddon. The Romans had been having trouble with the area, and specifically with the Jews, long before Artorius was born. His aforementioned ancestor, Marcus Artorius, who jumped from the tower, had been present at the destruction of the Second Temple in AD 70. At that time, the VI Ferrata was stationed in Roman Judea, which was renamed 'Syria' when the Romans finally decided they had had enough of the Jews, destroyed Jerusalem and rebuilt the city as Aelia Capitolina under Hadrian around AD 135.

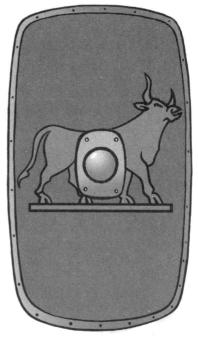

Plate 8. The VI Ferrata Banner.   Plate 9. VI Ferrata Shield.

Antoninus Pius sent the VI Ferrata to Mesopotamia for a brief period in the 140s but had to bring it back to Roman Galilee in AD 150 to settle increasing disturbances in the area, re-establishing the camp at Megiddo. In addition to protecting a major trade route from the Jordan Valley to the Mediterranean, the VI Ferrata was responsible for securing Egypt, the area that produced much of the food for the Roman provinces. The region was of great strategic importance, and army after army fought to control it over millennia, as they continue to do to this day. Artorius probably transferred to the VI Ferrata while the legion was fighting the Parthians in the Middle East, helping Lucius Verus take the Parthian capital of Ctesiphon. Following the conclusion of the war, Artorius returned to Megiddo with his legion. This new posting would have placed Artorius among the legions responsible for keeping the peace both in the Jezreel Valley and possibly as far away as Jerusalem. Here he would have learned the difference between Christians and Jews, and of the internecine strife that troubled both.

The whole area was filled with religious associations for the many Jews who lived there. These were descendants of the people who had fled north following the destruction of the First Temple in Jerusalem by the Babylonians in the fifth century BC. Earlier, in the 1100s BC, the Prophetess Deborah had advised the Israelite ruler Barak to attack the Canaanites under Siserah from Mt. Tabor, just to the east of Megiddo.[7] Barak won, but Deborah was credited with the victory. The tombs associated with her, and with Barak, were located there. The great Jewish hero, Joshua, also supposedly fought several battles in the valley a couple of centuries later. The proximity to the Jordan River, which figures so prominently in the Jewish religion, was at the opposite end of the valley from the Mediterranean, so there was pilgrimage as well as trade traffic through the region. However, the Romans had so much trouble with the Jews that all traffic was carefully monitored.

The area also featured a plethora of Christian holy sites. On the opposite side of the Jezreel Valley from Megiddo was Nazareth, the town where Jesus grew up and began his ministry, due west of Mt. Carmel and the city of Bethlehem. Northeast was the Sea of

Galilee, where Jesus performed many of his miracles. East was the Jorden River where Jesus was baptised. In other words, there were a host of reasons for Christians to make pilgrimages there.

Artorius' life at Megiddo, when he and his unit were not out on patrols, would have been like that of any centurion in a typical Roman fort. As yet, the VI Ferrata's camp at Megiddo is still the only permanent Roman fort discovered in the region, perhaps in all the Middle East, that dates to the second century. Archaeologists knew the fort had to be somewhere near the Arabic city of Lajjun ('legion'), but until recently they were not sure where. Aerial studies, ground penetrating radar, and other techniques eventually pinpointed a site where archaeologists started finding roof tiles stamped with the emblems of the VI Ferrata, as well as other detritus from the legion. The fort they uncovered beside a city and atop a relatively low-lying mountain, was a monster – a true legionary fortress. Measuring around 500 by 300 metres, it probably held about 5,000 soldiers. To put that in perspective, most of the forts that date to the second century held between 200 and 800 men. The fort at Megiddo was bigger by several orders of magnitude, an indication of its importance.

The fort controlled a massive region, the entire province of Syria-Palestina, which extended south of what had been the original city of Jerusalem. To a young man, now twenty-two, coming in from several years at the temporary training camps made by soldiers in the III Gallica, the enormous, highly organized structure may have seemed intimidating, especially since he wasn't one of the soldiers to simply garrison it, but rather one of its officers.

As with most Roman forts of the period, the VI Ferrata's headquarters was shaped like a playing card, with straight sides and rounded corners. Outside the walls was a defensive ditch that flattened out so that traffic could pass at the gates, which were symmetrically positioned opposite each other along the walls. Atop the inner wall of the ditch were crenelated ramparts. What is visible now are the bricks that surrounded rubble fill, but in Artorius' time the walls would have been plastered and painted with lines to mimic actual bricks. Watchtowers were placed at each corner and on either side of each gate. The fort was so huge that it had additional towers along its walls as well. This style of building would be mimicked centuries later by the types of moated castles in which Arthur and his knights lived in the medieval tales and in which the nobles who listened to them dwelt in real life.

If you have visited at least one Roman fort from this period, you have essentially seen them all (see Figure 1). They were built to a pattern that placed the headquarters at the centre with the commanding officer's quarters beside it. The granaries were placed on opposite sides of these buildings, while workshops, the infirmary and other necessary buildings lined the other two sides. The barracks filled in the rest of the rectangle. Each set of barracks contained rooms for eight men, the basic tent group when on the march. One century – about eighty men – to a building, with the centurion's quarters at the end farthest from the commander's quarters. There were six centuries to a cohort and ten cohorts to a legion, with the first cohort being twice as big as the others.

Some forts show evidence that these buildings may have been two storeys in height, which is probably how the fort at Megiddo

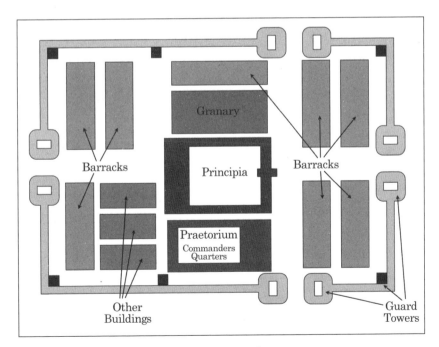

Fig. 1. Plan of a Typical Roman Fort. (W. Kinghan)

was designed and which was also true of many medieval castles. Each barracks in the fort had an entry room and a backroom, with the latter containing four sets of bunks. The infantry stored their gear in the first room. The backroom would have been extremely dark, which would have enabled nightshift soldiers to sleep even in the light of the desert sun. The thick, plaster-covered walls would have kept the rooms cool. The colour scheme was simple, inside and out. About two to three feet of reddish plaster lined the lower part of the wall, with everything above painted white, the whole topped off by red roof-tiles. A door and window were cut in the wall to the first room, but only a door in the wall of the second. Recently, scholars have begun to speculate that cavalry units occupied the lower levels when necessary and kept their horses in the first room. The centurions' quarters were far more lavish, including extra areas such as a dining room, designed for entertaining guests.

The *principia,* or main headquarters, was positioned where the two main 'streets' of the fort crossed. The entry was a large, walled courtyard, where officers would have gathered to receive orders. Further in, beyond a cross-hall, stood a chapel where the legion's standards were kept. There was a straight line of view from the chapel across the courtyard and through the main entrance. Considered the heart of the fort, this room was always guarded.

On one side of the chapel were the administrative offices. The Romans loved bureaucracy and had paperwork – whether on wood, papyrus, or wax tablets – down to a science. Records were kept in an adjacent room. To the other side of the chapel the standard-bearers served as the bankers for the legion. They tracked the soldiers' pay, savings, expenses, and anything else to do with the financial workings of the legion. Money was secured in an iron chest in this room, which was, understandably, also heavily guarded. High windows allowed natural light into the rooms of the principia, and iron grills separated the chapel, administrative, and banking areas from the cross-hall.

Parade grounds, baths, forges, and shops were located outside the fort's walls. While many forts had a vicus (village) grow up outside one of its gates, where the personnel who supported the legion lived, the headquarters of the VI Ferrata had an entire city that sat on a nearby hill, the top of which had been levelled off. Approached by a causeway, it was surrounded by plastered, crenelated walls with a series of watchtowers. The city's defences consisted of overlapping panels that conformed to the contour of the hill rather than a precise geometric shape like those of the fort. The placement of the watchtowers was more asymmetrical, and the layout of the town more haphazard than the fort, though it followed the same grid pattern the Romans loved so much and that many of our modern cities use to this day.

The streets outside the city and fort were lined with tombs and altars that featured inscriptions, placed so that the names of the departed could be easily read. The dry climate allowed for interment as well as cremation, and both appear to have been practised at the fort occupied by the VI Ferrata.

One of the main things that legions did, apart from train, was build and maintain infrastructure. Given the desert terrain, the primary concern for this large population center was water. Fortunately, there was an abundance of water in the Jezreel Valley, so it was simply a matter of using Roman engineering to get the water where it needed to go. The roads, particularly the one that formed the trade route that the fort guarded, were well maintained. While Artorius was serving at the fort, these are the types of activities his century would have undertaken.

The reign of the Emperor Antoninus Pius came to an end with his death on 7 March 161. He was succeeded by co-Emperors Marcus Aurelius and Lucius Verus. In that same year, Verus decided to argue with the Parthians about Armenia and marched on them with the III Gallica and detachments from the VI Ferrata and some of the Danube legions. Younger centurions would have been chosen from the Ferrata for this task, leaving the veterans to guard the critical Jezreel Valley. This pitted Artorius against the very adversaries his time in the IIII Gallica had trained him to fight.

The first outbreak of what became known as the Antonine plague was reported. Circa 165, Artorius' old legion, the III Galicia, marched on the Parthian capitals, including Seleucia, on the west bank of the Tigris (not to be confused with other cities by the same name. It was here, while Artorius was with the VI Ferrata, that the Antonine plague struck.

Scholars have generally agreed from contemporary descriptions that the disease was smallpox. It spread along the Roman roads and trade routes, arriving in Han China around 166, when a delegation sent by Lucius Verus reached their distant trading partners via Vietnam, possibly by ship from India, with whom the Romans had been trading.

Smallpox itself is thought to have originated in Egypt around 12,000 to 10,000 BC. The Hittites accused the Egyptians of using it against them on the battlefield, and outbreaks do correspond with some frequency to places and times when the world was at war. The first hard evidence for the disease shows up in mummies of Ramses V and others between 1570 and 1085 BC. China records it in 1122 BC and Sanskrit texts of roughly 1500 BC tell of its presence in India.

A similar plague hit Athens in 430 BC and is also thought to have been smallpox. The disease transmits from person to person via exposure to coughing and sneezing in close quarters, and to contaminated items such as clothes and bedding. Cramped living conditions and the tendency of poorer people to share and recycle bedding and clothing accounts for the extreme number of deaths among the lowest levels of society.

The modern smallpox vaccine was developed because it was noted that dairy farmers were immune to the disease. This was thought to be because of their exposure to cowpox. Surprisingly, despite its name, cowpox is less common in cows than it is in other mammals.

The Antonine Plague wiped out entire towns and villages in Italy, and about a third of the population of Rome. What we do not have are contemporary accounts of deaths among the people on the farm-villas in Campania. Is it possible that what was true about dairy farmers over a millennium and a half later was also true of Romans on their farms? We know of herds of cattle, horses, goats and even camels travelling with the legions to provide food for the soldiers. If cows were for the meat, you would also get the hide, which can be used to fashion clothing; but live cows give milk. The same is true for sheep, goats, and horses, all of which the Roman soldiers were responsible for caring for. It would be interesting to know if the soldiers who survived were either raised at a rustic villa as Artorius had been, and if soldiers who cared for the legion's herds were less susceptible to the disease.

Alas, no such records were kept, but we have one huge hole in the middle of the map where the disease spread – the territory where steppe riders cared for sheep and cattle, drank fermented mares' milk, and otherwise incorporated a number of dairy items into their diet – which necessitated them milking the animals and, in all probability, coming into contact with cowpox.

At its height, the contagion was killing 2,000 people a day and the suggested number of fatalities is estimated at 5 million. It was described over two centuries after its eventual disappearance by the historian Ammianus Marcellinus as having 'polluted everything with contagion and death, from the frontiers of Persia all the way to the Rhine and Gaul'. Curiously, it never seems to have crossed the Channel to Britannia.

Marcus Aurelius dealt as best he could with the pandemic that threatened his Empire. He gave out stringent commands for the isolation of the sick and seems to have understood far earlier than most western physicians the importance of cleanliness. More than this, he brought his own faith to bear on the situation, invoking the god Apollo whose oracle he almost certainly consulted for help in dealing with the pandemic. He is also said to have 'zealously revived the worship of the gods' (*Historia Augusta*) and appears to have issued commands to his legions to place dedicatory inscriptions throughout the Empire calling upon Apollo and Jupiter for protection.

The altars and inscription found in Rome itself, throughout Asia Minor and as far as the borders of Roman Britannia, appear to have been erected during the period when the plague was at its height, and to have faded out more or less when the pandemic ended. Given the period, this is almost certainly a call to pray for delivery from the invisible enemy of the plague.

Despite this, the disease hit the Roman army hard, killing almost a third of its soldiers, so that Marcus Aurelius was forced to postpone a planned offensive against the Marcomanni, who were challenging him along the Danube.[8] Soldiers had to be nursed back to health, and new men transferred from posts in less vulnerable areas to fill gaps in the ranks of the Danube legions. In the meantime, Artorius moved again, probably because of this situation, joining the II Adiutrix c. 167, as it returned to its base at Aquincum (modern Budapest) in Pannonia.[9]

The II Adiutrix

The II Adiutrix was one of Marcus Aurelius' premier legions, based on the north-eastern frontier of the Empire. It was stationed in Pannonia Inferior at Aquincum (modern Budapest) when Artorius joined it.[10] The legion's name 'Adiutrix' meant it was a 'helper', and that its prime function was to assist other legions. Its symbols were Capricorn and Pegasus. (see Plates 10 and 11) It had been among the legions that joined Lucius Verus in Parthia, fighting alongside the III Gallica and the VI Ferrata from the years 162 to 166, the year before Artorius joined it. The legion was hard hit by the plague, and they required new officers to get its detachments back to the Rhine. This is likely how Artorius became attached to this legion.

The II Adiutrix returned to its base at Aquincum (modern Budapest), bringing the plague with it, placing Artorius directly in the line of the deadly disease. But if he caught it, he didn't succumb to it, given his illustrious career.

The headquarters of a legion did not need to be in the capital of a province. When not based in such a location the *legatus* of the legion was the commander. But something different happened at Aquincum. In this case, the governor of the province outranked the *legatus*. When there was more than one legion in a province, the governor was placed with the premier legion. It was in fact possible for a governor to take control of all of the legions in his province. Then, if something happened to the governor, whoever was in control of all the legions in the province became *acting* governor with two Senators as *legatus legioni* acting as subordinates to him. Such was the case in the Marcomannic Wars, (AD 166–180) when three provinces that once made up Dacia came under the control

Plate 10. II Adiutrix Banner

Plate 11. II Adiutrix Shield

of one governor. This also happened when Claudius Albinus took command of three British legions prior to his bid to be emperor in AD 197. In that year he effectively became governor of Britannia. A similar event affected Artorius' own later career, as we shall see.

When an emperor was present, he commanded all the legions in the province plus any others he called upon. This is how Lucius Verus came to be in command of all the legions in the war with Parthia, and how Marcus Aurelius had command of the legions along the front between the Roman Empire and the Marcommani, Quadi, and Iazyges, which was marked by the Danube River.

The II Adiutrix's main task was defending the north-eastern border of the Empire from invading Germanic and Sarmatian peoples. The absence of a good portion of the legion to combat the Parthians left the border weak, and the ensuing struggles blossomed into the conflict known as the Marcomannic Wars. These wars are also sometimes called the bellum Germanicum et

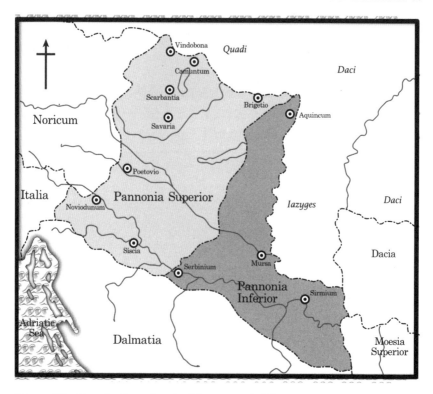

Map 3. The Danube Front for the Marcomannic Wars.

Sarmaticam, showing that the Romans distinguished between the Germanic tribes and the Iazyges and other Sarmatians tribes.[11]

Just prior to Artorius joining the II Adiutrix, the legion had dealt with attempts by the Suebian tribe known as the Quadi to cross the border into the Empire. The Quadi belonged to the Marcomannic Confederation, as did a Sarmatian tribe, the Iazyges. The Marcomanni, 'people on the borderlands', faced the II and III Italica and the II Adiutrix in Noricum.[12] By AD 167, when Artorius transferred in, the legion was fighting the Quadi along the border of Pannonia Inferior from its headquarters at Aquincum, while the V Macedonica, the legion commanded by Marcus Aurelius himself, moved across the border of Dalmatia to establish a camp in the Iazyges' territory, north of the Danube at Potaissa in modern Turda in Romania.

With the II Adiutrix, Artorius fought against the Germanic Quadi. He had some strange allies. These were Christians, who aided the II Adiutrix in battle by praying. Artorius himself had become used to the sect during his time in the VI Ferrata and probably thought nothing of their strange behaviour. Christians were generally not a militant group, as the Jews were at this time. In any case, the Romans were willing to accept help from whatever quarter they could, and since their prayers appeared to result in the legion's success, Artorius would have seen no harm in them. By AD 173 the Quadi had cornered the XII Fulminata, which almost died because of a heatwave and because their supply line was cut. Either the busily praying Christians, or an Egyptian wiseman who managed to establish a direct connection to Mercury, supposedly caused lightning to strike the Quadi. The ensuing rain solved the water problem, and the newly christened 'Thundering legion' routed the Quadi. By the following year, the Romans had soundly defeated them, but Artorius was not there to see it, having already moved on to the V Macedonica and a place in history.

Judging by the images on Trajan's Column, the Quadi, who were bearded, generally wore tunics over trousers along with cloaks, though some appear to have run into battle shirtless. The Romans beheaded those they captured. This last detail is curious since the Romans usually took prisoners and turned them into slaves. Beheading in general was reserved for the execution of a Roman citizen, with crucifixion preferred for non-citizens. That the II Adiutrix beheaded the Quadi suggests that the insurgents were regarded as a client state rather than as foreigners attacking across the border, and high-ranking prisoners would have been ransomed by auction back to their people. This would have set up a strange dynamic for Artorius. The higher he rose through the ranks, the more he would have been required to entertain such prisoners, and from necessity he would have become familiar with the language and culture of these people, some of whom he may have already encountered earlier in his life. Now he could have found himself condemning former acquaintances to death.

In AD 167, incursions into Dacia by the Vandals and Iazyges caused Marcus Aurelius to move the V Macedonica out of Moesia Inferior to Potaissa in Dacia Superior. As officers continued to fall to the plague a great need arose for anyone who had experience fighting this type of adversary. Then Lucius Verus himself died, probably of the plague, in January AD 169, and Marcus Aurelius took his body back to Rome to preside over his funeral. But by the summer the Emperor was back, leading the V Macedonica against the Iazyges, which brought more men into the plague-ridden area and ultimately causing more to die.

In AD 171, Artorius transferred again, this time to Marcus Aurelius' premier legion, the V Macedonica. Now a seasoned officer with twelve years of service, he would have held a very senior post. His experience with the Parthians was desperately needed in the Macedonica, fighting the Iazyges and their heavy cavalry. So, he put down the Pegasus of the II Adiutrix and picked up the Bull of the V Macedonica (see plate 12), a move that was to bring him to a place and time that would change his life.

The V Macedonica

While Lucius Verus imported his legions into a single province, Marcus Aurelius scattered his over several. Sending some of his resources to aid Verus had left the Emperor so seriously stretched that in AD 168 Ballomar, king of the Marcomanni, was able to invade as far into Italy as Aquileia. This was the emergency the

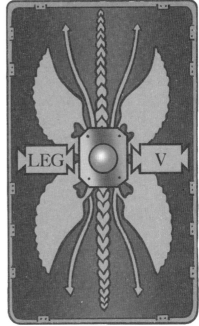

Plate 12. V Macedonica Banner.   Plate 13. V Macedonica Shield.

Romans were attempting to address when Lucius Verus died. Marcus Aurelius immediately scrambled to secure his position. He called in outside legions to free Aquileia and raised the legions I and II Italica. In AD 171, when Artorius transferred to the V Macedonica as a centurion, the emperor struck a truce with the Quadi and the Sarmatian Iazyges, allowing him to concentrate on the Marcommani.

In AD 172 the Romans marched against the Marcomanni on the north side of the Danube. We are unsure which legion was used, though it was probably either the I or II Italica, but the campaign collapsed when the Quadi broke the truce, followed by the Iazyges. Their combined forces surged across the Pannonian Plain and into Dacia, and the Romans pulled back to their side of the Danube. The legions XIII Gemina and V Macedonica had to do their best to hold onto Dacia, which lay north of the Danube, while the II Adiutrix held the line against the Quadi.[13] Artorius took part in a unique engagement against the Iazyges, which became a much-lauded event, and was the point at which his career began to take off. It would certainly have brought him to the attention of his superiors in a most dramatic fashion.[14]

By this time the Iazyges were living north of the Danube, on the further bank of the river from the V Macedonica's base at Potaissa.[15] The procedure for the Danube legions was to send out detachments, led by centurions, to patrol the area.[16] The soldiers of the V Macedonica routinely patrolled the southern bank the Danube at the conjunction with the Tisza River, precisely where the historian Cassius Dio places a unique battle between the Romans and the Iazyges.[17]

The fighting began with the infamous steppe manoeuvre, the feigned retreat. This involved two sides of the opposing army holding the line while the centre fell back. The object was to get the Romans to follow the fleeing horsemen, and then close on them from the sides with the steady units. Then the centre would turn around and attack the trapped infantry. The Romans pursued the apparently fleeing Iazyges onto the frozen Danube, and the Iazyges turned and charged, with the flanks sweeping around to encircle the Romans and attack their exposed backs.

Normally, this attack resulted in lots of dead Romans and barely scathed Iazyges. On this occasion things went differently. The officer in charge had apparently drilled his century in a modified version of a fighting technique based on the infantry square, which the Romans had employed successfully against cavalry in the war with the Parthians in Armenia.[18] Instead of facing the Iazyges in parallel lines, the Romans stood back-to-back in a square, *pili* pointed outward. They planted their shields in the ice with the boss at a 45-degree angle to the base and pressed down on it with one foot while jamming the nails of their caligae (sandal-like boots) into the ice to prevent slipping. The Romans then pointed their *pili* at the cavalry and took the charge – twisting sidewise to let the horses slip between them.

As soon as the Iazyges were beside them, the Romans grabbed the reins of the horses and pulled the animals off balance. The battle might have been more even, but the centurion in command had also drilled his men in a modified form of Graeco-Roman wrestling, where everything was fair, except poking out an opponent's eyes. This particular century, then, fought using everything, including their teeth, to trap and pin their opponents. As a combat technique, it was as effective on the ice as it had been on sand in the testudo formation.

Cassius Dio describes it vividly:

The Iazyges, perceiving that they were being pursued, awaited their opponent's onset, expecting to overcome them easily, as the others were not accustomed to the ice. Accordingly, some of the barbarians dashed straight at them, while others rode round to attack their flanks, as their horses had been trained to run safely even over a surface of this kind. The Romans upon observing this were not alarmed, but formed into a compact body, facing all their foes at once, and most of them laid down their shields and rested one foot upon them, so that they might not slip so much; and thus they received the enemy's charge. Some seized the bridles, others the shields and spear shafts of their assailants, and drew the men toward them; and thus, becoming involved in close conflict, they knocked down both men and horses, since the barbarians by reason of their momentum could no longer keep from slipping. The Romans, to be sure, also slipped; but in case one of them fell on his back, he would drag his adversary down on top of him and then with his feet would hurl him backwards, as in a wrestling match, and so would get on top of him... The barbarians, being unused to combat of this sort, and having lighter equipment, were unable to resist, so that few escaped.[19]

These were far from normal military tactics, but sound instead like the inspired reaction of a quick-thinking centurion. The result of the affray was that the small unit of Romans captured a larger force of Iazyges, and the Iazyges' king promptly sent envoys to Marcus Aurelius to sue for peace.

Even if Artorius was not the ingenious centurion who concocted this strange set of battle tactics, he would certainly have known the man who did; but given that he finally advanced to the rank of *primus pilus* around the time of this battle, and that he was a senior centurion in one of the two legions who supplied the detachment in Dio's account, there is a very good the chance that the clever officer who annihilated the Iazyges on the frozen Danube was indeed Artorius. In addition, he later circulated in the same social circles with Dio's father, providing an opportunity for Dio to have heard the tale from Artorius himself.

Artorius' long journey was about to get even longer. After training with the III Gallica, he turned in a good performance in the Valley of Jezreel with the VI Ferrata, where he would have become familiar with the burgeoning Christian religion, particularly the Essene form practised in Nazareth. The losses in the legions along the Danube almost certainly caused his transfer to the II Adiutrix, where he avoided the plague and marched to the Danube to battle the Quadi back and forth across the frozen river. He would certainly have combined that knowledge with what he had learned against the Parthian cataphracts and used it to great effect against the Iazyges after he joined the V Macedonica, and his performance against the horse riders from the Pannonian Plain would finally earn him what he had desired for so long: the rank of *primus pilus*.

4

RISING THROUGH THE RANKS

We are not sure what level of centurion Artorius had achieved before becoming *primus pilus*. Since he appears to have been out on patrol on the frozen Danube prior to the advancement, it seems unlikely that he was one of the top centurions as these would have operated more from the base fort. In any case, the responsibility he shouldered upon becoming *primus pilus* of the V Macedonica was enormous. To understand how great it was, we first need to look at the basic structure of the Roman legions and what a normal job for those of different ranks would have been.

The Legion

The core unit was a century which, given its name, supposedly had a hundred men, but more often numbered around eighty, due to injuries and sickness. Sixty was the minimum number of men in a century. As we saw, the V Macedonica had been hit hard by the Antonine Plague and had seen serious fighting over the years Artorius had been with the II Adiutrix, so its numbers should have been greatly reduced. The legion was commanded by Marcus Aurelius himself and, given the added challenge of fighting while also protecting the Emperor, it was probably close to full strength. In addition to a centurion, who gave commands from the back left of the century, there was an *optio*, a *signifer* and a *tesserarius* in the front line. The *optio* was the second in command of the century. The *signifer* marched in the front centre and carried the standard for the unit. This, often bearing symbols of awards or honours the century had earned, served as an assembly point for the soldiers if they became disoriented in battle. While someone was designated to take over carrying the standard if the original bearer fell, it was considered a major dishonour for a century to allow its *signifier* to be killed. The *tesserarius* was third in command of the century and when not on the battlefield handled most of the paperwork and background organization of the unit.

Six centuries formed a cohort. The most senior centurion in a cohort was also the unit's leader, the *praefectus cohortis*.[1] This is the rank with which Artorius could have started out if he had chosen to pursue the Equestrian *tres militae*, a path that would have landed him in a magisterial position – but he had other plans.

The legion was made up of nine cohorts of this nature. The tenth cohort, the one commanded by the *primus pilus*, or First Spear, was a different story. The First Cohort, as this special cohort was known, was twice the size of the regular group. Instead of six centuries it had five, each of which held twice the number of men, up to two hundred soldiers each. These were commanded by the top five centurions in the legion, with the most senior being the *primus pilus*. He was ninth in command of the legion as a whole, behind the *legatus* (general), which in Castus' case was Marcus Aurelius himself; the senior tribune (from the Senatorial class); the Camp Praefect (an Equestrian who tended to be a former

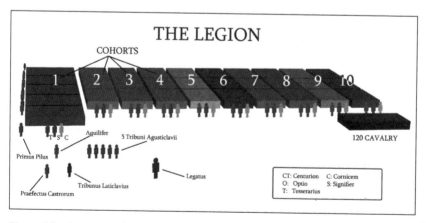

Fig. 2. The Structure of a Roman Legion. (W. Kinghan)

primus pilus), and five lower-ranking tribunes who were chosen from among the Equestrians.[2] This last is the second rank Artorius could have held in an administrative military cursus. But he chose a different path, and around AD 174 became *primus pilus* of the V Macedonica.

Primus Pilus

Obtaining this long-sought rank gave Artorius back his Equestrian status, and after one year he could have gone into the civil service, providing he had amassed enough wealth to maintain his social status. Perhaps he had not yet achieved this goal, or perhaps he simply enjoyed an active life. In any case, he chose to stay in the army, and this probably accounts for the way in which his career suddenly took an unusual turn.

In addition to the infantry, the cavalry for the legion was now also part of Artorius' responsibilities. This included any auxiliary units, which were made up of mounted draftees from different peoples who had allied themselves with the Romans. The regular Roman cavalry was commanded by a *duplicarius*, which means the officer got double the pay of the average rider, assisted by a *sesquiplicarius* who received pay and a half. He had assistants called *principales*, and *decurions* who led *turmas*, which were roughly the cavalry equivalent of centuries. Another type of auxiliary troop, called a *numerus*, wasn't organized on the Roman pattern.[3] Their value lay in the unique fighting styles of their peoples, something that was about to become extremely important for Artorius and directly involved the Sarmatians.

As *primus pilus*, c. AD 175, Artorius was included in the war councils with the Emperor as plans were made for the V Macedonica to attack the Iazyges. We should not forget that he may already have had a working knowledge of the Sarmatian culture, maybe even their language, from his early education and the presence of slaves from the same people. His time with the III Gallica and VI Ferrata had trained him to fight heavy cavalry akin to that used by the Sarmatians, and he had had recent experience on the terrain with the II Adiutrix and during his time with the V Macedonica.[4] He had a lot to bring to the table of that war council – not the least of which was his education in the Greek philosophy and culture from which his family was ultimately descended – both of which were revered by Marcus Aurelius and would have made Artorius stand out from the crowd.

The Romans continued to win battles against the Iazyges on the plain bounded by the Tisza and Danube rivers, and the Sarmatians, as they had been wont to do before and would do again, decided to switch their allegiance from the Marcommani and Quadi to the Romans. While the treaty was being negotiated it would have been Artorius' duty to entertain the ambassadors. Once again, his knowledge of their culture and language would have made him perfect for the job.

The Iazyges had two kings, Banadaspes and Zanticus, whose names appear to be titles. Banadaspes was in charge of the cavalry (Ban = Leader, aspes = horse), while the 'Zan' in Zanticus' name may have identified him as the leader of the people. The same construction appears in the name of Vannius (the king of the Iazyges who fought Tiberius), the fifth-century leader of the Alans, Sangiban of Gaul, and in the name of Lancelot's father, King Ban, in the Arthurian legends. The Romans were familiar with the concept of two kings since Romulus ruled alongside Tatius in their own history. They had also just come through a period with two emperors, Marcus Aurelius and Lucius Verus. The double office holder concept went as deep into their society as the position of *duo viri*, the magisterial office held by Marcus Artorius at Pompeii.

As part of the treaty, the Sarmatians returned 100,000 hostages to Marcus Aurelius, many of them civilians. Hostage taking was a common practice since there were no concentration camps in ancient times. High-ranking hostages were often placed at the courts of opponents of Rome in exchange for nobles of similar rank, so that they could learn their customs. Such a case resulted in Arminius, a Germanic officer under Varus during the time of Augustus, learning the Roman tactics well enough to defeat three legions in the Teutoborg Forest, a catastrophe that almost collapsed the Empire. Known as the 'Varus disaster' the event haunted imperial Rome throughout its history. This may be why

Plate 14. Sarmatian
prisoner from a
second-century
Roman Mausoleum.

Marcus Aurelius requested heavy cavalry rather than nobles in the treaty he struck with the Iazyges.[5]

One of the big mysteries of the time was how the Romans got a cavalry unit the size of a legion from the Tisza plain to Britannia. But this is what happened, and the probability is that this task fell primarily to Artorius, who as *primus pilus* in the Emperor's legion would have been assigned to escort the possibly disoriented Sarmatians to their new post.

Escort Duty

Artorius would have been well equipped to carry out this task. His knowledge of Sarmatian culture was almost certainly extensive by this time, and if he was indeed the centurion who defeated them on the Danube, and if he also played a significant role in the treaty struck with them by Marcus Aurelius, he would have earned their respect. Mounted, the Iazyges would have made good time compared to the legions: about 20 miles per day at leisure, roughly 50 miles per day at speed. Yet their herds of cattle and sheep, numbering well over ten thousand just to feed them, their yurt-like tents, which they carried on carts, and their weapons, since their horses could carry them and their armour for only so long, were the same problem the Parthians had. In other words, they could only travel as fast as their baggage train, possibly using the extra time for hunting to help feed the massive unit.

Ammianus Marcellinus (c. 330-c. 391) who had been a soldier and fought against the Sarmatians and the Roxolani, describes them perfectly in his *Res Gestae*:

> They have no hovels, and they don't care to use the plough, but they feed on meat and abundant milk by sitting on the wagons which are protected by curved covers made of bark... When they come to a grassy location, they arrange the floats in a circular shape and feed the beasts. After consuming the pastures, they transport their cities away, if this term can be used. On the wagons the males join the females and on them the children are born and raised. These wagons are their permanent homes and wherever they go they consider them their homes. They push the herds of oxen before them and graze them with the flocks; especially they take care of the breeding of horses. (Book XXXI, 2, 18)

The Romans were simply not set up to supply what their new allies needed in terms of housing and stabling, never mind transport. The Sarmatian women and old men drove the wagons while children helped the riders manage the herds: milking the animals, slaughtering, and so forth. In other words, this was a transplantation of an allied people. There is no way the Romans could have undertaken this if the Sarmatians considered themselves to be captives or conscripts, the words so often used to describe them. They would indeed have seen themselves as allies, something which presents a quite different picture to the more usual one of defeated prisoners forced to join the legions and controlled every step of the way by their new masters. Their commanders, however, were most certainly Roman, as was the man designated with the task of getting them to Britannia: Lucius Artorius Castus.

These were a hardy folk. Though they called the grasslands home, they could travel the paths marked for them by Roman roads with relative ease, though they surely left a trail like a swarm of locusts passing through in their wake. The Romans were fortunate that the Sarmatians preferred to eat meat, relying on their own herds rather than stripping the nearby farmers of everything they owned. Still, the trampling to either side of the roads would have been significant. Yet those same roads would have enabled the carts, drawn by oxen, to keep pace with the rest of the settlers. They would have had some horsemen to help the Romans scout for stopping places, familiar with the needs of their people and likely mounted on some of the famed war horses that had been bred in the mountains and who handled terrain like goats rather than the plains-bred mounts that served as remounts and food.

Artorius would have had some mounted centurions and Roman cavalry with him on escort duty and papers authorizing the transport of the Sarmatians to ensure easy passage and to reassure the people through whose lands they passed that they were not an invading force. The route would have taken them west to the Adriatic Highway, through Dalmatia, after which they would have skirted the Alps, following the Roman roads west to Lugdunum (modern Lyon) in Gaul, a place to which Artorius would return at the very end of his career. From there they had to travel north to the coast and to Port Julius, where they would have used merchant ships to cross the Channel to Britannia. Somewhere along the way 2,500 of the 8,00 Sarmatians split off and proceeded south to the area around Lugdunum (see chapter 9). How many trips those ships made and how they convinced the horses and livestock to board them for the roughly eight-hour journey remains unknown, but Artorius is the one who worked out how to do it – knowledge that would serve him well in his next post.

Once in Britannia the huge party headed north to Eboracum (modern York), where they reported to the *legatus* (legate) of the VI Victrix and the governor of the province. From there they

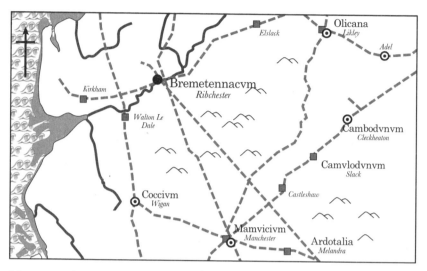

Map 4. Roads to Bremetennacum and Local Forts.

continued west across the Pennine Hills, until they reached the fort of Bremetennacum, which guarded an important set of crossroads, meeting in what is now Ribchester, in Lancashire, England.[6]

Artorius' arrival here would have created something of a sensation among the local populace; in the future it would become part of the legend that grew from his memory.

Settling the Sarmatians

The fort at Bremetennacum was originally built around the time Pompeii was destroyed in AD 79. Only Roman soldiers lived inside it, so all of the members of their baggage train and the other individuals who supported them occupied a *vicus* (village) outside the walls. Consequently, it is not surprising that the vicus at Bremetennacum dates from shortly after the time the fort was built.[7] Yet upon the arrival of the Sarmatians a new sort of camp would have had to be established, since 5,500 horsemen and their entourage would not fit in either the fort or the existing vicus.

Outside the fort to the North the remains of a number of timber buildings were uncovered. They are considered to be part of the vicus which stood next to an area levelled and covered in gravel towards the middle of the second century. This is best interpreted

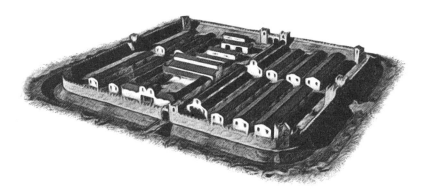

Plate 15. Bremetennacum. (W. Kinghan)

as a parade ground, almost certainly associated with the arrival of the Sarmatian heavy cavalry garrison. The site certainly extends beneath the present village. Indeed, the vicus appears to have extended along the main road to the north over Longridge Fell and as far as the Forest of Bowland. Remains of at least two bath houses were also found, with the addition of a circular *laconicum*, or steam room. All of this indicates the arrival of a large mobile force that was destined to settle long-term at the fort.

The landscape around Bremetennacum is largely flat – good land for herds and for pitching tents, and the Sarmatian cavalry could not possibly have been housed inside the fort, which held only five hundred men. Not only was the fort of insufficient size, but there was also no way the Romans were going to get steppe horses to stand packed three or four to a stall. We can assume therefore that use was made of the flat plains around the area, to build and maintain an enclosure that could stable an extensive herd.

The nature of the nearby area still known as the Fylde was ripe for development, aided by the presence of a Roman road that passed across it from Ribchester to Kirkham. As R. I. Richmond, the greatest expert on the area, states: 'The Fylde therefore presents the most suitable land for settling the Sarmatae: there was hardly another area like it in Northern Britain, and its existence no doubt decided the site for the settlement.'[8]

Though the climate was probably wetter than that which the Sarmatians were used to, they had just come from terrain where the entire Danube had frozen solid enough to fight a battle on it. In contrast, the Romans who came with them had little tolerance for Britannia's climate. Among the remains of personal letters found at the fortress of Vindolanda, on Hadrian's Wall, are several requesting extra socks and trousers to help against the cold. Artorius himself probably had no more love for the cold than he had had for the unbearable heat he had endured in the Middle East, given that he chose a much more moderate climate in which to retire. As for trousers, the Sarmatians already came equipped with those and the heavy leather coats and boots to go with them. They also, in their herds, had the raw materials necessary to make more. Their nomadic lifestyle lent itself well to their establishment in Britannia.

The Rise of Bremetennacum

The commander of Bremetennacum was given a strange title: *praepositus numeri et regionaris* (something like commander of the foreign group and the region where they were settled).[9] Bremetennacum is the only place in Britannia where this rank is documented. By the late third century the title would drop the *numerus* reference and simply become the commander of the fort and the region, an issue that has puzzled classicists and archaeologists alike over the years.[10] Since the vicus became known as *Bremetennacum veteranorum Sarmatarum* (Bremetennacum of the Sarmatian veterans) c. AD 200, the Sarmatian *numeri* had probably become Roman citizens by this time and were allowed to retire to the site. What is clear is that they settled there and became established enough for the region to be named after them.

Some soldiers were known to serve in the legions for as long as thirty or forty years.[11] *Auxilia* served a standard twenty-five years, and the *numeri* were modelled on them. The Roman army discharged its soldiers every other year, so twenty-five and twenty-six were the most common number of years for terms of service.[12] There is every reason to believe that the Sarmatians who were recruited in AD 175 were discharged around AD 200, which may account for the reduction in the rank of the commander at Bremetennacum at this time.[13]

Plate 16. Sarmatians, Dacians and Scythians as pictured by Albert Kretschmer and Carl Rohrbach.

While it is accepted wisdom that the Sarmatian-Iazyges did not become citizens upon the completion of their twenty-five years of service,[14] the number of inscriptions bearing the name Marcus Aurelius that show up in Britannia, starting around AD 200, suggest otherwise. Anyone taken captive under a particular Emperor was forced to take his name upon discharge, followed by the cognomen of his choice. That these former soldiers did not understand the

Roman naming practices is demonstrated by the fact that some took a *praenomen* as a cognomen, as in the person named Marcus Aurelius Lucius, who is described as 'a horseman'.[15] Another bears the cognomen Castus, suggesting that this name was important to the Sarmatians, and pointing clearly to Artorius' association with them.[16] Veterans could earn citizenship by serving in the Roman army for three to four years after their discharge, and there is no reason to think the Sarmatians stopped fighting. This is highly likely to be what they did, retiring to the *vicus* at Bremetennacum, and giving it its name.[17]

Several other inscriptions refer to the Sarmatians. When they were drafted into the Roman army, they were all expected to take the name of the Emperor – in this instance, Marcus Aurelius. The only way to distinguish them would have been by the cognomen of their choice, which would become permanent upon the completion of their twenty-five years of service. This explains the inordinate number of inscriptions to men named Marcus Aurelius in Britain, including Aurelius Severus,[18] M. Aurelius Ianuarius and M. Aurelius Victor.[19] M. Aurelius Victor's tombstone depicts an apparently naked horseman wielding a sword; the horse's tail is long and appears to be wrapped.[20] The horse's short mane is also consistent with Sarmatian practices rather than with Roman cavalry.[21] This may be the same Aurelius Victor mentioned in an inscription from Halton Chesters.[22] Another Aurelius Victor is mentioned in an inscription from Risingham, which can be dated to c. 278.[23]

While Hadrian granted citizenship to entire families,[24] the citizenship of the horsemen was only extended to one wife, and no children were included in the grant. Children born *castris* ('in camp', that is, in the vicus at Bremetennacum)[25] and boys who came in with the warriors, could also become Roman citizens if they joined the army at the fort, thus supplying recruits, and it's quite possible that the Sarmatian families followed this tradition.

Something curious occurs with the forts around Bremetennacum after the arrival of the Sarmatians. The garrisons of the other forts protecting the area move on, with the Sarmatians taking their place, creating the 'region' which Bremetennacum is known to have controlled.[26] Certainly such an enormous group could not have been

Plate 17. Dupondius showing Marcus Aurelius and the submission of the Sarmatians.

settled at one fort designed to hold less than one tenth its number of warriors, despite the extensions to the vicus uncovered in recent excavations. After the civil war between Albinus and Septimius Severus, which we will discuss later, in which roughly half of the Sarmatian *numeri* died, the outermost circle of forts, including those at Kirkham, Elslack, Olicana (Ilkley) Camulodunum (a candidate for Camelot) and Manvicium (Manchester) were re-garrisoned, and by the late third century, when the commander's rank no longer contains the title 'of the *numerus*', the rest of the forts around Bremetennacum were once more at full strength, suggesting that the Sarmatians were no longer covering for them.

There are at least three specific references to Bremetennacum in the records that have survived from the period of Roman rule in Britain. In the *Notitia Dignitatum*, which dates from the fourth century AD and lists the forts in Britannia along with the legions attached to them, the *numerus* of the fort had become the *cuneus Sarmatarum*; in another document, known as the *Antonine Itinerary,* it was *Bremetonnacum*; in the *Ravenna Cosmography*, which lists place names across Britannia it is *Bresnetenaci veteranorum*.[27]

Several inscribed tombstones were discovered in the immediate area during early archaeological excavations in and around the area of the fort. Several of those buried there are shown to be of

Sarmatian origin, and the fact that these are Roman-style cremation burials rather than those typically practised by the Sarmatians themselves, indicates just how embedded in Roman lifestyles they had become. Though now lost, one inscription (CIL vii, 229) in particular, gives us pause:

> By this earth is covered she who was once Aelia Matrona, who lived 28 years, 2 months and 8 days, and her son Marcus Julius Maximus who lived 6 years, 3 months and 20 days, and her mother Campania Dubitata, who lived 50 years. Julius Maximus, of the Sarmatian cavalry unit, attendant to the governor, placed this as the memorial of a husband to an incomparable wife, to a son most dutiful to his father and to a most attached mother-in-law.[28]

As this stone is no longer extant to be dated, we cannot be sure when it was erected, though the mingling of Roman and Sarmatian names tells us it was after the arrival of the *numerus* from across the Channel from Gaul. Though we can only speculate at this point, it's even possible that the man who raised the tomb, clearly out of respect for the memory of his family, could well have been active when Artorius was again in Britannia in AD 181 (see below). The name Campania Dubitata also suggests someone from the area where the Artorii were often domiciled, though again we cannot be certain of this.

A second tombstone, also lost, but recorded by Mommsen as C.I.L vii, 230, reads:

D [IS] M [ANIBUS]
[e]q (possibly trooper)
AL [AE] SARMATA [RUM]

'To the shades of the departed [name missing] .... Trooper of the Sarmatian cavalry regiment...'[29]

Importantly, the stone bore a relief that represents the owner of the grave dressed in the scaled armour of the Sarmatians, stabbing a fallen adversary with his long *kontos*.

Plate 18. Sarmatian
Warrior on a Tombstone
from Bremetannacum.

Several other inscriptions refer to Mars, who is known to have paralleled the nameless Sarmatian war god. Finally, though it dates from a period after that in which Artorius was active in the area, a monument dedicated to Maponus, a god of Gallic origin widely worshipped in Britannia and named by the Sarmatians Oitósuros, twinned by the Romans with Apollo, reads as follows:

> To the holy god Apollo Maponus, for the safety of our sovereign lord and of the regiment of the Sarmatian horsemen of Bremetennacum, Gordian's own, Aelius Antoninus, born at Melitene, Centurion of the VI legion, Victrix [erected this pillar].[30]

This tells us that a serving officer born in Melitene, modern day Malatia on the Euphrates river, erected a monument to a god who was more of Britannia than Rome. He names the place where it stood as Bremetannacum and the serving regiment as Sarmatian horsemen and dates the period as during the reign of the Emperor Gordian (AD 238-244). This shows that the Sarmatians were still very much in evidence nearly seventy years after they were escorted there by Artorius, and that they were part of the actions against a new enemy, which we shall examine in Chapters 6 and 7.

Tracking inscriptions that refer to the heirs of the Sarmatians who adopted Marcus Aurelius as a name into the third century shows that some went on to serve in the XX Valeria Victrix, while others remained in the VI Victrix. These were still horsemen, some of whom are depicted in steppe garb.[31] Those who now appear 'naked' in the carvings were probably originally shown in scale-mail, as are the Sarmatians elsewhere in the Empire, but the details have faded from the carving with the passage of time.[32] We shall explore the fate of the remaining Sarmatian conscripts, and how the area where they were based also associates them with stories of the later Arthurian period in a later chapter.

Once he had seen to it that the Sarmatians and Iazyges were settled into their new homes, a task which could have taken as long as two years, including travel, Artorius was free to return to normal duties. Also, around this time, he become eligible to do something the average Roman soldier could not: he could legally marry. He may have entered into an arranged marriage, perhaps with a father-in-law who needed a male heir, similar to the way Arthur is said to have married Guinevere, daughter of King Leodegrance in the later legends, thus forming an alliance between his own kingdom and that of Northumbria. Though we cannot know for certain either way, Artorius may have married either in Britannia, or back in Italy, where he was to move next to take up an even more prestigious post. A marriage could also have brought him the income he needed to leave the military, assuming he failed to earn a high enough post on his own. But Artorius need not have worried. Already unusual, he was about to distinguish himself far above most of the Equestrians of his day and to become a legend whose actions would be remembered long after his death.

5

PRAEPOSITUS

In AD 177 Artorius made a huge and important move in his career. He was reassigned to a Roman naval fleet, or *classis*. Not just any *classis*, but the Empire's premier fleet, stationed at Misenum (modern Baiae) near the city of Puteoli, where the Artorii had their luxury seaside villa. This fleet was the size of a legion, numbering roughly 5,000 men, about the same size as the unit of Sarmatians Artorius had just escorted to Britannia. He also moved into a very unusual position, one that wasn't in the regular hierarchy of the fleet: *praepositus*. This rank could mean one – or all – of five things:

1. He commanded the fleet in the absence of the *praefectus classis* (admiral).
2. He commanded the detachment at Puteoli.
3. He commanded the detachment at Ostia.
4. He commanded the detachment at Rome.
5. He commanded naval forces on land.

The first would involve him staying in Misenum when the praefect needed to be somewhere else. Since this was during the reign of Commodus when things were frequently turned upside down, it is entirely possible that there was no civilian praefect in charge of the fleet, so that the highest-ranking Equestrian officer, the praepositus (in this case Artorius), would have been in actual command. This would have put him in charge of the protection of the massive merchant ships that ferried grain from Egypt to the heart of the Empire. Artorius would have also overseen the repair and building of ships, the training of sailors and all the other activities of the port.

The second option would have been for him to be in charge of the two cohorts permanently stationed at Puteoli. Given the nature of his career to date, and that his family had a luxury villa there, this is a reasonable post for him to have been granted. The purpose of these cohorts was primarily to deal with any fires that broke out in the area, though they probably also helped maintain the famous Flavian arena on the site.

The third option meant that Artorius would have been in charge of the two permanent legionary cohorts at Ostia, which at the time oversaw the transport of cargo up the Tiber River into Rome, as well as dealing with any outbreaks of fire.

The fourth option was to be the commander of the naval forces in Rome. There the legion had its own barracks near the Coliseum, fought simulated naval battles and maintained a canopy over the arena to protect audiences from the weather. They also moved weapons through the city and probably again served as fire-fighters.

The fifth position, which would have seen Artorius overseeing naval forces on land, should have fallen to a lower ranking officer, supplying Marcus Aurelius' troops in the Marcomannic Wars. However, the Danube, Black Sea, and Ravenna fleets seem to have taken care of this, which means it is unlikely that Artorius held that position.

In the first instance, Artorius' men would have been at sea when they were not training at the base. Contrary to Hollywood depictions, the Roman navy had nothing to do with slaves rowing galleys under the sting of the lash. The navy was a separate branch of the military. The members were known as 'marines' and they had to be free men. If a man was a slave, he had to be granted his freedom before joining. This same rule applied to the legions on land, and the various fleets were considered to be legions on water.

In Artorius' time there were eleven other fleets, situated mostly on the frontier, while the Classis Misenensis was stationed in the Portus Julius harbour at Misenum on the northwest point of the Bay of Naples (see Map 5). The second praetorian fleet was the Classis Ravennatium, which, as its name implies, was harboured at Ravenna on the Adriatic.

The crews of the naval ships over which Artorius had control were called a 'century', but unlike the century on land, the number of members related not to the unit but rather to the size of the vessel, with the smaller boats only serving as *vexillations* (detachments). The smallest boat, the *scapha*, from which we get our modern word 'skiff', was mainly used to ferry people from a larger vessel to another, or to a beach.

Next in size was the *navis oneraria* (literally 'burden ship'), a sailing vessel that carried cargo. It had one bank of oars in case the wind died or blew in the wrong direction. One massive sail was set amidship while a much smaller one was on the bow to aid with steering. These vessels moved cargo, mainly on rivers but also from seaport to seaport if using them was more economical than using one of the larger ships.

There were also a host of specialized craft, smaller and with fewer oars, designed to navigate specific types of waterways, such as canals, rivers, and coastal estuaries.

Merchant ships were massive, lumbering vessels that required the protection of navy warships. In addition to moving wine, oil, and other commodities to the farthest ports of the Empire, they carried the grain that was the lifeblood of Rome. Another member of the Artorii, buried at Puetoli, and a native of Alexandria, served in the Misenum Fleet; he was typical of many sailors who seem to have been recruited in disproportionate numbers from Egypt. This is probably because the men born in Campania and similar provinces were predestined for a land-based legion, as Artorius was for the III Gallica, while one born in the Egyptian province would be more likely to be drafted into the navy. The ships also carried their precious cargo to Ostia, much nearer Rome, during the years the grain trade passed through that port, where various Artorii served in various capacities, including as shipbuilders. These were the main type of ships that would have transported the Sarmatians to Britannia, a technology lost to the West from the fall of Rome until the time of William the Conqueror, though there may have been one that King Arthur used to get his knights back and forth to the Continent.[1]

In fact, while the later medieval Arthur uses a small craft to get Excalibur from the Lady of the Lake, there are no sea battles, which makes sense since most of the boats pictured in the art are depicted as rather small and are certainly incapable of carrying armoured horses along with their knights.

In later tradition, the Arthur of legend appears to have the option of travelling by ship at the back of his mind a good deal of the time. He repeatedly transports his knights back and forth to the Continent to fight Roman legions, battle giants, chase after Lancelot and Guinevere and so forth. This type of troop movement between Britain and the Continent indicates the presence of a standing navy, something that is absent from most of Europe from the early fourth until the tenth century. Some scholars have argued that Riothamus, the figure championed by the historian Geoffrey Ashe as the historical Arthur, may have come from Brittany rather than Britain because of the problem of getting horses across the Channel. Other nominees for a historical figure behind the tales stay rather firmly rooted to the land, be that Dyfed (Wales), Cornwall, Yorkshire, Ireland or somewhere else. At best, they sail with a few knights along a waterway in a riverboat. They are not moving over a thousand horsemen and armoured knights across the English Channel.

Yes, there are Saxon burials in boats that date to the sixth century, while warriors from Northumberland were able to sail to the Isle of Man, Ireland and elsewhere in the seventh century. Vikings are largely everywhere by the ninth century, and by the tenth century ship-to-ship battles are recorded, indicating that Britain at last had a navy capable of battle at sea again. But from the early fourth until the tenth century, no ruler in Britain commanded a fleet capable of shipping over a thousand horses. Yet in the late second century, Artorius did just that.

The next set of ships was named after the number of banks of oars they had on each side. There were *biremes, triremes, quadriremes, quinqueremes,* and *hexaremes,* with two, three, four, five and six banks of oars respectively. The flagship of each fleet was initially a *hexareme.* The bulk of the fleet was made up of *triremes, quadriremes,* and *quinqueremes,* while the faster and more agile *biremes* tended to be used to chase pirates.

The thoroughbreds of the Roman fleet were the *liburnians,* named for the Liburniae, who invented them and gave their name to Liburnia, the province that Artorius would eventually govern. They were light and wickedly fast, estimated to attain speeds of seven knots by oar and a stunning fourteen knots by sail, a little over 9 mph and 18 mph respectively. They were prized by Senators and high-ranking travellers for their ability to make journeys mercifully short. All the warships were outfitted with one main sail and a foresail, modelled after the *oneraria* (commercial ships for transport). They also had a ram that jutted out from their bows beneath the waterline to be used in ramming enemy vessels.

Rome had no naval competition in the Mediterranean in the second century, so the *quinqueremes* and *hexaremes* fell into disuse. The biggest problems for Rome mainly consisted of pirates attacking merchant and grain ships from the islands around Greece and Crete, while the Moors were increasingly active off Mauretania and the Iberian Peninsula. The faster and more agile *biremes* were required to confront them.

As for the military personnel, the *praefectus classis* ('admiral of the fleet'; also known as the *procurator classis*) was chosen from the Equestrian class, just as with the procurator in charge of Egypt. He had to be extremely wealthy, holding at least 200,000 sesterces (£295,0000, $350,000) annually, twice as much as Artorius had made as a *primus pilus.* A *praepositus,* the naval equivalent of the senior tribune in a legion on land, reported directly to the praefect, who chose him when he was not himself the officer in charge, in which case he reported directly to the Emperor. In the Classis Misenensis, because it was a praetorian fleet and its officers were appointed by the Emperor, this office was held by an Equestrian rather than by a member of the Senatorial class. This is yet more evidence that makes Artorius an Equestrian of this rank.

Next in rank was the *nauarchus*, the naval equivalent of *a primus pilus*, who commanded a squadron of ten ships. The title also applied to executive officers. Each ship was commanded by a *trierachus* (captain). Parallel to him was the centurion who commanded the marines, as opposed to the rowers, who were distinguished from the fighting men. As in the legion, this centurion had an *optio*. A *beneficianus*, rather than a *decurion*, oversaw the administrative work needed for the unit.

The organization on each ship was closer to that of the auxiliaries because of the different sizes of the vessels and the different uses to which they were put. Every ship would have a *gubernator* (pilot or helmsman), a *celeusta* who supervised the rowers, and a *proreta* who stood lookout on the bow. Larger ships would have additional specialists, such as an *iatros* (ship's doctor).

The Misenum Fleet

Roman history is constantly overshadowed by its myths. As Virgil recorded in the *Aeneid*, the Romans believed they were descended from the Trojan hero Aeneas. But the greatest hero of Troy was Hector, and one of his closest companions was Misenus, who travelled with Aeneas to Italy as his *buccinator* (trumpeter). The Roman buccina was a curled brass horn that was used to give orders in normal Roman military life as well as on the battlefield,[2] so this was an important reference for the legionaries.

In one of those ill-fated contests between mortals and Greco-Roman gods, while the fleet was docked at Cumae, Misenus challenged the sea god Triton, who played a conch shell, to a musical battle. Misenus, naturally, lost and was drowned as punishment. This death occurs at a critical point in the epic. It causes Aeneas, uncertain how to celebrate his fallen friend, to seek the Golden Bough, which he takes to the Sibyl at Cumae. She tells him to cremate and bury Misenus' body on the peninsula before his soul enters the Underworld. Aeneas obeys, and from this story came the name of the Misenum Fleet.

Adjacent to the site where Misenus' ashes were scattered, near Puteoli, are the Campi Flegrei ('burning fields'). The entire area reeks of sulphur, and new volcanos are still forming to this day – vents of a super-volcano – which accounts for the roughly semi-circular shape of the bay. It may also be the reason for the choice of this site as the last resting place of Misenus' ashes. One of the vents is Vesuvius, which is still active. The geothermal activity made it possible to construct naturally heated Roman baths, one of which was built by Nero and is still in use to this day. It is certain that Artorius himself would have made use of these baths, given their proximity to the naval base.

Also on the curve of the volcano is Mount Etna, where according to Italian tradition Morgan Le Fey watches over the wounded King Arthur and from where she casts the *Fata Morgana* ('Deed of Morgan'), a mirage that appears as fairy castles above the horizon in the Strait of Messina (not to be confused with Misenum). While Arthur's Seat in Edinburgh is an extinct volcano (It last erupted sixty-five million years ago), there is no reason to believe that this inspired the connection of Arthur with volcanoes; however, it could have been a memory of Artorius' time in the region during his posting to the Misenum fleet.

This enchanted coast, particularly the north-western end, became the site of numerous luxury villas, including one belonging to the Artorii family. The massive port at Naples received the grain shipments, which were then transported to Rome under the watchful eye of the Misenum fleet. It was at Misenum that Caligula lined up boats to create a 'bridge' over which he could ride his horse across the bay. Later, as we saw, Nero used an officer from the same fleet to murder his mother, Agrippina, who was associated with the Artorii closely enough to raise a memorial to one of the family. In other words, the location has connections with both history and legend.

The harbour at Misenum was in three parts. The first was the Portus Julius where the on-duty ships docked. The second was a large lake, Lucrinus, and a beach where the soldiers trained. The third was a lake, Avernus, where the ships were taken for repairs. Because of negative bradyseism, whereby the gradual uplift of parts of the earth's surface and the filling or emptying of underground chambers of magma in the area, much of what was visible in Artorius' time is now underwater. It is still possible to walk around Lake Avernus and view the ruins of the temple of Apollo that once stood on its shore. Such an excursion gives you a true sense of how intimate and interconnected the harbours were.

Avernus was also believed to be the entrance to the underworld and is portrayed as such by Virgil. The name comes from the Greek word *aornos* (ἄορνος < a - 'no' + ornis 'bird'), meaning 'without birds', since according to tradition any bird flying over the lake was destined to fall dead, possibly as a result of the volcanic gases that fill the air. The site had a dark and unsettling atmosphere. Indeed, the shape and alignment of these lakes with the other volcanoes in the area suggest that they are yet more vents of the super-volcano, with the three used by the Misenum fleet now filled with seawater.

The Misenum Fleet was one of the two praetorian fleets, which meant that it was directly available to the Emperor at all times. This is part of why it was divided among several ports along the

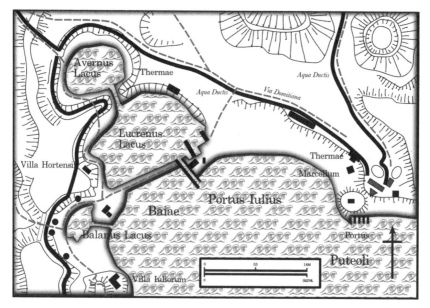

Map 5. The Naval Base at Misenum.

coast of Italy, including Ostia and Puteoli. Its main port was, as its name implies, at Misenum. There, it was required to have ships in place at any moment in case the Emperor wished to embark.

The fleet gave its name to the Misenum Sea, which included the area between its port and the islands of Corsica and Sardinia, yet during the time of the Adoptive Emperors the smaller ships of the fleets were mainly used on the Tigris and Euphrates to support the Parthian War, and on the Danube and the Tisza in support of the Marcomannic Wars. In addition to running supplies to the Middle East and along the Adriatic Sea, docking at Split on the coast of Liburnia, the Misenum Fleet, particularly in the time of Marcus Aurelius, protected the all-important trade routes, frequently crossing paths with the other praetorian fleet, based at Ravenna. The classis Ravennatium had 250 ships and also drew many of its crewmembers from Egypt. The Misenum fleet would have had even more vessels, given its premier status. The II Adiutrix, in which Artorius had served, was created from the Classis Ravennatium, and Septimius Severus used the Ravenna fleet in the East from AD 192 to AD 193 and the Misenum fleet in his battles against the self-styled Emperor Pescennius Niger. In other words, the two fleets intertwined rather than keeping to specific territories and were also much in demand.

Puteoli

The connection between the Artorii and Puteoli dates back to at least Republican times (509 to 27 BC). From there they conducted business with the bankers of Pompeii and circulated with the Senators and imperial families, who had their pleasure villas in the region, moving between there and their inland homes.

We cannot be sure where the villa rustica that belonged to the Artorii family was, but it would have been fairly close to Puteoli so that produce could be easily transported to the maritime villa. This would have been far simpler than their main home. Entering through the main gate you would have stepped into a courtyard, off which were four rooms used for horses and storage. On the far side of the courtyard was the entrance to the main part of the villa. This included a reception room behind which would have been the *tricinilum* (dining room). To the far right and far left were two rooms that may have served as a kitchen and an office. Between these was an *ala* (hallway/wing) that led to the rear portion of the villa. Here there would have been bedrooms and a stairway leading to a second storey where slaves would sleep.

The maritime villa on the other hand was a far more spectacular affair (see Plate 19). Massive and opulent, the main entrance faced the nearest road. From there you stepped into the atrium, which featured a ceiling open to the sky with the roof slanted to collect water in a pool beneath it. The family altar was located to the right as you entered. The patriarch's study, where he received his clients, was located to the left of the entrance. Small rooms that served as bedrooms were positioned in even numbers to each side. As in the villa rustica, a triclinium opened off this space for dining in an indoor space. Directly opposite the main door was an opening to a magnificent garden that may have had a water feature in its centre.

This space, as in the larger *villa urbana* (city villa), such as that where the Emperor Commodus practised fighting with his gladiators, was surrounded by a colonnade leading to several smaller rooms. Then, depending on the topography, a huge space

Plate 19. A Typical Roman Coastal Villa at Brejun, Croatia (Begović Dvorzak).

with a pool stretched out as an architectural surprise in what would otherwise have looked like a more modest house. Here the colonnades were open to the ocean views. Balconies and other viewing features were incorporated around the edge, and benches and other conversation areas surrounded the pool. Statuary would have decorated this open-air space, and there would have been a splendid triclinium for outdoor dining. To the rear would have been the kitchen. Storage rooms were likely underground. Some extremely wealthy owners had fishponds and private baths. The slaves may have slept underground in these villas, which could be three storeys tall.

The Artorii appear to have acquired their villa shortly before or during the reign of Augustus, and in Castus' childhood it would have been owned by his grandfather, Marcus Artorius Pricillus Vicasius Sabidianus.

With the exception of Capua, Puteoli had the most magnificent amphitheatre outside of Rome (see Plate 20). This was where the Emperors went to watch the Games when they were not in the City. The Flavian amphitheatre at Puteoli still survives. Built at the same time as Rome's famous Coliseum, Puteoli's arena was the third largest in Italy.[3] Some of the mechanisms and cages that hauled wild animals from the underground to the arena floor are well preserved. The proximity to the harbour and the established shipping routes between the northern coast of Africa and Puteoli made it far easier to hold spectacles with exotic beasts at this arena than at the Coliseum and Capua. Seating at least 50,000 people, it used massive sails, which were operated by cohorts from the Misenum fleet, to shield the audience from the sun and rain.

These sails, along with the wood used in all buildings, made the city extremely susceptible to fire. Since there were so many wealthy people in it, and the harbour itself was so valuable to the Romans, the primary duty of the cohorts stationed there was almost certainly firefighting.

Fortunately, the ocean was right there with plenty of water. In addition, there was easy access to the major aqueduct that supplied the city with water. Chains of men would have stretched from the water source to the fire, passing buckets back and forth until the

Plate 20. The Coliseum with mock naval battle and sliding roof.

flames were extinguished. With two cohorts to do the work, it's unlikely that any of the wealthy residents ever had to join in the effort.

The fleet itself, being made of wood, was also highly flammable, which is why personnel dedicated to firefighting were stationed on each vessel as well as at the ports. This training would serve Artorius well when he took charge of the massive port of Spalato (modern Split) in Liburnia. When Ostia ceased to be the main grain trade port, Puteoli once more became the premier destination for the vital shipments.

Julius Caesar switched the designated destination for the grain trade from Puteoli to Ostia, transporting food to Rome via the canal through Tarrachina. Tiberius made improvements to the harbour and added a forum to the city. Two cohorts of the Misenum Fleet were stationed there in their seemingly universal roles as guards and firefighters.

There was a problem with the location of Ostia, though: the port tended to fill with silt. In AD 113 Trajan attempted to address the issue by dredging the port and rebuilding the harbour in the shape of a hexagon. The Romans, however, couldn't do anything about the waves that were far larger than those in the Bay of Naples. Try as they might, their walls were no match for Neptune. By the third century they gave up and switched the grain destination back to Puteoli, which means that Artorius, if he were stationed there, would have ended up commanding cohorts in the declining port of Ostia. He had family there as well. As elsewhere, the Artorii of Ostia held municipal offices and intermarried with the well-to-do and politically powerful. The post would have been important, but unlikely to be prestigious enough to set Artorius up for the promotions that were to follow. That means we need to look at a third possibility for his base of operations: Rome.

Commodus and the Coliseum

Rivalling Caligula and Nero, Commodus was one of the most insane Emperors the Roman Empire produced. According to Cassius Dio, the reign of Marcus Aurelius' son did not begin badly, and following the death of his father in AD 180, things went smoothly for a time. Then, for some unknown reason, Commodus started to lose his mind. Believing he was a reincarnation of Hercules, he spent a great deal of time at the Coliseum in Rome and other arenas wherever he travelled, proving his strength and heroic nature to his citizens by taking part in the games.

The new Emperor trained in a small, private arena at the villa of the Quintilli, whose previous owners he murdered in order to acquire the property. The arena he would have trained in when he visited the seaside villas on the Bay of Naples was at Puteoli. That meant that as of 180 AD, whether Artorius was in Puteoli or Rome, he was directly under Commodus' nose – and yet, somehow, he survived.

Perhaps Commodus had not gone completely insane yet while Artorius was there, and memories of this capable officer seem to have stuck with the Emperor. Whatever the case, Artorius managed to curry favour with his new master, as we shall see when we explore his ascent up the next rung of the ladder.

It seems likely that Artorius' placement in the Misenum fleet brought him into contact with Commodus. Both would have spent some time in the greatest arena of the time, the Coliseum.

An architectural wonder, it had four tiers of seating. Starting at the bottom was where the Emperor and Senators sat. The next tier up was for the Equestrians. The third was for freedmen, and the fourth for women and Roman citizens who were not part of the other groups. The area above the arena itself was open to the elements, and slaves worked in the cells and tunnels beneath the structure to raise animals and usher gladiators onto the wooden, sand-covered arena floor.

This was also where you would find the sailors, manipulating the Velarium, the massive set of sails that shielded the audience from sun and rain. In the time of Commodus, the Circus Maximus had such a shade on it, and the sailors operated these though pulleys and ropes in both structures. This may explain why two cohorts from the Misenum Fleet and two from the fleet at Ravenna were stationed in Rome.

Perhaps for this reason the barracks for the sailors of the Misenum fleet, the Castra Misenatium, were placed near the Coliseum. Those for the Classis Ravennatium were across the Tiber. The sailors from the two fleets, in addition to operating the Velarium, participated in mock naval battles, where the floor of the amphitheatre was flooded as part of the games. Their ships were probably those used on the canals between Rome and Ostia since they were small and would fit in the Coliseum, in addition to being in proximity to the venue.

The sailors drilled on their ships, using the beat of drums and chanting to keep time, techniques that were employed in altering the position of different portions of the Velarium. And in command of all of this was a *praepositus*, almost certainly Artorius. A type of bronze 'stamp' presumably used to identify goods shipped to or from Artorius' home, and bearing his name, was discovered in Rome in 1825 and is currently housed in the Louvre in Paris. It utilizes the same spelling variant we find in 'gladi' on the main inscription from his mausoleum, as we shall see. In this case, what should read' Lucii Artorii Castii,' 'to Lucius Artorius Castus', the label reads 'Luci Artori Casti', which dates it to the same period as the main inscription and proves that Artorius was, for at least part of his career, in Rome.[4]

Plate 21. The Artorius Stamp (base) © Musée du Louvre/ AGER Service d'étude et de documentation.

Plate 22. The Artorius Stamp (top) © Musée du Louvre/ AGER Service d'étude et de documentation.

Marriage

Since we have an inscription to Lucius Artorius Pius Maximus, who seems to have been a direct descendant of our Artorius, we may assume that at some point in his life he got married and had children. Given the marriage laws of Rome, now that he had passed the rank of *primus pilus* he was no longer forbidden to marry by his military rank. As praepositus of the Misenum

Fleet he not only had his first opportunity to marry but was required to. Ostia provided little in the way of high society where it would be suitable for an officer of such high standing to seek a bride. Rome, with Commodus beginning to slip into madness, was downright dangerous. But Puteoli, with the family villa to impress a potential father-in-law and a crowd of wealthy neighbours, would have provided Artorius with the perfect hunting ground.

For a Roman of Artorius' status, love would not have entered into the equation. The law said that he had to marry a woman when he was between thirty and fifty years of age. In the case of most men with military careers, they tended to marry in their late twenties or early thirties, and their brides seem to have been in their early twenties. With Artorius at somewhere near the middle of the expected age for him to take a wife (he would have been thirty-six or thirty-seven at this time), he certainly did so, just as Arthur was required to take a queen.

The three things that defined marriage in ancient Rome were citizenship, property, and children. Artorius was a citizen, and his Equestrian rank made it extremely unlikely that he would go looking for a non-citizen to marry. Given his career to this point, he was almost certainly lacking in the property department. Since he built his own villa in Dalmatia, his wife does not seem to have brought any property to the marriage – at least nothing significant in the way of land. That leaves children. Artorius probably did something the rest of his family was infamous for doing - marrying for political advantage.

Once Artorius or his family located a suitable bride, the father of the bride and groom had to give their consent. The bride would have brought a dowry with her, just as Guinevere brought the Round Table (made for her father, Leodegrance) to Arthur, and it would have remained in her control instead of passing to her husband. To avoid paying high taxes upon leaving the military, Artorius needed to sire three children, something his wife would have been in favour of since she obtained the *jus liberorum*, expanded legal control over her own life once she bore three children to her husband. If Artorius was stationed at Puteoli, this was the best chance he had in his career to take a wife and father three or more children.

In the second century there was a family of Greek origin in the area called Secunda. They had connections with Puteoli while another family, the Secundina, had ties to Rome. In two Artorii inscriptions at Salona that mention Artorius' Dalmatian relatives, we find a Secundina and her eight-year-old son, Marcus Gellis, who were possibly Artorius' daughter and grandson.[5] Rather than being descended from the Secundina, this woman's name likely comes from the Artorii's habit of numbering people. That means there was a first daughter, who would have been called Artoria, while the next child would have been Secundina, 'the second little one', followed, at last, by a son, named Artorius after his father. This would have fulfilled both our Artorius' and his wife's obligations to the state. We know that they were successful, unlike Arthur and Guinevere, who are generally seen as childless, because the line continued in Dalmatia for at least a hundred years after this, until the time of Diocletian.

We cannot be certain one way or the other whether Artorius' wife and family accompanied him on the next, and most significant, leg of his career, which was to take him once again to the very edge of the Empire. Given his years of service, and his experience in all aspects of legionary life, it seems likely that he would have left his family behind, at least until he was settled in his new home. Once this was done, he could send for his wife and children to join him, probably setting them up in the well-appointed quarters granted to a commander of his high rank.

Whatever the case, the next episode in his extraordinary career was to take him back to Britannia and an encounter with destiny that would take him out of history and into legend.

6

THE BATTLE FOR BRITANNIA

Roman Senators in the military rose through the ranks following what was known as the cursus honorum: Senatorial tribune, praetor, consul. Equestrians followed a different path: the tres militiae. This consisted of being a *praefectus cohortis* (commander of two cohorts, about 1000 infantry in an auxiliary unit), an Equestrian tribune, and a *praefectus ala* (commander of either five hundred or one thousand cavalrymen). After that, they followed the elite Equestrian path: *tribune cohortis* of a fire brigade or a city police unit in Rome, *tribunus cohortis* of the Praetorian Guard (personal protectors of the emperor), and *primus pilus iterum* (a second term as *primus pilus*). Then there was the route Artorius' career took: *praepositus, praefectus, dux*. We have discussed his role as *praepositus* and will consider what *dux* means in the next chapter. Here we look at Artorius' role as *praefectus*, one of which he was extremely proud since he listed it as one of the two mentioned in the smaller inscription. (See plate 2)

Before the rule of the Emperor Claudius, it was possible for an Equestrian *primus pilus*, such as Artorius, to be advanced directly to the rank of military tribune, but by the end of the second century, a tour as *praefectus cohortis* was required prior to the promotion.[1] After serving as a *primus pilus*, Artorius should have taken the post of *praefectus cohortis* of either *auxilia* (foreign/non-Roman, yet allied, troops, who did not have citizenship) or *numeri* (such as the Sarmatians who were sent to Britannia).[2] He followed the latter route.

Victory over the Marcomanni came in AD 178 while Artorius was serving as *praepositus* of the Misenum fleet, but military action on the Danube continued around the time of Marcus Aurelius' death on 17 March 180. Commodus then became Emperor and instructed his generals to make the same deal with the Marcomanni, Quadi and remaining Iazyges that Marcus Aurelius had crafted in 175.[3] Whether this was the cause, or whether there was some other reason, in 181 Lucius Artorius Castus was sent back to Britannia – and into legend.

Return to Bremetennacum and the Wall

It was to protect the south from the fierce northern tribes that the Emperor Hadrian initially commanded the building of the Wall that bears his name to this day. Begun in AD 122, it took 10,000 men a total of eight years to complete and underwent many rebuildings, repairs, and extensions during the Roman occupation until it finally stretched for c. 75 miles (120 km) east to west from Maia (Bowness) on the Solway Firth (with a later spur running down to Maryport in Cumbria) to Segedunum (Wallsend) on the Tyne. At the time of its completion, it measured 10 feet (3.48 metres) in width and varied in height between 15 to 30 feet (4.6 to 9.1 metres). There were twenty-eight forts along its length with a dozen or more fortified watchtowers set between each of them. Even in the Middle Ages, the Wall was still seen as a dividing line and served as the point where the medieval Arthur of the chronicles battled the Picts, the descendants of the Caledoni, the people of the north.

Though the purpose of the Wall was primarily defensive, it had gates leading from south to north, indicating that it also acted as a checkpoint and customs station for civilian and mercantile movements. Effectively, it marked the border of the Empire in the north and the strong military presence based there never declined until the legions were withdrawn in AD 410. The strategic roads leading to it and garrison forts that supplied it were to be of later assistance to the defenders of Britain in the fifth and sixth centuries: Arthurian times. There are still Arthurian associations with several of the forts upon the Wall, which may well stem from the presence of Artorius Castus and the Sarmatians stationed there. Indeed, in part this is what led one of the greatest experts on the Sarmatian people, Tadeusz Sulimirski, to suggest that the Sarmatians were broken into units of five hundred men stationed throughout the length of the Wall – an observation made prior to the overwhelming evidence for their presence at Bremetennacum.

Within the military zone below the Wall, a number of pottery sherds bearing a figure recognised as a smith god, wearing a conical hat and bearing a hammer, have been found. These have been tentatively identified as Roman or Romano-Celtic deities, such as Tyrannis or Alletio, but another possible source would be the Alano-Sarmatian troops posted to the wall. Almost all have been dated to the late second century AD. The existence of a nameless warrior/smith god, often identified with Mars or Seleucius and worshipped by the Sarmatians, mean the images may have been inspired by the presence of the Sarmatian troops stationed along the Wall. Their discovery points to a degree of domestication and continuing Sarmatian presence in the area after Castus had left Britain.[4]

Helmut Nickel, keeper emeritus of the department of Arms and Armour at the New York Metropolitan Museum, and one of the first to recognize the parallels between Artorius and Arthur, noted that some twenty miles (thirty-three kms) west of Camboglanna, which could have been the original Camlann, lay the fort of Avallana or Avallava. He suggested this as a possible location for Arthur's 'Avalon', since it was 'just about as far as a seriously wounded man could be transported'. He continues:

If the mortally wounded 'historical Arthur' could have been brought to the harbour-fort at Avallana and shipped south to safety, this might have become the nucleus of the transport-to-Avalon story. If the ship arrived without him, because he had died on the way, or if the ship did not arrive at all, because it was sunk in some storm, it might have been the motif for the legend that he just disappeared and might be still living in the Otherworld. On the other hand, if the assumption is true that Arthur's knights were Sarmatian cavalrymen, then it should be pointed out that it was a Sarmatian custom to bury their important dead in riverbanks, in order to make the site unrecognizable after the next spring flooding, this way preventing any robbing of the grave. [5]

The fort of Avallana and its connections to Arthur's Avalon will be discussed in Chapter 9, when we explore the various candidates for this mystical site. But while Artorius may have embarked at one point in his career from Avallana, perhaps for the battle at Dumbarton Rock, which we will consider shortly, we now know that he survived his tenure in Britannia, so this parallel to Arthur's death is no longer viable. The coincidence of two place names that contain a powerful resonance with later Arthurian tradition may have evolved from Artorius' presence on and around the Wall, and as we shall see Avallana is not the only site associated with him and with the Sarmatians.

The Ala II Asturum, which was raised in Spain and served in Germania, may have been at Bremetennacum for a while in the 160s, possibly as the result of an uprising among the Brigantes, which caused Bremetennacum to convert to a cavalry fort, though their presence is open to debate.[6] It has been suggested that the unit based at the fort may not have been from the VI Victrix at all but was possibly a roaming unit, much like the Sarmatians would eventually become, and even more like the mobile force attributed to a later fifth/sixth century Arthur. Whatever the case, a detachment from the VI Victrix, potentially this cavalry unit, certainly occupied the site under Marcus Aurelius and Lucius Verus.

The model for the Sarmatian enclave in Britannia is close to what Artorius had become familiar with in Syria during his initial years as a centurion, an officer in charge of a village or city and the surrounding territory. He would have known the benefits of encouraging the Sarmatians to maintain their cultural identity. The steppe tribes tended to assimilate rapidly to any culture that they viewed as having conquered them, losing much of their devastating fighting ability.[7] Instead, the Iazyges became an elite fighting force. Artorius, who knew their culture and abilities, and who had unprecedented latitude in his command in light of the complete disaster Britannia became during his time there, can almost certainly be credited with achieving this feat.

Given the abandonment of other forts in the same region at this time, Artorius would have become, to all intents and purposes, 'commander of the region' even though he only rendered his title as *praefectus*. The term 'region' is important. Of the four times 'region' is referred to in Latin inscriptions in Britannia, once is in the rank of a centurion who erected an altar at Bath,[8] one is a tombstone describing someone from the region of Lindum (*regionis Lindensis*) and two are from Bremetennacum.[9] The inscriptions at Bath and Bremetennacum are unclear as to where the region is situated, but given the Roman naming practices, it probably refers to the area around the place where the inscription was found, though some years later.

As we have also seen, there are several (undated) inscriptions from the area that refer to Sarmatian horsemen or a Sarmatian cavalry unit. In any case, it's evident from the lengthy period of their occupation there that the Sarmatians remained as a more tightly knit group and in closer association with the fort than was typical for *numeri*.

The Knights of Sarmatia

One of the most distinctive aspects of the Arthurian legends is the appearance of the Knights of the Round Table. King Arthur's men were armoured cavalry who fought with swords, lances and shields. While in Britannia, Artorius commanded Sarmatian *numeri* from the fort at Bremetennacum.[10] *Numeri* were auxiliary troops that supported the legions rather than an actual part of them. Akin to the troops Arthur fielded when he, as the 9th-century historian Nennius describes in his compilation of earlier documents, fought alongside Rome's allies, the kings of the Britons, in the fifth or sixth century.

The Romans certainly respected (and feared) the Sarmatians. The poet Ovid, in a collection of poems written in exile, painted a less enamoured picture of them in the first century:

> One sees them scamper about, bareback, quivers and bows at their backs, their arrows dipped in venom, their faces covered over with hair, and the hair on their heads so shaggy they look rather like human bushes. They all carry knives at their belts, and you never know whether they're going to greet you or stab you, cut out your liver, and eat it.[11]

Despite their unprepossessing appearance (at least to Roman sensibilities) their fighting skills were legendary and left a deep impression on their enemies. They were skilled horsemen, able to shoot with their short, recurved bows from the saddle with deadly accuracy, using arrowheads dipped in venom, as well as fighting with long lances. Their use of scaled body armour, made of overlapping plates of bone or metal, depending on the wealth of the rider, as early as the fourth century BC, and likely earlier, made them formidable opponents. It is here, also, that we may see the alternative origin of their name as 'the covered people'– those who wear armour. Examples of Sarmatian armour are to be seen on the previously mentioned tombstone from Bremetennacum,[12] and armoured horsemen of the steppe type also turn up on tombstones at Chesters (see Plate 24), where some of the unit's members were buried.

Despite recent statements[13] that there is virtually no physical evidence for the presence of Sarmatian people beyond Bremetannacum, and in particular along Hadrian's Wall, archaeological investigation by Giuseppe Nicolini in 2019-20 shows that beads and bracelets of Sarmatian origin have been unearthed at a number if Roman forts along the Wall, specifically at Vindolanda, Segedunum and Chesters. These offer clear evidence of the Sarmatian presence in the area where, as we shall see, Artorius and his cavalry fought, appearing in fact exactly where we would expect to find them.[14] The recent discovery of a Sarmatian sword with its typical circular hilt top, adds to this conclusion.

Plate 23. Sarmatians in Scale armour from Marcus Aurelius' Pillar. (Helmut Nickel)

John Colarusso, one of the greatest living experts on the culture and myths of the Caucasian races, proposed that the name 'Sarmatian' means free man (c.f. ninth-century Ossetian *sarma*, free man). The name Iazyges is based on the Iranian word for worship/ worshipper, as in Yazidis, Yazd, Yazdigerd. The Sarmatians in general and the Iazyges in particular might have had a theological impulse to interpret the name Artorius as Art Hor, which could be rendered as 'fire priest – sacred', hence 'Arthur'.[15] This could have made the name Artorius resonate particularly with them.

A third interpretation, suggested by Ilya Yakubovich, offers Syawa-arma-tya, or 'black arms', a possible reference to the heavy tattooing common among the related Pazyryk people, similar to the Picts or 'Painted People' against whom the later Arthur pitted his warriors. Curiously, the Saxon historian Bede, writing some five hundred years later, described the Picts as originating in Scythia. If this were true – though there is little solid evidence to support it – this would make the two forces confronting each other neighbours from adjacent parts of the Empire.

Still another possibility was offered by Herodotus and other Greek and Roman historians, who considered the Sarmatae and the Sauromatae ('lizard people') to be members of the same race. They wore scaled armour, which could have made them look reptilian – especially when mounted on their fast-moving horses. They certainly resembled the legendary dragons, which are common to both Scythians and Britons.

The Roman historian Strabo (63 BC-23 AD), who wrote extensively about both communities, suggests the existence of a strong Celtic presence among the people of the steppes, even referring to one group as Keltoskythai, Celtic Scythians. If this linguistic or cultural link really existed, then it would certainly explain the overlap between Sarmatian and Celtic traditions in Britannia during and after the lifetime of Artorius. Such a mix would also make the transmission of folklore from the Sarmatians to the Celtic peoples easier than it would normally have been.

Roman military units carried their own personal standards into battle, as well as those of their legions, and this is true particularly of *numeri* like the Sarmatians. The member of the unit from Bremetennacum depicted on a tombstone found at Chester, is shown wearing steppe garb and carrying a dragon-shaped standard.[16] Another tombstone, this time at Bremetennacum itself, shows a standard-bearer, also in steppe garb, bearing the more traditional Roman cavalry device.[17] (see Plate 18 on p.95)

The standard most often associated with the Sarmatians happens to be a bronze dragonhead with a windsock-style tail attached to it.[18] This type of standard was called a *draco* and its bearer a *draconarius*.[19] Such banners would have been used by Artorius' Sarmatians when they rode into battle, and victories won under these dragon-headed banners could have given rise to the connection between the name 'Artorius' and the cognomen 'Pendragon' ('chief' or 'head' dragon) which later became attached to Arthur's family.[20] In the Medieval manuscripts which tell the

Plate 24. Reconstruction of a Sarmatian warrior with Dragon banner from Chesters Roman fort. (W. Kinghan)

stories of the Arthurian legends, there are several illustrations that depict Arthur's knights riding under such a banner, and one shows Merlin himself carrying the draco, the dragon-head, or Pen-dragon, banner. (see Plate 31 on p.179)[21]

The draco was eventually adopted throughout the Roman army. Other steppe banners of a similar type featured the heads of wolves and other animals, but the dragon-head standard the Sarmatians carried may well have appeared in Britannia during the time of Lucius Artorius Castus.

The *numerus* of 5,500 horsemen dressed and equipped like medieval knights and flying a dragon-head banner would have been central to Ulpius Marcellus' campaign against the invading Caledoni, whom we shall meet shortly. That they appear to have been commanded by an officer named Artorius is intriguing enough, given the stories that developed later about Arthur and his knights fighting against the Picts (the descendants of the Caledoni) along Hadrian's Wall (cf., Geoffrey of Monmouth, ix.6). The existence of a later British poem, *Areith Awdyl Eglur* ('The Sovereign's Chair'), attributed to the sixth-century Celtic poet Taliesin, seems to support this, referring to Arthur fighting 'along the Wall' (*mur*) and in 'a walled enclosure'. (See Chapter 10 and Appendix 1 for a full version of the poem). Curiously, the mention of the warrior 'who was no Arthur' in Y *Gododdin*, also refers to a wall: 'He used to send black crows to the wall.'

The Caledonian Invasion

When Artorius took his place in his new post, he found Britannia in a complete mess, militarily speaking – not unlike the disaster the fifth or sixth century the later Arthur stepped into when he fought 'alongside the Kings of the Britons' and the much later medieval story that has the newly crowned King Arthur battling twelve rebellious kings.

Back in the second century AD, while the II Augusta did its best to keep the peace in southern Wales from its base at Isca (Caerleon, one of Arthur's traditional courts), and the XX Valeria Victrix handled conflicts in northern Wales from Deva (Chester), the VI Victrix manned Hadrian's Wall from its headquarters at

Eboracum (York), as well as the regions to both sides of the Pennine Ridge and as far north as the Antonine Wall.[22] Ulpius Marcellus stepped in as governor in AD 178 to bring order to the soldiers of the VI Victrix, who were apparently rebelling.[23] The Caledoni took advantage of the situation to breach the Antonine Wall and start raiding to the south.

Stretched thin compared to the other legions, the VI Victrix's position was a disaster waiting to happen. That catastrophe came around AD 182 or 183, just after Artorius transferred in as *praefect*, when Caledonian tribes were reported as moving to breach Hadrian's Wall, possibly intending to attack the headquarters of the XX Valeria Victrix at Deva (Chester). Cassius Dio, writing of this, gives us a very Roman view of the wild tribespeople from the north.

There are two principal races of the [Northern] Britons, the Caledonians and the Maeatae... The Maeatae live next to the cross-wall which cuts the island in half, and the Caledonians are beyond them...They dwell in tents, naked and unshod, possess their women in common, and in common rear all the offspring. Their form of rule is democratic for the most part, and they are very fond of plundering; consequently, they choose their boldest men as rulers. They go into battle in chariots, and have small, swift horses; there are also foot soldiers, very swift in running and very firm in standing their ground. For arms they have a shield and a short spear, with a bronze apple attached to the end of the spear-shaft, so that when it is shaken it may clash and terrify the enemy; and they also have daggers.[24]

The Caledoni attacked the western side of Hadrian's Wall, but the Roman defences held. The staging post for troops destined to serve on the Wall was Bremetennacum, considered to be a place of tremendous wealth and political as well as military importance, as we saw.[25] The portion of the Wall supplied with troops by Bremetennacum included Camboglanna (Castlesteads) and Avallana (Burgh-by-Sands).[26]

Collingwood and Wright identified Camboglanna with the fort at Birdoswald, but recent research indicates a more persuasive identification with Castlesteads, just southwest of Walton, in eastern Cumbria, located a few hundred yards south of the line of the Wall. It is 8 miles from Stanwix at Carlisle and 7.5 miles from Birdoswald to the East.[27] Camboglanna is important because it has been suggested as the site of the later fifth/sixth century Arthur's last battle: Camlann. At Camlann Arthur supposedly died, and we know that Artorius lived after his time in Britannia. This has led to the suggestion that this battle was fought by someone else, perhaps the group called 'Arthur's Men', who are referred to briefly in an early Welsh poem from *The Black Book of Carmarthen*. In this poem Arthur is represented as the leader of warriors, fighting a battle at a place called Llongborth (Ships Port):

At Longborth I saw
Arthur's men
Hewing with steel,
Followers of the Emperor
The *Llywiaudirllafwr* [Director of Toil].

The naming of Arthur as 'Emperor' and 'Director of Toil' suggest not only the power exercised by this man, but also perhaps his association with the Romans. Memory of a leader who was 'the Emperor's man' could very easily have become 'the Emperor' over time. Longborth has been identified as Portchester, part of a line of forts along what was known as 'The Saxon Shore'. The fifth/sixth century Arthur is believed to have fought a series of actions against the incoming Saxons from Germany, Fresia, and Jutland.

Before Artorius' arrival in Britannia, Camboglanna had been garrisoned by the Cohors IV Gallorum equitata, but they appear to have been wiped out by the Caledonians and were only replaced when Septimius Severus rebuilt the fort in AD 210.[28] Into the time gap between these two garrisons rode Artorius' men: the Sarmatians.

At this time, the Romans had re-garrisoned many of the forts between the two walls, although they did not send new men to the Antonine Wall itself. This allowed the Caledoni to breach the more northern defences in AD 183. and flood south, across territory held by the Dumnoni, Selgovae, and Votadini. There is evidence of war-related destruction at both Blatobulgium (Birrens) and Burnswark, near the western end of Hadrian's Wall, as well as at other forts both on and just south of there. Fighting may also have occurred at Aballava at this time. A Roman road between Birrens and Newstead could have carried the invading Caledoni farther into Roman territory, but something stopped their progress, as shown by an inscription at Luguvalium (Carlisle), which tells how a cavalry regiment slaughtered a 'band of barbarians' (*manu barbarorum*) at the site.[29] To this day local villagers tell ghost stories of a Roman cavalry unit fighting barbarians in the area where the medieval tale of *Sir Gawain and the Carle of Carlisle* is set. Could Castus and the Sarmatians have been responsible?[30]

The Battle List

Given that the correlation between the names Arthur and Artorius is backed up by over a score of parallels between Lucius Artorius Castus' actual biography and Arthur's fictional biography, the odds of there being no connection between the historical figure and the legendary hero grow increasingly slim. To see just how extensive the list of parallels is, we must take a closer look at one of the most famous sequences in the biography of the later Arthur, from the work attributed to the 9th-century monk Nennius and known as the *Historia Brittonum*.

The most hotly contested passage in this work is a list of twelve battles that Nennius says Arthur fought against the Saxons, and few studies of Arthur have failed to discuss it.[31] For the longest time the list has posed problems for Arthurian scholars who have attempted to identify the sites named in this account of Arthur's military career.[32] There is absolutely no guarantee that the battles belong together, though independent sources do connect some of them with a leader named Arthur.[33] All occurrences of the name Arthur in Britannia post-date Artorius' service there. Yet a comparison between the biography of Lucius Artorius Castus and Nennius' account certainly offers some striking parallels. Excluding Badon (attributed to Ambrosius), the list consists of:[34]

1. One battle on the River Glein,
2. Four battles on the River Dubglas in the region of Linnuis,
3. One battle on the River Bassas,
4. One battle in the wood of Celidon/Cat Coit Celidon,
5. One battle at castle Guinnion,
6. One battle at the City of the legion (more properly, the 'City of the legions'),[35]
7. One battle on the River Tribruit,
8. One battle on Mount/Hill/Rock Agned or Breguoin.[36]

The locations have been mostly traced to places in the north where Artorius served. Celticist Kenneth Jackson's linguistic analysis of the identifications produces the following list of likely names:[37]

1. The River Glen in Northumberland, though the River Glen in Lincolnshire is also a possibility,[38]
2. The River Dubglas, which could be any of a number of rivers,[39] though the River Douglas in Lancashire and the Douglas Waterway south of Glasgow are excellent possibilities,[40]
3. The River Bassas unidentifiable,[41]
4. Cat Coit Celydon, a wood 'within range of Glasgow and Carlisle, perhaps the moorlands round the upper Clyde and Tweed valleys',[42]
5. Castle Guinnion unidentifiable, though other scholars have suggested fort Vinovia near modern Binchester,[43]
6. Chester for *'urbe legionis'*, though recent research makes York the more likely location,[44]
7. 'The Strand of the Pierced or Broken (Place)' for the Tribruit, with no named location suggested,[45]
8. Fort Bremenium (High Rochester) for Breguoin,[46]
9. Badon (which has a number of possible sites, including Dumbarton Rock)

One thing that can be said with confidence is that the list is certainly not chronological. The end rhymes of the battle names indicate that Nennius took the list from a rhyming-poem, which unfortunately no longer exists.[47] No one selects battle sites so that their names will rhyme when a subsequent poet talks about the great deeds of a commander. Nennius could well have taken names from unrelated sources to fill in a gap in an existing source. Or the poem may have actually said that the commander was named Arthur. While such a combination of 'leader' with 'battles' as a title has not been identified as a fifth- or sixth-century figure, the second-century Lucius Artorius Castus most likely fought a series of battles that does fit the battle list during what the Romans referred to as the Caledonian invasion.

As we mentioned, at the time of the AD 183-185 Caledonian invasion, Artorius was praefect of fort Bremetennacum. Jackson's etymology for Bremeno could just as easily indicate Bremetennacum, with a root referring to Bremen, who may have been a people or a god as we shall see in a moment.[48] The archaeological record indicates that a battle did occur there at this time, shown by extensive damage to buildings outside the fort.[49] Prior to that, in AD 183, Ulpius Marcellus, the then governor of Brittania, was temporarily recalled to Rome to deal with a legal matter, and the Caledoni took the opportunity to mount one of their most concerted attacks. The Roman forts – Trimontium (Newstead), Habitancum (Risingham), Cappuck (Oxnam Water), and Bremenium (High Rochester; another candidate for Bremeno) – all collapsed along Dere Street, the Roman road that still forms a main artery north to southeast of the Pennines.[50] At Trimontium, the *Ala Augusta Vocontiorum* may have been the unit that the Caledoni destroyed. At Habitancum, *Cohors IIII Gallorum* equitata was probably the unit that next fell to the invaders, since the *Cohors I Vangionum Milliaria Equitata* and *Numerus Exploratorum Habitancensium* were brought in to re-garrison the fort after it was later rebuilt by Septimius Severus.[51]

The Latin name for Cappuck is unknown, but the garrison the Caledoni destroyed was probably *Vexillatio Raetorum Gaesatorum.*[52] The fort itself lies to the southwest of Walton, in

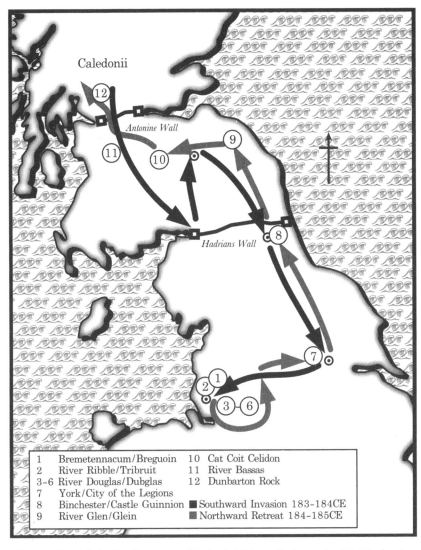

Map 6. The Caledonian Invasion. (Linda A Malcor. Redrawn by W. Kinghan)

eastern Cumbria, and was located a few hundred yards south of the line of the Wall. It is 8 miles from Stanwix at Carlisle and 7.5 miles from Birdoswald to the East.

Both *Cohors I Aelia Dacorum milliaria* and *Cohors I Delmatarum equitata* garrisoned the fortlet in the late second century.[53] One may have been the unit destroyed by the Caledoni and the other a replacement unit. Or the destroyed unit may have been the

Cohors I Lingonum Equitata, which garrisoned the fort in the mid-second century. Lingonum refers to the Lingones, who might be responsible for the Linnuis reference in Nennius.

Several dedication slabs show extensive rebuilding at the site in the early third century.[54] That the XX Valeria Victrix was helping to bolster the Roman defences just north of Hadrian's Wall is evidence of how hard the legion VI Victrix had been hit. The positioning of an inscription baring the words, LEG. XX. V.V. FECIT, surrounded by symbols of the XXth legion, bears testimony that the gate and walls had to be rebuilt from the ground up following the invasion.[55]

Cassius Dio says that the invaders broke through Hadrian's Wall itself, perhaps still following Dere Street.[56] This would put the breach at Onnum (Halton Chesters), which was re-garrisoned by *Ala I Pannoniarum Sabiniana* in the third century, suggesting that something had happened to the second-century garrison.[57] Yet nearby Cilurnum (Chesters) was among the forts that Septimius Severus had to repair,[58] while the aqueduct and water supply system had been repaired under Ulpius Marcellus.[59]

The Caledoni attacked the eastern side of Hadrian's Wall, this time heading for Eboracum (York) and the headquarters of the VI Victrix. The defences failed, and they breached Hadrian's Wall, by-passing the territory controlled by the Carvetii and attacking Eboracum,[60] where they killed a Roman *legatus* (general).[61]

The acting governor, during Ulpius' absence, was M. Antius Crescens Calpurnianus.[62] Nennius recast this story as happening to Septimius Severus, who did indeed die at York, but of a disease rather than as the result of a battle.[63] Whereas Cassius Dio says that the barbarians 'cut down a general together with his troops' (describing a battle presumably near York during the invasion of 184),[64] Nennius says that Severus was 'killed at York with his generals'.[65] The phrasing is close enough to spark speculation that the 'Annals of Rome' which Nennius is believed to have worked with, was a copy or fragment of Cassius Dio's *Roman History*.

Between this incident and the return of Ulpius Marcellus, who won his case in Rome and came back to Britannia as governor AD 184-185 after Perennis, the head of Commodus' Praetorian

Plate 25. Hadrian's Wall today. (John Matthews)

Guard, dismissed all of the legates of the British legions,[66] something happened that turned the tide for the Romans. The fighting was no longer south of Hadrian's Wall but moved into southern Scotland, north of the Forth-Clyde Isthmus. Ulpius immediately ordered a punitive campaign against the invaders intended, if possible, to exterminate them.[67]

While some scholars have assumed that this pattern of destruction in northern Britannia took place in AD 197, the historian Peter Salway argues, quite correctly, that the damage actually occurred AD 183-185.[68] An eye shield of the type used by Sarmatian cavalry and a variety of beads that have been identified as Sarmatian have been found at Chesters (Cilurnum) from this period, suggesting that the Sarmatians of Bremetennacum helped to supplement the garrison of the fort or perhaps fought through there, pursuing the Caledoni, thereby causing the damage to the fort on the way north, with the damage to Halton Chesters done on the way south.[69]

At Bravoniacum (Kirkby Thore), a building tile of uncertain date and from an unidentified unit baring the cognomen 'Castus' inscribed on it, is recorded.[70] The name Castus does appear quite frequently in the third century, so there is no reason to connect the stone with Lucius Artorius Castus on the basis of the name alone. But while there may have been some battles fought in the region of nearby Maiden Castle (not to be confused with the Iron Age fort in Dorset) in the second century, the case is stronger for the main conflict taking place along Dere Street.[71]

Consider then, the following scenario, based on the battle list Nennius ascribed to Arthur and the biography of Artorius.

Battle Is Joined

After sacking Eboracum (York), the Caledoni continued south through territory controlled by the Brigantes. The invaders used the Roman roads, turning west at the first major fork and crossing the Pennines, almost certainly heading for the headquarters of the XXth at Deva. The fort Olicana (Ilkley) lay along the most likely road and was 'restored' sometime between February or June 197 through 2 May 198, which suggests that the Caledonian invasion did indeed follow this route from Eboracum and past Olicana some ten years earlier.[72]

The road they took led them straight to the crossroads guarded by Bremetennacum. Nennius says that one of Arthur's battles happened at the Mount/Hill/Rock of Breguoin, which can be identified with Bremetennacum itself. Despite modern criticism, Kenneth Jackson showed that the development from Bremenium to Breguion is perfectly natural, explicable, and to be expected, showing that the sites were named after the same tribe and probably conflated.

Bremetennacum is only our modern rendering of one of the ways in which the region was defined, and the name did apply to the entire region, not just the fort.[73] This rendering is based on 'Bremetennacum veteranorum' in the Notitia Dignitatum, 'Bresnetenaci veteranorum' in the Ravenna Cosmography and 'Regio Bremetenacensis'. The 'Breme' part of the name does not come from a Latin stem.[74] Some authorities have speculated that it was a name of a sub-tribe of the Brigantes, who may have supplied the name for the fort at Bremenium on Dere Street as well; others have held that it was based on the name of a nearby river. The 'tennacum' part means 'holding'. So, the name works out as '[Strong]hold of [the] Breme(n).' If the battle of Breguoin, which may have had something to do with the Brigantes whom the Sarmatians were policing, occurred in 184 at Bremetennacum, Lucius Artorius Castus was there, as *praefectus* of the VI Victrix. The fort continued to hold at least through the 180s,[75] at which point it may have been re-garrisoned for a time by a vexillation from the legion XX Valeria Victrix,[76] perhaps because the Sarmatians were elsewhere.

Our contention is that Artorius and his Sarmatians defeated the Caledoni at Bremetennacum and pursued them west along the Ribble River to the tidal estuary (Nennius' 'Strands' of the Tribruit river). The Dow River flows into the estuary near Freckleton, which served as a Roman port. The Douglas River joins the Ribble near this point as well. That gives the three rivers at an estuary that some think could be identified as the Tribruit. Although Jackson disagreed with the etymology that gave rise to this identification,[77] the Ribble does empty into the sea within a reasonably short distance of exiting the limestone landscape and pass that was guarded by Bremetennacum.

The name that Jackson eventually came up with for the etymology of Bremetennacum could just as easily describe the estuary of the Ribble as any other place where three rivers meet a beach.[78] At the estuary near where the Douglas and the Dow join the tidal portion of the Ribble, another unit of Sarmatians could have defeated the Caledoni again. It's possible that the Caledoni were trying to attack the Roman port at Freckleton, which originally sent supplies through the fort at Kirkham. But by the time Artorius was *praefectus* of Bremetennacum, Kirkham had been abandoned.[79] The nearest fort would have been Bremetennacum itself, which would have been responsible for safeguarding the port and the supplies shipped through it. (Perhaps here we may recall the later Arthur's defence of Longborth, i.e., Ships Port, mentioned in the poem quoted from the *Black Book of Caermarthen* on p147.)

The Caledoni would next have fled south along the Dubglas. The four battles listed by Nennius as being fought at the Douglas River, in modern day Lancashire, would have been within the region controlled by Bremetennacum. Jackson decided that Lindsey in Lincolnshire was a probable source for Nennius' 'Linnuis,' but he points out that there is no Douglas River in Lindsey and none of the battle sites are connected with southern Britannia.[80] Yet Jackson's etymology would give the 'original' form as *Linnens and require a shift of a 'd' to an 'n'. Plus, there is still the problem that there is no river with this name in the area. This raises the possibility that 'Linnuis' is an unattested location.

Unlike Nennius, the 12th-century writer Geoffrey of Monmouth, in his *Historia Regum Britanniae,* one of the most important sources for the later 'historical' Arthur, has the battles on the Douglas occur *after* the battle at the 'City of the legions' (York).[81] This could mean that the Douglas referred to is the Douglas Waterway south of Glasgow, with the battlefield somewhere southwest of the place where the Douglas joins the Clyde. This alternative scenario would move these battles later in our hypothetical sequence.

So far, the Sarmatians were precisely the troops who should have been best used to respond to an invasion in this region. But at this point something occurred that caused them to leave their normal area of operation. Artorius probably chased the Caledoni along the Douglas River then angled them back across the Pennines toward Eboracum (York). The fighting seems to have swept south and east, into the area around Lindsey, before heading back north, but the archaeological record is mostly silent about this. If Linnuis is in fact Lindsey, the association with the battles on the Douglas may have been added as a gloss at a later date, possibly by Nennius himself, just as he added the gloss Cat Coit Celidon, to the ancient woodlands in southern Caledonia.[82]

The Caledoni themselves appear to have turned to face the Sarmatians at Eboracum.[83] Though writing much later, there is no reason to discount Geoffrey of Monmouth's preceding Arthur's invasion of Scotland with a battle, which is exactly what we find here, against Saxons, Picts, and Scots at York.[84] Artorius won again, and the Caledoni retreated along Dere Street with the Sarmatians in pursuit. Evidence of a Sarmatian presence in the area may be seen in a number of stamped tiles (now lost, from a bathhouse), found at Bainesse near the site of ancient Cataractonium (modern Catterick) which bear the stamp ESAR',[85] possibly '*Equitatum Sarmati*'.[86] This suggests that the repair was accomplished by a unit deployed from Bremetennacum rather than by the local garrison. Curiously, Catterick is one of the possible sites for the location of the battle described in the ancient British epic, Y *Gododdin*.[87] If Artorius and his Sarmatians did win a battle there, memory of that victory may have led to the comparison four centuries later between the warrior Gwawrddur and Arthur as described in Y *Gododdin*.

At fort Vinovia (in Durham near Binchester), Artorius engaged the Caledoni again, giving rise to Nennius' battle at castle Guinnion.[88] The battle must have taken place away from the fort since the site itself does not show evidence of destruction, but the unit garrisoning it was replaced by the *Ala Hispanorum Vettonum civium Romanorum*,[89] suggesting that the original unit was destroyed or scattered in a battle.

The Caledoni are known to have continued back into the region above Hadrian's Wall with at least one Roman commander still giving chase, where they were when Ulpius Marcellus arrived back in Britannia and gave orders for the punitive campaign against the invaders. Artorius seems to have continued to chase the invaders north.

The Caledoni now headed for a site near Flodden, northwest of Wooler in Northumberland. The site happens to be on the Glen River, which corresponds to Nennius' Glein River. Crawford points out that '*in ostium fluminis glein*' could mean a 'river-junction.'[90] This is precisely what is found on the Glen of Northumberland near this famous battlefield.

By now the remnants of the Caledonian forces must have been in a panic and intent simply on returning to their homeland north of the Antonine Wall. If so, Artorius was still pursuing them, possibly now under orders from Ulpius Marcellus to exterminate the invaders. The Sarmatians caught the Caledoni in the Cat Coit Celidon, the Caledonian forest, and defeated them again. The few who survived fled for home. During this flight they may have turned to fight one further battle at a river known as Bassas. This river remains unidentified, but Jackson suggested that it could be in southern Scotland.[91] The cognomen 'Bassus' crops up repeatedly among the troops on Hadrian's Wall,[92] at fort Alone (Watercrook) near the Lune River in third-century Cumbria[93] and as the name of a pre-third century *praefectus castrorum* at Caerleon,[94] though there is no known connection between any of these men and a river.

The last battle on Nennius' list has proven to be a headache for scholars over the centuries: Badon. Billed as Arthur's final victory against the invaders, in this case the Saxons, Badon, which Geoffrey of Monmouth identifies as the southern city of Bath, simply doesn't fit the list of northern battle sites. Nor would it have been a possible site for Artorius' final battle against the Caledoni for the same reason that it makes no sense with the other sites on Nennius' list. This suggests that Badon belonged to a separate battle tradition, one that Gildas describes as occurring in the year he was born, for which many speculative dates have been given in the fifth and sixth centuries. Gildas also tells us that the battle took place in 'the early part of the year'.

That fits with the Artorius sequence, where his final battle was likely in January or February of 185 AD. That it was a great battle was probably enough to land it on Nennius' list by what is known as the Attraction Principle:[95] that when two events in a narrative have elements in common, the lesser known one will be recast as belonging to the hero of the original story. In the case of Badon, Arthur was more famous than whoever actually commanded, someone Gildas does not in fact name, but who was probably a man named Ambrosius Aurelianus,[96] so the battle was 'attracted' to Arthur's list of accomplishments. Nennius tacks it onto the end of his list, and Geoffrey of Monmouth slots it in before a more promising battle that finishes off his sequence of Arthur's struggle against the Picts and Scots (or Irish in later sources): the Battle of Alclud.

Gildas says that a Roman *legatus* and his legions defeated the invaders, which is consistent with Artorius, who was not a *legatus* at the time but who was soon to oversee all three legions currently occupying Britannia as a *dux*. Intriguingly, both Nennius and Gildas agree that this Roman's battle was a tremendous slaughter and that it involved a naval blockade.

Nennius and Gildas both give the site of the battle as the western terminus of Hadrian's Wall during the time of Septimius Severus, who attacked by leading troops from York. So, at this point, a nameless *legatus'* tale was attracted to the better-known figure of the Roman Emperor. Severus in fact never fought such a battle. No one did so at the western terminus of Hadrian's Wall. But Geoffrey of Monmouth tells of such a battle at the western terminus of the Antonine Wall, exactly where Artorius and his Sarmatians were chasing the Caledoni.

In Geoffrey's story, Arthur uses a naval blockade at Alt Clut (Alclud, i.e., Dumbarton Rock) to prevent his enemy from escaping while he and his cavalry slaughter them. Artorius certainly had the know-how to use a naval blockade and the Roman ships to accomplish it at his command. It was something no battle leader in the fifth or sixth century could have done, particularly at such a northerly location in deep winter. Yet Artorius and his Sarmatians, who had fought in conditions that caused the Danube River to freeze solid, definitely had the skills necessary to defeat an enemy under such conditions.

Gildas appears to be drawing on a variant of the legend of the Battle of Alclud that was in circulation at the time of Magnus Maximus (c. 383-388), whose own story of trying to usurp the imperial throne paralleled Arthur's campaign to the Continent and eventually to be crowned Emperor. So, by the fourth century the story had already been attracted to that of the infamous Magnus Maximus,[97] though Gildas pushes the time backward to that of Septimius Severus, smack in the range of Artorius' lifetime.

It is our contention that either peace or the extinction of the Caledoni invaders came at the hands of Artorius and the Sarmatians in early AD 185, while Ulpius was still governor. When he was replaced by acting governor Marcus Antius Crescens, coins were issued to celebrate a victory in Britannia.[98]

In 185, something else of note happened: Artorius took some Sarmatians on an expedition to Rome.[99] Both Dio and Herodian mention in their histories that the 'lieutenants of Britain' sent 1,500 'javelin men' or 'kontus men' to Rome to warn Commodus of an assassination attempt by Perennis, a Pretorian praefect with designs on the post of Emperor.[100] The 'lieutenants' were the praefects who had been serving under the legates Perennis had just sacked, and their complaint may have been about that. Since Xiphilinis, the eleventh-century Byzantine monk who wrote the summary of Dio's histories, gets 'pilum' (the javelin-like weapon used by Roman infantry) correct elsewhere, the weapon referred to here and those who wielded it, must be something different. There is only one option. The troops could only have been those who carried the *kontus*: the Sarmatians of Bremetennacum.

Since the Sarmatians had no idea where Rome was, someone had to lead them, and that someone had to be Artorius. The speed with which the warning gets from Britannia to Rome also argues for mounted troops rather than foot soldiers. Herodian says that along the way these men intercepted coins bearing the image of Perennis' son.[101] Whitaker speculated that the coins were issued by Perennis in response to his son's victory against the Sarmatians in Pannonia. Since these would have been blood relatives of the Sarmatians of Britannia who made up the expedition, personal revenge may have underscored their need to warn Commodus of the plot to assassinate him. The arrival of the delegation from Britannia foiled Perennis' intentions and resulted in his death, together with that of the soldier named as Maternus, who seems to have been preparing his own plot, possibly in collusion with Perennis. Commodus would certainly have been grateful to the commander who warned him of the assassination attempts, and even brought a force of his own, presumably to offer protection to the Emperor. If so, Commodus would soon have a chance to repay him.

Meanwhile, while Artorius and his Sarmatians were in Rome in AD 186, the VI Victrix fell to pieces and revolted. The future Emperor Pertinax was sent to replace the acting governor of Britannia, Marcus Crescens, ostensibly to bring order to the VI Victrix. His harshness, though, led to him being attacked by his own men on Hadrian's Wall and he begged to be allowed to return to Rome. Britannia suddenly needed a new governor, and Commodus found one in a very unusual place.

Throughout the Caledonian invasion and beyond, there had been one well-defended territory, which stood out among the less viably run areas across the rest of Britannia. This was the region controlled by the forces stationed at Bremetennacum, and it was to the capable praefect, Lucius Artorius Castus, who commanded it, that Commodus turned to bring peace to the island.

7

DUX ARTORIUS

Artorius now stood ready to assume the most significant role in his already extraordinary career – that of *dux*, commander of the three legions serving in Britannia. How this came about is as tangled and complex as anything we've seen in this account of his life. It pushed his career to even greater heights and gave him a place in history that has remained long hidden, but which became the foundation for some of the most important legendary traditions of Britain.

As we have seen, following the governorship of Ulpius Marcellus (c. AD 178–c. 184) Pertinax, the future Emperor and currently a prominent Senator, took over as governor of Britannia. For roughly eighteen months his term was plagued by people trying to kill him and by his killing people in response. Pertinax at last asked to be allowed to return to Rome, and Commodus, having discovered a candidate to replace him, granted his request. At this point there is a four-year gap in the list of the Roman governors of Britannia. But someone took over the reins, and everything suddenly went completely quiet in Britannia for those four years (AD 187 to 191).

We suggest that the reason no one has found a Senatorial governor in charge of Britannia after Pertinax is because the governor wasn't a Senator. He was an Equestrian, a *dux* who commanded all three legions of Britannia. This is exactly what Artorius' inscription says he was: '*Duci legionum trium Britannicimiarum*' (*Dux* commanding the three legions of Britannia). We propose that

Castus was a *de facto* governor, following Pertinax. This gives us a man called Artorius commanding all of Britannia and creating a time of peace between two periods of intense struggle, which ended in a civil war – something that is readily attributed to the figure of the fifth/sixth century Arthur.

As we have seen, Artorius' campaign against the Caledoni, like Arthur's against the Saxons, consolidated Britannia, following a period of infighting. In Artorius' case, this included an attempted mutiny by the VI Victrix (whose centurions were later executed by Pertinax), while the II Augusta sought to name 'Priscus, a lieutenant,' as emperor.[1] This should have resulted in the legion being disbanded – a normal process following a rebellion in the ranks. The fact that they were not may well be due to Artorius' connection with them. In any case, his victorious campaign against the northern tribes preserved Britannia for the Romans at a time when this quadrant of the Empire was as shaky as it had ever been. It was almost certainly this action – as well as the incident of warning that prevented a direct attack on Commodus – that recommended him to the Emperor.

The Mad Emperor

The words '*dux* of the three British legions' in the account of Artorius' life from the inscription tell us that, aged approximately forty-eight, he attained this new and superior rank. This was unusual for the time – perhaps for any time in the history of the Empire. It meant that, while he was only an Equestrian and not a Senator, he was being given a degree of authority in the farthest reaches of the Empire that was extremely rare for anyone of his existing social status.

We must assume this was due to his catching the eye of the Emperor. Commodus himself certainly had considerable knowledge of military life, having served as joint ruler with his father from AD 177 to 180 and accompanying Marcus Aurelius throughout the Marcommic Wars; incidentally giving him first-hand experience not only of the steppe warriors but in all likelihood of Artorius himself, who was *primus pilus* of the V Macedonica at the time, and involved in the same affray.

Curiously, Commodus was born a younger twin on 31 August 161 with the *praenomen* Lucius. His family name Aurelius was followed by the *cognomen* Commodus, which honoured Lucius Verus, whose original name was Lucius Ceionius Commodus. On 12 Oct 166, at the ripe old age of five, Commodus assumed the title of Caesar, along with his younger brother, Marcus – his elder twin, Titus, having already died. Marcus passed away three years later, and three years after that, at age eleven, Commodus added Germanicus to his name, commemorating Roman victories against the Quadi, one of the Germanic tribes that constantly rebelled against Roman domination. In AD 175, with Artorius serving as *primus pilus* of the V Macedonica, Commodus added Sarmaticus to his ever-extending list of names (each one taken in honour of a significant event) in celebration of victory over the Iazyges. In 177, aged sixteen, he became the youngest consul in Roman history and later the same year was elevated to co-emperor alongside his father. This was the first time an emperor had succeeded his biological father since Titus succeeded Vespasian in AD 79. Though he became increasingly deranged during his life – including, as did so many other emperors, awarding himself the status of demigod – he seems to have effectively handled the chaos already spreading throughout the Empire. During his reign there were significant areas of reduced conflict, including those in Gaul and Britannia, which we will explore below, but Commodus' increasingly dictatorial behaviour resulted not only in several insurrections, but also finally in his assassination in AD 192, marking the end of the great Nerva-Antonine dynasty.

However, June 177 saw him become co-ruler with Marcus Aurelius and assume the name and titles of Imperator Caesar Lucius Aurelius Commodus Augustus. When Marcus Aurelius died on 17 March 180, Commodus temporarily changed his name to the *praenomen* Marcus followed by Aurelius Commodus Antoninus Augustus in honour of his late father and step-grandfather. In 182 he added still more names: Germanicus Maximus, and then Britannicus – following Artorius' victory over the Caledonians. By 185 the name Felix preceded that of Augustus, and occasionally Hercules Amazonius was thrown into the mix because of Commodus' increasing obsession with the demigod. By 191, Commodus bore the weighty titles and names of Imperator Caesar Lucius Aurelius Commodus Augustus Antoninus Germanicus Maximus Sarmaticus Britannicus Hercules Amazonius Romanus Exasperatorius Invictus Felix Pius. This phenomenal moniker unpacks to Emperor Caesar (his title) Lucius Aurelius Commodus (his name) the Highest Antonine, Ultimate Conqueror of the Germanians, Conqueror of the Sarmatians, Conqueror of the Britons, Hercules of the Amazons, the Supreme Roman, the Invincible, Fortunate and Holy. (One wonders if he was compensating for something).

That he shared the *praenomen* Lucius with Artorius, and that two of the latter's victories supplied additional titles, Sarmaticus and Britannicus, should not be lost on us. Neither should the fact that Hercules was, according to Herodotus, the greatest hero of the Sarmatians. An inscribed altar from Dura Europos on the Euphrates shows that Commodus' titles were passed on to the farthest reaches of the Empire. Auxiliary military units received the title Commodiana, while Commodus himself claimed still more titles: Pacator Orbis (Pacifier of the World) and Dominus Noster (Our Lord). This latter title would in time be used conventionally by all Roman emperors, beginning around 100 years after Commodus, who seems to have been the first to use it.

This was the man who, in 187 AD, gave Artorius the task of bringing Britain back to its proper position as part of the Empire. As Emperor, Commodus could, of course, appoint whoever he wished to whatever rank he wished. To Castus, he awarded the rank and title of *Dux*.

Leader of Battles

Dux, which is the base for the English word 'duke', meant that whoever held it was usually functioning either outside his assigned territory or in a rank above the level of one he was permitted to hold. A *dux legionis* was an underling who commanded a legion, and a *dux vexillatio* commanded a large vexillation ('detachment') of troops. This evolution in the meaning of *dux* actually started under Marcus Aurelius. By the Severan period (AD 193-211), a *dux* belonged to the Senatorial class, but prior to that an Equestrian such as Castus could hold the rank.[2]

A Senatorial *legatus* who commanded two legions instead of one would be a *dux*. Or a Senatorial *legatus* who took his troops, say, from Gaul to Germania would also be of this same rank. Artorius' inscription says that as *dux* he commanded all three British legions, and since this was the total number of legions in the province of Britannia, such a position could only have been possible for someone who held an even more prestigious post: that of governor. Although some members of Artorius' *gens* did rise to become Senators, he wasn't among these, since his next rank is *procurator centenarius*, a purely Equestrian office. That leaves us with an intriguing possibility: that Artorius was the first (and only) Equestrian governor of Britannia, meaning that someone with his name united all of the military units of the island under his command – something the later Arthur is said to have done.

The 9th century writer Nennius, from whom we get most of our information about the fifth/sixth century Arthur, appears to suggest that there was some disparity between his social and military rank: 'he fought alongside the kings of the Britons but he himself was not one of them.'[3] If we apply this to Artorius, it suggests a Roman commander rather than a king, though it could also mean that he was someone who held an equal status to that of an overall ruler. Our new analysis of the Artorius inscription suggests that such a difference existed for him also.

The clues left by Artorius' own words on the inscription lead us to this conclusion. The doubled 'g' in LEGG in the main inscription indicates a plural. Twice *dux legionum*, or *dux* of more than one legion? Which is it? The interpretation depends on the missing word, and the following word on the inscription, which ends in an 'm', gives us the clue we need to answer the question. One more bit of evidence is needed to confirm our suspicion, and that is provided by the word that follows the missing word: *Britanicimiarum*.

Little debate has occurred over the word '*Britanicimiarum*' in comparison to the rest of the Artorius inscription. The assumption has been that it's simply a spelling error for *Britannicarum*.[4] Yet there may once again be no error. *Britanicimiarum* could simply be a variant spelling, and the translation would therefore be rendered 'British.'[5] That gives us '*dux* of the [MISSING WORD] British legions.'[6] The one thing that everyone agrees on is that in the late second century there were three legions in Britannia: the II Augusta, the XX Valeria Victrix, and the VI Victrix. Translated into Latin, 'three legions' gives us 'LEGG TRIUM'. Does the reconstruction fit the space? The inscription is currently mounted between a doorjamb and a wall and hung to fit that space rather than to show what the distance would be between the letters in the original inscription. The magic of computers, though, has enabled us to reconstruct the inscription with the correct spacing. Letters from one part of the inscription can be moved to another and resized to fit the height of the letters in the new line [See Plate 3]. DUUM isn't long enough. But TRIUM renders:

DVCI LEGG TRIUM BRITANNICI/MIARVM

This expands to *Duci legionum trium Britanicimiarum*, which translates to *Dux* of the three British legions.[7] With the plural, this means Artorius held the rank of *dux* twice, though we still don't know for how long.

How did he achieve this? This returns us to the issue of what *duci legionum* means as a rank. We know from the *Historia Augusta*, a set of Roman histories written by Aelius Spartianus and Iulius Capitolinus, that during the reign of Commodus, officers of Equestrian class sometimes occupied ranks previously reserved for Senators. This was likely a consequence of the two severe crises of the second century, the Antonine Plague, which as we saw carried off a large number of people, and the Marcomannic Wars, which accounted for the deaths of a number of high-ranking officers and left Senatorial positions open that had to be filled by Equestrians, something Perennis, at the time still Commodus' *praetorian praefect* (leader of the imperial bodyguards), was quite happy to do. So, though an Equestrian *dux legionum* wasn't possible under Marcus Aurelius, it was under Commodus, who was off pretending to be Hercules rather than tending to matters of state.

This is important, because a Senator who ruled a province was called 'legatus Augusti propraetore', but sometimes the governor of a province could also be called '*dux*', as in the case of Sextus Cornelis Clemens, '*dux trium Daciarum*', 'governor of the three Dacias' who ruled in the years AD 170-172 under Marcus Aurelius.[8] An Equestrian who, for exceptional emergency reasons, ruled a province, was called '*duci legionis*' or '*legionum*', if more than one legion was in the province. Artorius says his rank was '*duci legionum*' while in Britannia.

An Equestrian governor of Britannia? How could Artorius have possibly obtained such an exalted position? Beyond the evidence of his own inscription, the answer lies in one of the most tangled moments in the history of ancient Rome.

Dio has this to say about the incidents at the heart of the matter: '[Commodus] also had some wars with the barbarians beyond Dacia, in which Albinus and Niger, who later fought against the emperor Severus, won fame; but the greatest struggle was the one with the Britons.'[9]

As we have seen, the province of Britannia had been in turmoil for well over a decade. Looking again at these events, we may remember that the uproar among the soldiers in the VI Victrix was the primary reason why Marcus Aurelius settled the 5,500 Sarmatian heavy cavalry on top of them in AD 175.

The II Augusta mutinied almost as frequently as the VI Victrix did. The XX Valeria Victrix seems to have been missing entirely, though they may have been in Scotland or Ireland as we will discuss shortly. Several tribes in Britannia were also causing trouble; not only the Caledoni, but also the Brigantes, Ordovices, and Iceni, all of whom were south of Hadrian's Wall, were in an uproar. Artorius would have been a good choice to deal with the Brigantes. Not only were the Sarmatians settled on top of them, but also their kings would almost certainly have fought alongside Artorius to defend their lands from the Caledoni, just as Nennius describes the kings of the Britain doing with Arthur.

There are few details that the surviving early Arthurian texts have in common, but several of the manuscripts give biographical details that are generally consistent with each other. They tell of a man named Arthur who was a warrior in Britain at some time in the past. The earliest accounts say that he was a soldier, not a king, and that he held the title '*dux bellorum.*' Literally, 'leader of wars' or 'duke of battles', but the rank of *dux* had a more specific definition in a military context, as we have seen.

The stories of the fifth/sixth century Arthur give a sense that such a man was the historical leader of a group of mailed horsemen who fought on armoured horses using swords, lances, and shields. Arthur commanded his troops from a fortress, which is variously identified as Caerleon, the probable origin of the otherwise fictitious Camelot, and other locations. When mentioned, Arthur's standard is usually said to be a dragonhead banner, which may account for his cognomen, Pendragon, as we saw. He fought battles in Britannia, defending the 'civilized' areas of the island against 'barbarian' invaders, who are sometimes identified as the Saxons, though Geoffrey of Monmouth and those who followed his work included tales of Arthur's battles against Picts, Scots, and Irish. Gildas, identifies the sixth-century invaders as Picts and Scots in his *De Excidio Britannia* (c. AD 540).[10]

In the *Vitae Sancti Gildae* (Life of Saint Gildas), written in the twelfth century, Arthur fights in southern Scotland, killing the saint's brother.[11] Eventually Arthur and Gildas are reconciled, with Arthur 'doing penance through the remainder of his life, simply for having slain in battle one who had risen in arms against him'.[12] Similarly, Ulpius Marcellus, who we remember was the governor of Britannia during the Caledonian invasion, gave orders to completely destroy the Caledonians rather than simply decimating them. That puts Artorius in the position of slaying all 'who had risen in arms against him' in southern Scotland. This may account for the seemingly exaggerated story of Arthur killing nine hundred and sixty men by his own hand at the battle of Badon, as recorded by Nennius, a statement that does not have to be interpreted literally, but just that he gave orders for no quarter to be given in the battle.[13]

The pattern of destruction between AD 183 and 185 is attested by archaeological finds, such as the Sarmatian eye shield for a horse found along the route taken by the Caledoni back across

Hadrian's Wall, along with pieces of scale armour found nearby and a variety of Sarmatian beads and necklaces found scattered among the forts on the Wall. They tell us that Artorius was almost certainly the victorious commander who prevented further disaster for the Romans, and that the troops he used were the Sarmatian cavalry from Bremetennacum.

In the *De Excidio,* Gildas refers to the leaders of the Roman military as 'Romanorum reges' ('Roman kings') who 'possessed the empire'.[14] These Roman leaders included Emperors, who filled a role in the military structure of the Empire analogous to that filled in sixth-century Britain's military structure by kings. While Gildas made a distinction between '*rectores*' (governors) and '*duces*' (leaders of armies), he made no such distinction between '*duces*' and '*reges*' (kings).[15] For Gildas, calling someone a Roman '*rex*' (king) or a Roman '*dux*' ('commander who crosses provincial boundaries') was essentially the same thing.[16] Given the interchangeability and attested overlap of these two words in the sixth century, it is perfectly understandable for stories about a *Dux Artorius* to become tales about a *Rex Arturius* (King Arthur). Other renderings of Arthur's name include Arthurius and Arthurus/Arturus, variations that could derive from a Celticization of Artorius.[17] All of this makes Artorius the most likely historical source from which the later legends of King Arthur, with all of the variants of his name, sprang.

York

One question that is often asked is was there a real Camelot? As far as the name goes, despite the number of places with the prefix 'cam' the answer is probably no, but whatever answer one accepts, if Artorius was indeed running things from AD187 to 191, as we believe, he must have had a base of operations. The main contender for this seems to us to be Eboracum (York), situated to the northeast of the Sarmatian base, but connected by a Roman road through the Pennines.

Construction on the massive legionary fortress at York had begun at roughly the same time as those at Deva and Ribchester itself in the mid-70s AD. Originally built of wood, it took almost a century, starting under the reign of Trajan, to be replaced with stone. It was still underway when the Caledoni sacked it and would have been in the same state when Artorius served there, only reaching completion when Septimius Severus based his reconstructive operations along Hadrian's Wall there after Artorius' death. There is enough evidence to suggest that York, rather than London, was the capital of Britannia in the second century.

There is no text that lists Londinium as the governor's headquarters. The evidence comes entirely from a tomb raised to the procurator of Britannia, Gaius Julius Alpinus Classicianus (c. AD 60) during the Boudiccan rebellion,[18] and a legatus Augusti iuridicus (an 'imperial lawyer' sent to advise a governor on civil law), who put up an inscription there to honour Trajan's victory over the Dacians in c. AD 105.[19] The problem with these examples is that they are early and do not claim that Londinium was the headquarters of the governor. At the time of Boudicca's rebellion, it was an important port, but it had not yet achieved the status of *civitas*. It was mainly a military base of operation. Government operations appear to have been transferred there only after Camulodunum (Colchester), another candidate for an historical Camelot, was destroyed by the Iceni in AD 60-61, contemporary with the date of the inscription mentioned here. The governor at the time was Gaius Suetonius Paulinus, who isn't mentioned in the inscription. Under Agricola's command, as described by Tacitus, the Romans pressed north and founded bases at Deva (Chester) and Eboracum (York). It would be odd to leave the governor in the south when all the action he needed to oversee was in the north, and this is where another inscription comes into play.

This Greek inscription, dating from the late first century (c. AD 84) and found at York, states that the governor's headquarters was there.[20] This is consistent with the references to the 'important figure' killed in the Caledonian invasion, and with Septimius Severus later setting up his headquarters at York, where he eventually died after rebuilding Britannia, following the civil war with Albinus. As to what the governor's lawyer was doing in Londinium when the governor himself was in York, we simply don't know. Perhaps he had family there. Perhaps he wanted to put up his monument to Trajan at a busy port so people would actually see it instead of putting it in what was essentially a war zone. There could be any number of reasons, and the presence of a lawyer does not guarantee the presence of a governor. But the existence of the governor's headquarters does require that the governor be present. Since the governor ultimately controlled all of the legions in his province, and one was usually stationed at the governor's headquarters. Artorius, serving as *dux* of the three British legions, almost certainly would have governed from York.

The fortress at York was located north of the Ouse River and followed roughly the same pattern of all the legionary forts, such as the one described for the VI Ferrata, which we discussed in Chapter 3. Artorius would have occupied the quarters designated for the *legatus*. At this time, he may or may not have had his wife and children with him. We know from the letters discovered at Vindolanda fort on Hadrian's Wall itself, families did follow the highest-ranking officers to their posts. If Artorius had young children, which was entirely possible given that his marriage probably took place during his time as praepositus of the Misenum Fleet and children presumably followed soon after, he may have left his family in Campania in the comfort of the inland villa owned by the Artorii. This is consistent with Arthur leaving Guinevere at Camelot while he rode out with his knights, which at least once resulted in her kidnap by a rival lord. The same abduction pattern occurs in the Nart Sagas.

Artorius would have spent much of his time at York at this point, so the kings of the Britons, the commanders of the Sarmatians, and the legati of the XXth and IInd legions would know where to find him. The four years he commanded, as far as we can tell, were marked largely by peace, something that happened during the time of the later Arthur in the fifth/sixth centuries after he supposedly became King or battle leader of Britain.

The other option is that Artorius developed a travelling headquarters – or as it would come to be called, a 'court'– such as that recounted in many of the later Arthurian legends. Artorius appears to have moved from trouble spot to trouble spot, following the model of the Emperors Lucius Verus and Marcus Aurelius, thereby helping to keep the peace. This factor was recognized by some of the earliest authorities on the later Arthurian period, who declared that the British leader was at the head of a mobile force – if only to explain his ability to fight over such a large area of the country.[21]

Against Armed Men

Most of the ink spilled over the Artorius inscription concerns the two words following the listing of his appointment as *dux*. The words that we can see are: ADVERSVS ARM [....]. S. Mommsen, followed by Malone,[22] chose '*Armoricanos*' (Armoricans) for ARM because Cassius Dio and Herodian both recount disturbances in Gaul in AD 185, events that could plausibly involve Artorius. Although the Rhine legions wound up conducting the trials of the soldiers who rebelled, the legions of Britannia sent vexillations, under the command of Caunius Priscus, to Gaul, as well as to Armorica, to put down the uprising.

The alternate reading, that ARM- stands for *Armenios* (Armenians), isn't possible. While there were disturbances in Armenia in the second century, there are several problems with this reading. First, the disturbances were addressed by Lucius Verus (c. AD 162-166), who quelled rebellion in Syria. This puts the conflict far too early for Artorius, who became a *dux* in the late second century, to have been involved in the fighting. Second, the fighting was against the Parthians, not the Armenians. And third, since Rome was having serious problems with its legions in Britannia, it's hard to imagine that several cohorts would have been taken from Britannia and transferred all the way across the Empire to fight in Armenia when there were several perfectly good legions who were not having problems already in the area.[23]

This brings us back to the question of what the ARM- in the Artorius inscription could actually mean. If neither Armenios nor Armoricos works, and since Caunius Priscus rather than Artorius is the most likely officer to have been sent to Armorica, there has to be a third possibility, another word starting with ARM-.

We do not have to look far. There are multiple armed men causing trouble all over Britannia, and the Latin for 'armed men', in the accusative, is ARMATOS. The use of *'armatos'* in an inscription is confirmed by CIL 02, 05439. The phrase *'adverus armatos'* is used by Tacitus (*Annals*: 59: *'sed palam adversus armatos bellum tractare'*) and again by Livy (*History of Rome*: l.5, c, 27; *'sed adverus armatos et ipsos'*). The word fits the gap in the Castus inscription exactly, which makes the line read:

DVCI LEGG TRIUM BRITANICIMIARVM ADVERSVS ARMATOS

This translates to '*Dux* of the three British legions against armed men.'

Therefore, we offer *armatos* (armed men) as the third option for the expansion of ARM-. Similar inscriptions read *'adversus rebelles,'* ('against rebels') or *'defectores'* ('defectors'), or *'hostes'* ('enemy hosts'). If *armatos* is the correct reading, the reconstruction would look as below.

Aside from the fact that this fits the broken part of the inscription better than either of the others, we have to keep in mind the multiple disturbances in Britannia, the Caledoni raiding south of Hadrian's Wall, destroying almost half of the VI Victrix until someone, in all probability Artorius, chased them back north

Plate 26. The *Armatos* Reconstruction by Alessandro Faggiani.

of the Antonine. Then there were the repeated rebellions among the VI Victrix and the II Augusta.

History is silent as to what the third British legion, the XX Valeria Victrix, was doing at this time, but there is evidence for a Roman presence in Ireland, which was what Agricola had originally planned for the legion stationed at Deva (modern Chester), and which may have involved therm.[24] A survey of Roman ruins in Ireland reached the conclusion that while there was no Roman invasion per se, there was definitely a toe-hold presence there, including military protection of trade sites.[25] If the XXth wasn't moving between the Antonine and Hadrian Walls, trying to clean up the mess left by the Caledonian invasion, it may have made a foray into Ireland. Whatever they were up to, they don't appear to have spent much time at Deva, since the fort boasted only a skeleton crew at the time, and they were certainly not causing the kind of trouble that drew attention to their fellow legions since none of the accounts of the period mentions them. The discovery of the 'Ring of Artorius' at a site near Chester (see Chapter 1) adds an intriguing connection to the story.

All of this suggests that Artorius was employed keeping 'armed men' in their places, mainly in territory controlled by the VI Victrix. This is indeed what he seems to have done. There are no further reports of rebellion in the British legions after AD 187, and even the tribes seemed to have settled down to an uneasy peace. If we are right in our belief that Artorius was acting governor of Britannia for the years between AD 187 and 190, to which all existing evidence points, he must have done a great job – the troubled province was re-established and there were no further outbreaks of rebellion or raiding reported during this period.

Leaving Britannia

After two terms of two years each as *dux*, keeping the peace in Britannia, Artorius was rewarded, presumably for a job well done, by being made governor of the province of Liburnia (roughly equivalent to present-day Croatia). It was an important post, though a good deal less active and dramatic than his time in Britannia. Perhaps it was felt that he had earned a rest.

To depart the island province of Britannia, Artorius had to leave by boat, and like Arthur, who did the same, he never returned. His point of departure could have been from any of a number of places. He probably stayed at York until his replacement, Decimus Clodius Albinus, arrived. Albinus belonged to the II Augusta, so Artorius could just as easily have departed from the legionary base at Caerleon where that legion was stationed. It's interesting to note that Caerleon is often cited as one of Arthur's courts, which would fit well with the notion of Artorius having a group of commanders who moved with him.

From his landing on the Continent at Port Julius, Artorius would have taken to the road if he wanted to travel overland to his new post, or he could have sailed all the way to the Mediterranean and then up the Adriatic to the main port at Spalato (Split) in Liburnia, where he would spend the last known part of his career.

8

. LIBURNIA

We next find Artorius in Liburnia, which he had visited when he was a centurion in the V Macedonica and *praepositus* of the Misenum Fleet. Located between the Krka and Raša rivers on the eastern coast of the Adriatic Sea, the Liburnian territory was conquered by Rome in 33 BC. As we saw, the seafaring skills of its people gave rise to the ship named after them that was so important to the Roman navy. During the Marcomannic Wars the Roman supply line ran through here and, after the Romans triumphed, the port remained valuable for trade. Some Sarmatians, now at peace with the Romans, lingered inland beyond Spalato, so it would have been useful to have a procurator in charge who could communicate with them and who understood their culture. Artorius' focus, though, was now on the port and the ships that used it.

Breath-taking scenery in the area included small islands off the coast that were frequented by wealthy Romans. This part of the Adriatic was mostly calm as a result of these natural breakwaters, and the weather was far superior to what Artorius had endured in Britannia. It must have seemed like the Elysian Fields or Heaven to him – depending on which religion he followed.

Procurator Centenarius
Liburnia was a Roman province from the mid-second century to the end of the 330s. We aren't sure whether it was a province in

its own right or a sub-province of Dalmatia, but the governor of Dalmatia, bordering on Liburnia, was at the time of Artorius' arrival probably Cassius Dio's father, Marcus Cassius Apronianus, who held this post at some point after AD 185.[1]

The rank of *procurator* frequently gets translated as 'governor', but procurators could claim several jobs. Some ran mines, some inventoried weaving-houses, dye-houses, or linen-houses, some oversaw mints. Still others ran imperial estates. In Artorius' case, because of the addition of '*iure gladii*' to his title, we are sure that he was a high-level magistrate in charge of all Liburnia. *Ius gladii* literally means 'Power of the Sword' and carried the authority of inflicting death sentences, even on Senators. It was an authority held only by supreme magistrates, usually Senators but occasionally, as in Egypt, by Equestrians.[2] That Artorius had this authority indicates that Liburnia was functioning much like Egypt, as an Imperial rather than Senatorial province, probably because of the importance of its port. Artorius' compensation for this position was the princely sum of 100,000 sesterces (£140,000, $175,000) per year, a salary that, added to the wealth he'd already amassed, enabled him to maintain the financial requirements of his Equestrian rank, provide for his growing branch of the Artorii, purchase or construct a villa, and build a tomb for his entire immediate family.

Magistrates at this level had to supply their own staff, so they regularly took friends and family members with them to their posts. Artorius could have been doing this for several decades, so it's not surprising that we find references to other Artorii in Liburnia and surrounding provinces, as well as a possible Artorius Fortunatus in Britain, contemporary with or post-dating Artorius Castus' tenure in that region, but not predating it. Surveying the list of names regularly used by the Artorii, the most common *praenomen* is Caius. A brother, half-brother, stepbrother, or another relation by that name may well have been accompanying Artorius since he became *praepositus* of the Misenum Fleet and throughout his service in Britannia. As we have already noted, this Caius may be the source from which we get the stories of the Celtic Cai and the Arthurian Sir Kay.

Building a Life

We're not exactly sure where the border between Liburnia and Dalmatia was. This is important because governors were not allowed to own land in the province that they governed. Since Liburnia had been carved out of Dalmatia, Artorius may have been a sub-governor under Cassius Dio's father, placing his villa inside the boundaries of Liburnia. If the estate was on the Dalmatian side of the border, then Artorius was a governor in his own right.

We also do not know if he bought his villa from someone else or received it as a reward for decades of honourable service or, like his mausoleum, built it from scratch. Its extent is uncertain, but Professor Naned Cambi of the University of Split noted that it probably covered the area between the coastline of Pituntium (modern Podstrana) and the cliffs 8 miles (12.88 km) distant at Mosor, on which the remains of an Illyrian-Roman fort were discovered.[3]

Roof tiles found at the site of the villa bear the stamp of one Ambrosius, who had his brick-making business near the gates of Spalato. The remains of a press found on the land once occupied by the villa tell us there were olive trees on the property, along

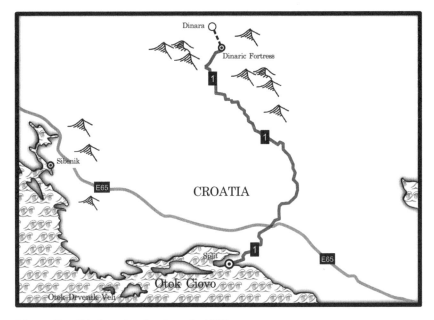

Map 7. Possible location for Artorius' Villa.

with a vineyard that stretched across the hillside rising from the sea, the ridges for which can still be seen today. The Artorii were known to have shipped both of these products to Marseilles around the time of the eruption of Vesuvius and later to Florence. Whether Artorius himself exported his products or kept them for private use is unknown. Beyond the hill with the vineyard is the Adriatic Highway. There the land flattens out into terrain suitable for raising horses, so Artorius probably engaged in that activity as well.

His villa would have been luxurious enough to match the family's seaside villa on the Bay of Naples. In an interesting connection with the Arthurian legends, the villa was used by Ausonius, the father/grandfather of Paulinus Peleaus, whose own biography was scrambled with that of the Maimed King and the Fisher King of the Grail romances, who was named Pelles or Pelleas.[4] This curious parallel offers yet another link between the world of the Sarmatians and the Arthurian legends.

Paulinus in fact got caught up with the Alans, cousins of the Sarmatians, when Alaric sacked Rome in AD 410.[5] A third of Alaric's force, the steppe nomads were probably responsible for the decision to bury Alaric in a river when, as per the custom we described earlier, he died soon after. They also were not very good at following his orders about not taking any loot because they turned up in Narbonne at the wedding of Athaulf, Alaric's successor, with a large amount of treasure that included branched candlesticks, silver platters and golden cups, possibly the treasure taken from the sacking of the Second Temple of Solomon in Jerusalem in AD 70.

When the Alans separated themselves from Athaulf's forces, Paulinus stayed with them, apparently against his will. Athaulf took his army over the Pyrenees into Hispania (Spain), where he died of a wound to the thigh like the Maimed King of Arthurian tradition. The Alans stayed in southern Gaul, raiding and selling off their treasure – with Paulinus' help as translator – until they decided to settle down. Or possibly the treasure ran out. In any case they stayed on to support the future Emperor Constantius III against another group of Alans from northern

Gaul led by a king named Sangiban, who raided south with the usurper Constantine III of Britannia.

Once Sangiban's Alans were informed that they were supporting the wrong emperor, they switched sides and joined their brothers in battling the usurper. Threat to the empire settled, Sangiban took his Alans back north and Paulinus' Alans remained in the area of Burgundy, where Sarmatians appear to have been already stationed from an earlier time. This, points to further connections of Arthurian and Sarmatian history, as we shall see in Chapter 9. In any case, Paulinus was finally left to his own devices and built a shack on the coast near Marseilles, where he took up fishing, or so he wrote. Here, then, we have a Maimed King figure and a 'Fisher King' associated with steppe cavalry.

Of one thing we can be sure: Artorius' family continued to live in the Liburnia area and to occupy the villa he had built for at least another 300 years. Professor Cambi notes that 'among the inscriptions found at Podstrana, the name of the manager of the estate is present, as is that of Ausonius, the regent of the Roman province of Dalmatia ... from the fifth century... Ausonius presided over a property dispute, which was quite possibly connected to the heirs of Lucius Artorius Castus.'[6]

Artorius clearly had his wife and possibly grown or nearly grown children with him at this point because he refers to them in the larger inscription. Given the presence in historical records of a woman who may be Artorius' daughter, a boy who could have been his grandson and another woman who could be his niece in Dalmatia, near where his own tomb was found, he probably did precisely this. Records mention Lucius Gellius Artorius, who died at eight years and eight months, who was the son of Gellius Felix and Artoria Secundina.[7] The inscription bearing their names was found in the region of Salonae, an area that includes the city of Spalato, as well as the ruins of an extensive Roman citadel, close to Artorius' villa. Given the proximity of this inscription to those of Lucius Artorius Castus, Artoria Secundina (perhaps a 'second' Artoria in a given family) was possibly his daughter and the boy Lucius a grandson who was named after him. Artoria Erontima (or Frontina), whose inscription also comes from Salonae, could be another daughter.[8]

Artoria, daughter of Caius Artorius and Flora, was buried in Noricum, part of a federation of Celtic tribes occupying what is today parts of Austria and the Czech Republic. The dating of the inscription that mentions her is still unclear.[9] That Caius' wife's name could have been Flora is intriguing as well, given the Artorii's adherence to the goddess of that name. Artorius Felicissimus, who lived to be sixty-one and who was buried near Narona, could be another close relative.[10]

Apparently, something untoward was happening in the region, though no source records exactly what it was. Most texts are preoccupied with Perennis' fall from power c.185-186. The previous governor of the area, Lucius Junius Rufinus Proculeanus, lasted less than a year. Perhaps Proculeanus ran afoul of Commodus? Or perhaps the governor fell victim to the plague? No military upheaval is reported, though it is possible that something of that nature was responsible for the governor's death – which might explain Artorius' posting to Liburnia in AD 191, at roughly the same time as Dio's father became governor of the neighbouring province of Dalmatia. It's likely that Dio knew Artorius. In fact, Artorius himself may have been the source of the account of the warning message sent to Commodus from Britannia and other stories recounted by the renowned historian, about places Artorius had served and events he had witnessed.

Xiphilinus, the eleventh-century Byzantine monk and epitomist of Dio's *History*, would have considered Artorius unimportant to the history of Byzantium and would, therefore, have almost certainly dropped his name from the summary of the fight on the frozen Danube and other accounts if they involved this figure who was barely known in the East if he was known there at all. We find the same phenomenon with the Grail stories, where the sacred chalice is associated with the Cup of the Last Supper in the West but not in the East. The difference in their social and political ranks could also account for Dio himself dropping Artorius' name from his account. In any case, as governor, Artorius would have socialized with Dio's family and certainly told tales of his lengthy career to the avid historian.

Artorius' years as procurator centenarius seem to have passed relatively peacefully. He was far from the lunacy of Commodus that gripped Rome; his northern neighbour, Pannonia, was unusually quiet, thanks to the presence of the future Emperor Severus as governor in the area. Dalmatia was at peace, and Liburnia flourished.

Then, in AD 192, Commodus was assassinated. Pertinax, the governor Artorius had replaced in Britannia, was named Emperor – and slain only eighty-seven days into his reign.[11] Didius Julianus purchased the Imperial throne, which was auctioned off by the army,[12] and sixty-six days later, he, too, was executed on the orders of the Senate by Septimius Severus, who made the journey from Upper Pannonia to Rome to find out what in the name of all the gods was going on.

Once there, he ascended to the Imperial throne and held a state funeral for Pertinax, which all Equestrians were commanded to attend. Unless Artorius was seriously ill or injured, he would have been present since there was no war in Liburnia or anything else happening that would have prevented him from making the journey to Rome. Afterwards, he returned to Liburnia, where he completed six terms as procurator centenarius and planned to retire. We know that Artorius served six times because of the VI, the Roman numeral for six, following his listing of the office on the inscription. We have no idea how long such a procurator was appointed for. Erring on the side of caution, we calculate that Artorius held the office in one-year increments. That means he would have started serving under Commodus in AD 191 and finished in AD 197 during the reign of Septimius Severus.

Building a Tomb

The problem with many Roman inscriptions is that they are more often than not moved from their original location to build something else, such as a house, a church, or a wall. Many were taken to construct Diocletian's palace in Spalato. This is a pity because where the ancients put something often had a great deal of significance. In the case of Artorius' inscription, though, we are very lucky since it remains, more or less, in situ.

We have seen how much we can learn from this inscription, but it has yet more secrets to give up. The 'D' and the 'M' in the upper left and upper right corners of the inscription stand for '*Dis Manibus*', 'To the spirits of the departed', and indicate that the inscription came from Artorius' actual tomb. Even if the 'D' and the 'M' had become separated from the inscription, we would still know where the text came from because of the context in which it was found: a graveyard wall belonging to the chapel of St Martin, close to where the smaller inscription was also recovered. Once humans establish a certain location as a graveyard, it tends to remain a graveyard, or at least hallowed ground, in the memories of the local populace, especially if the people buried there were aristocracy. There are unfortunate exceptions to that rule, such as poor Richard III of England who wound up under a parking lot in Leicester, but in many ancient Roman towns the rule held over the millennia. Today the ground on which Artorius' tomb once stood is still a cemetery in active use. The villagers of Podstrana, Croatia, have a deep-seated tradition that this is the spot where people were and are buried.

There are some other things they remember as well. The chapel associated with the graveyard is dedicated to St Martin of Tours. A Catholic saint, perhaps best known for being a Roman cavalry officer who cut off the bottom of his cloak to give it to a poor person, Martin has a story that not only echoes Artorius – it reverberates like a gong.

Living roughly two hundred years after him, Martin was born in Pannonia, the same region in which Artorius served in the II Adiutrix. As a boy he rebelled against his parents, becoming a Christian instead of a follower of Mithras, the preferred deity of the army and the most prominent devotion in the area at the time. This would have given Martin the same ambiguous religious framework as Artorius himself, who, as we have seen, may have either worshipped the Virgin Mary and Christ, or the goddess Flora and the god Mars. Martin was a member of the Roman cavalry and rode with the *Equites catafractarii Ambianenses*, a heavy cavalry unit based in northern Gaul that may well have been made up of Sarmatian riders, known to have established a semi-permanent foothold in the area.

Curiously, a second shrine to St Martin is found in the vicinity of another site associated with Artorius and the Sarmatians.[13] As for the story of Martin cutting his cloak, the Roman cavalry rider's cape was shorter than the cloak worn by the standard legionary because the shorter garment was more practical on horseback. Whoever dedicated the chapel on the site of Artorius' tomb to St Martin appears to have turned to the image of the long dead Roman officer for his choice of saint. But where is the image since it is not on the inscription?

The short answer is that the inscription was on the outside of the tomb, probably facing the water because of the heavy naval traffic, instead of the less-travelled road that led to the Adriatic Highway. The Romans believed that your spirit survived as long as someone remembered your story, which is why most people did their best to have at least their name inscribed somewhere, and wealthier people like Artorius went to the effort of have their entire biography carved in stone. The larger lettering of his name could be seen clearly from the water and his story by those who approached from his dock.

To see how the Artorii organized their tombs we have only to turn to the tomb of Castus' august ancestor Marcus Artorius Geminus, who lived in the reign of Caesar Augustus (27 BC to AD 14). His tomb was located in the southeast corner of the land belonging to the villa where Julius Caesar and Cleopatra raised Caesarion, something for which Geminus must have had the Emperor Augustus' permission. We have enough left of Geminus' tomb to reconstruct how it would have looked. Like Artorius' tomb, the inscription outlining Geminus' life faced the water, in this case the Tiber River rather than the Adriatic Sea. The name and other information he wanted to convey was in lettering of a uniform size, indicating its early first-century date. Since Geminus' name wasn't over the door, it remained unrecognized as his tomb for a long time. There is a slim hope that if the graveyard wall in Podstrana is fully excavated, more pieces of Artorius' inscription and the others in the tomb might be found. For now, all we can say with certainty is that they belonged to his family as those in Geminus' tomb belonged to his.

Outside the door of Geminus' mausoleum stood two statues, one of himself and one of his wife, so that we know what Geminus looked like. And a strange statue it is! In Roman art, only gods could be depicted as naked. Mortals had to be clothed, complete with shoes. Marcus Artorius is half-clothed and barefoot. Did he think of himself as a demigod? Did Augustus, whom he served, think of him as semi-divine? Whatever the reason, it was through him that the bloodline of the Artorii became mixed with that of several Roman Emperors. His upraised hand indicates that he was carrying some sort of weapon, or perhaps a standard. The pose is almost identical to that of the Augustus Caesar of Porta Prima, a suburb located roughly seven and a half miles (12 kilometres) north of the centre of the city along the Via Flaminia. Augustus' upraised arm gives the Roman salute, while Geminus' arm is too curved for that. The missing weapon, which would have been cast in bronze, is likely a pilum or other lance-like weapon. The drape of the tunic is essentially identical to that of Augustus, except that Augustus wears armour while Geminus is half-nude. Augustus' left hand contains a pilum, but Geminus' left hand appears to have carried something else, possibly a sword. While Augustus has a cherub atop a tree stump against his right leg, Geminus appears to have only had the tree stump or a stone block. The similarities suggest that Geminus' statue was copied from the Emperor's. The statue of his wife, which stood on the other side of the doorway to his tomb, shows her covered head to toe, the very model of a proper Roman matron.

Presumably, Artorius' tomb had a similar set of statues, now lost to the ravages of time. It's a safe bet that his wife's statue depicted her as a Roman matron. What would Artorius' have looked like, though? We can assume that his statue would have depicted him as a cavalry officer, the part of his career that was most important to him, since the second, smaller plaque bearing his name recalls those postings for which he wished to be particularly remembered. We can imagine Artorius with upraised right arm, holding a lance, and a left arm bearing a sword. He would, indeed, have looked every bit the hero he became. This image is also repeated in some artefacts that show Arthur as one of the Nine Worthies, such as a tapestry in the Historishes Museum, Bale, Germany (c. AD 1475).[14]

The other odd thing about the tomb of Geminus is a circular mosaic in the centre of the floor. It appears to be an image of Castor and Pollux, but one of the twins is missing. The tomb is within sight of the temple of the Divine Twins, one of whom was confined to Hades while the other was doomed to roam the mortal world. Eventually, Zeus took pity on them and placed them in the stars as the constellation of Gemini, after which Geminus was named.

The early Artorii generally cremated their dead, storing their ashes in urns. Inside Geminus' tomb, since interment was extremely uncommon as space for tombs was at a premium in Rome, several niches held the urns. Beneath each niche was a short inscription dedicated to the person whose ashes were in the urn. If Artorius Castus was cremated, this is where the smaller inscription would have been placed. While some scholars argue that this inscription came from a sarcophagus, we must consider the option of cremation. Artorius' grandfather, Sabidianus, had his body – or his ashes and those of his family members – either placed in urns or in a sarcophagus. The smaller plaque from St Martin's chapel in Podstrana that mentions Artorius has markings suggesting it is from a sarcophagus, but the placing of the letters lead us to suppose it was mounted beneath an urn. So, the scholarly argument continues. It must suffice that Artorius' remains, whether cremated or interred, eventually found their way into the tomb he had built for himself and his family. But before this he had one more adventure, one which would assure him of a place in the story of the Empire.

9

CIVIL WAR

Artorius probably never made it to retirement. If he were still alive in AD196, which isn't impossible since he would only have been fifty-four or five, historical events suggest that he could have been called back to active duty by civil war.

As mentioned in the previous chapter, yet another Lucius, this time Septimius Severus, stopped the chaos in Rome by forcibly taking the city with the Danubian legions and assuming the purple. But two rivals soon arose: Decimus Clodius Albinus in Britannia and Gaius Pescennius Niger in Syria. While Severus was able to take care of Niger, as we will discuss below, he needed specialist help dealing with Albinus' forces, which included at least some of the Sarmatians of Britannia.

Born in North Africa into an obscure family, Severus advanced through the Roman ranks, becoming first an Equestrian, then a Senator, and finally a Consul, before taking a series of posts as governor of various provinces, eventually winding up in Upper Pannonia next door to Artorius. The man was as ambitious as he was ruthless.

Whereas Commodus saw himself as a demigod, Severus went so far as to have himself worshipped upon his ascension, which is something neither Niger nor Albinus seems to have done. From the statuary he erected to himself we know that he thought of himself as the Sun-god, Sol Invictus, which led him to tolerate Christianity centuries before Constantine the Great recognized it as the official religion of the empire.[1] This is something else that makes it possible for Artorius to have converted from the worship of Flora to that of the Virgin Mary, echoing the later Arthur's supposed devotion to the mother of Jesus.

As well as Severus' devotion to Sol Invictus and his toleration of Christianity, he also acknowledged Mithraism, celebrating the god most popular with the army. All three creeds shared the holy date of December twenty-fifth. This had ramifications as to how Severus was viewed in Rome itself, as did the presence of his legions in the City, something that had been banned since the time of Julius Caesar. He replaced the Praetorian Guard and the City Watch with his soldiers and pronounced himself heir to Antoninus Pius and Marcus Aurelius, presenting himself as the next valid Adoptive Emperor, wiping Commodus, Pertinax and Didius Julianus from the imperial line as decisively as he was about to eliminate his rivals.[2]

In fact, he was founding a dynasty that would include his sons, Caracalla and Geta (whom Caracalla himself would kill and try to erase from memory), the brief interloper Macrinus (who took over from Commodus until he was himself assassinated), Elagabalus (who ruled as Marcus Aurelius Antoninus and was Caracalla's supposed son), and Severus Alexander (who was descended from Septimius Severus' wife and a cousin of Elagabalus), after which the Empire started to unravel. But in the last decade of the second century, militarily, politically, and religiously, Rome belonged to Septimius Severus.

In AD 193, Albinus, who had become the governor of Britannia following the unnamed governor whom we believe was Artorius, was proclaimed Emperor by his soldiers and, at the same time, Niger's soldiers declared *him* Emperor in the East. Severus sent word to both of them that they would be co-rulers with him, but in reality, he had no such intention. While Albinus bided his time in Britannia, Severus went after Niger.

Albinus, Severus, and Niger were all born in Africa, though Albinus, whose name may mean 'white', and Severus, whose name means 'severe', seem to be of Roman extraction while Niger may not have been. There is speculation that Niger, whose name of course means 'black', may actually have been an ethnically black Emperor of Rome. Certainly, his coins seem to support this hypothesis. While not a direct link to the Arthurian tradition, it is interesting to note that there were at least four knights of colour connected with the Arthurian legends: Sir Palamedes and his two brothers, Safere and Segwarides, and the hero of the less well-known Dutch romance of *Morien*.[3] The imperial contenders were reflecting the racial diversity that already existed in the army and that would later exist at Arthur's Round Table.

Unfortunately for Niger, Severus slaughtered him in Syria and set about destroying many of the legions and client kingdoms in the region, even breaking Syria into two provinces to further decrease the power of future commanders in that area. At the same time Severus recognized Albinus as Caesar, which kept him in Britannia for the time being by making him assume he would be Severus' heir in a return to the adoptive style of the Antonine emperors.

Once Severus had finished with his black opponent, he turned his attention to the white one, Albinus. He took a very strange route to reach his new adversary. Instead of shipping his soldiers to Gaul with the classis Misenatium, he travelled north through Dacia, Upper Pannonia, Noricum, Raetia, Upper Germania and into Gaul. Along the way he called up soldiers who were loyal to him, and Artorius, whose villa lay in Severus' path, would almost certainly have been among those raised. Severus could hardly have resisted the temptation to summon his former colleague. Artorius not only knew the British legions, particularly those which included Sarmatian cavalry, he'd also fought alongside many of the British kings Albinus had collected as allies as he moved his troops to Gaul in an attempt to meet Severus on a battleground of his own choosing. Such knowledge would have rendered Artorius invaluable, and Severus was not a man to overlook or fail to use such a resource.

The instant Albinus received word that Severus was gathering an army to march against him, he assembled the best of his units in Britannia and moved them to Gaul. Among these troops were the Sarmatians of Bremetennacum, who were to serve as his heavy cavalry.

Tinurtium and Lyon

Severus' forces first engaged Albinus at Tinurtium (modern Tournus, which is located southwest of Châlons and north of Mâcon),[4] in AD 197. In the ensuing battle it was reported that the British cavalry suffered heavy losses.

This detail tells us that Albinus brought a significant number of British horsemen with him. At the time, the only large group of British cavalry that suffered such a loss in numbers were the Sarmatians of Bremetennacum. Though some scholars think that all the Sarmatians of Britannia were wiped out in this civil war, the deaths probably totalled closer to half the contingent, judging by which forts had to be re-garrisoned following these battles, and which ones were allowed to remain empty.[5] Many of the forts west of the Pennines and south of the Wall were abandoned when the Sarmatians moved into Britannia, and the outer rim of them, about half, were reoccupied after the civil war. Taking the number of soldiers based at each fort, we can estimate that roughly 2,500 Sarmatians died in Albinus' ill-fated attempt to seize the imperial throne. Heavy losses indeed.

Severus, having served as governor of Upper Pannonia, might have had the knowledge necessary to defeat the steppe cavalry, but Dio makes a point of saying that the Emperor was not present at any of the battles except the last. The actual brains behind the initial defeat of Albinus' forces may well have belonged to the former commander of the Iazyges: Lucius Artorius Castus.

Following the battle of Tinurtium, something happened that enabled about half the Sarmatian cavalry to survive the civil war and return to Britannia: they switched sides. This was something the steppe horsemen were infamous for doing, and it had played a part in the treaty with Rome that sent the unit to Britannia in the first place. Just as the Round Table split in two towards the end of Arthur's rule, one side following the King and the rest his incestuous son Mordred, so Albinus' forces were now divided. The Romans had learned that explaining to the Sarmatians who the real Emperor was would make at least some of them defect to Severus' forces. It was knowledge that Constantius would use to great effect in the fifth century, and it probably resulted in

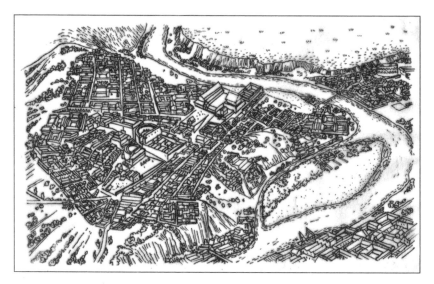

Plate 27. Lugdunum/Lyon. (W. Kinghan)

Albinus' downfall. Severus had a secret weapon: the best person in all of the Empire to persuade the Sarmatians to switch sides.

Following Albinus' catastrophic loss, he pulled south. Severus pursued him and engaged him a second – and final – time at Lugdunum (modern Lyon). Lugdunum was the capital of the province of Lugundensis,[6] Dio (76.6) gives the numbers as being 150,000 men on each side.[7] Unless there were far more *numeri* in the region than has been previously thought, this figure is impossible. Britannia only had about a third of this number in troops, even if Albinus completely stripped the military from the country, a massive abandonment of the frontier for which there is no evidence.[8] The three British legions had roughly 5,000 men and 120 horsemen each, a total of 15,000 men and 360 horsemen.[9]

There were only 37,550 auxiliaries in Britannia under Marcus Aurelius, though there was the potential to garrison 42,000 auxiliaries in addition to the regular legions.[10] The possibility of another group of Sarmatians, already based in Gaul, being called upon will be examined below, but Severus' route took him into areas controlled by six legions, giving him a total of 30,720 troops, 720 of which would have been horsemen.[11] The total number of *auxilia* in the entire Empire at this point was 150,000, and there is no way that they were all in Gaul.[12] The total number of mounted *numeri* in the Empire is unknown,[13] though the most substantial recorded number were the Sarmatians from Britain, who by AD 197 probably numbered around 5,000, losses over the years being offset by sons following fathers into the army as the vicus adjacent to the fort was established. Even if both Severus and Albinus withdrew all possible troops from the border defences, something neither of them either could, or would, have done, they could not have amassed the numbers Dio describes. Dio exaggerated the figures or the Byzantine monk who summarized his work simply read the numbers incorrectly.[14]

Dio (76.7) gives graphic details of the battlefield, 'covered with the bodies of men and horses'.[15] In addition, twenty-nine Senators and numerous Equestrians were executed under Severus for supporting his enemies. Given his usefulness to the Emperor and the fact that his family continued to be honoured after his death, going on to make advantageous marriages and hold important posts, it's unlikely that Artorius met such an end. If, however, Artorius fell in this battle, that makes his death prior to the year 200.

Avallo and Avallon

What happened next is still a matter of conjecture, although we cannot ignore the number of apparent coincidences that suggest our working out of the events is largely accurate. To understand this, we have to look at a theory originally proposed by Geoffrey Ashe in his 1960 book *From Caesar to Arthur*, in which, almost as an after-thought, he drew attention to a man named (or titled) Riothamus who lived in the fifth century AD. This man vanished rather than died and was known to have spent time in Burgundy in an area known as the Avallonnaise, centred in particular at a place named Avallo, or as it would come to be written, Avallon.[16]

Ashe later developed this thesis in a book called *The Discovery of King Arthur* (1985), in which he showed that Riothamus was a title rather than a name, meaning Greatest King, and proposed that this was the real Arthur.[17]

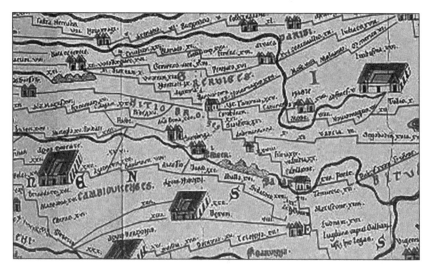

Map 8. Part of the *Tabula Peutingeriana* showing Avallo. (Authors' collection)

A particular focus of the argument included Riothamus' time in Gaul when he was apparently active in the fight against the Visigoths. A number of researchers have noted that there is a considerable amount of literary evidence that places Arthur in Gaul. According to Geoffrey of Monmouth in the *Historia Regum Brittanniae,* written around 1136, Arthur spent a total of nine years in the area, fighting against 'hostile provinces' in the region (Book ix Ch. 12 ff.). Another text, *The Legend of St Goeznovius* (*Legenda Sancti Goeznovii*) attributed to William, chaplain to Bishop Eudo of Lyons around AD 1019, writing over a hundred years before Geoffrey, not only describes Arthur as a king but also adds: 'This same Arthur, after many victories which he won gloriously in Britain and Gaul, was summoned at last from human activity.'[18]

Geoffrey may have picked up on this when he wrote his own book – he grew up in Brittany where St. Goeznovius flourished. Though Geoffrey's book is notoriously unhistorical, based as much on folklore and myth as on any kind of real history, we can still draw upon some of the details he included in his account of Arthur.

In book IX Geoffrey sends Arthur off to go to join his cousin, King Höel of Brittany, in subduing insurgents loyal to Rome.

In Geoffrey's narrative Arthur is opposed by a tribune named Frollo, under the Emperor Leo I – both fictitious characters – which makes Arthur the enemy rather than the ally of Rome. Such a reversal, which happens regularly in folktales, is something that almost certainly occurred as time blurred the historical facts.

Geoffrey tells us that the armies separated, Höel going south to Aquitaine and Gascony, where they fought against Guitard, leader of the Potevins, while Arthur remained in central and eastern France in the area known today as Burgundy, fighting a Visigothic enemy.[19] Later in the book he describes how Arthur, wounded in a battle against his bastard son Mordred, was carried off, over the sea, to a place called Avalon, there to be healed of his wounds.

Later still, in Geoffrey's follow-up book the *Vita Merlini* (c. 1150), he added several more important details. He tells us that Avalon is known as the Fortunate Island:

It produces all things of itself; the fields there have no need of the ploughs of the farmers and all cultivation is lacking except what nature provides. Of its own accord it produces green grapes, and apple trees grow in its woods from the close clipped grass. The ground of its own accord produces everything instead of merely grass, and people live there 100 years or more.[20]

Having described this remarkable place, Geoffrey continues:

There, nine sisters rule, by a pleasing set of laws, those who come to them from our country. She who is first of them is more skilled in the healing art and excels her sisters in the beauty of a person. Morgen is her name, and she has learned what useful properties all the herbs contain, so that she can cure sick bodies. She also knows an art by which to change her shape, and to cleave the air on new wings like Daedalus; when she wishes she is at Brest, Chartres, or Pavia, and when she will she slips down from the air onto your shores [i.e., Britain]. And men say that she has taught astrology to her sisters.[21]

Much of this description comes in a discussion between Merlin and the bard Taliesin – who may have contributed his own clues to the distant memory of Artorius. In his dialogue with Merlin, in which he describes the creation of the world and many other wonders, he says:

> There [to Avalon] after the battle of Camlan we took the wounded Arthur, guided by Barinthus to whom the waters and the stars of heaven were equally well known. With him steering the ship we arrived there with the prince, and Morgen received us with fitting honour, and in her chamber, she placed the king on a golden bed and with her own hand uncovered his honourable wound and gazed at it for a long time. At length she said that health could be restored to him if he stayed with her a long time and made use of her healing art. Therefore, we entrusted the king to her and returning spread our sails to the favouring winds.[22]

Despite numerous efforts to identify Avalon with various places in Britain – the most familiar being the town of Glastonbury in Somerset – none have been positively established. Yet Burgundy, where Geoffrey places Arthur during his Gaulish wars, does possess such a place: Avallon, in the area known as the Avallonnaise, now part of the Départment of Yonne in France. In Artorius' time it lay within the Roman province of Luguvalium, and its original name was Aballō, ultimately derived from Gaulish *Aballū/*Aballon, which translates as 'place of the apple tree' or 'place of the apple tree goddess', from the proto-Celtic *abalnā*.[23] This is exactly the etymology given for Avalon as it appears in the medieval texts of the Arthurian legends, where it is a place of apple orchards. Of course, it would be easy to dismiss this as no more than a coincidence, were it not for a number of historical connections.

One of the most recent explorations of the Riothamus theory is a book by independent researcher Marilyn Floyde. Geoffrey Ashe's thesis led her to explore the region of the Avallonnaise, with some intriguing results, which she presented in her short book *King Arthur's French Odyssey* (2009).

It should be said at this point that the present authors do not subscribe to the Riothamus theory, but some of Marilyn Floyde's conclusions seem to us to point to another possibility – one that connects the Burgundian Avallon and its environs with the mythical Avalon – and with the story of Artorius' final adventure.

Both Ashe and Floyde point out that while Geoffrey of Monmouth has Arthur fighting *against* the Romans, the fifth-century accounts of Riothamus declare that he was fighting *for* them. The fifth-century historian Jordanes, one of the best sources for the history of the barbarian tribes in the area, along with Gregory of Tours in his *History of the Franks,* written c. 550 AD, both mention Riothamus, describing him as a leader of the Britons. Jordanes offers us a glimpse of him fighting against Euric, a Visigothic king who is said to have routed 'Riothamus king of the Britons, before the Romans could join him'.[24] From here, the Britons are described as fleeing, with Riothamus gathering as many men as he could and heading into Burgundy, then still loyal to Rome.

This is the last record we have of Riothamus, and we assume that he perished somewhere in Burgundy. Floyde points out that Riothamus is described as leading a well-disciplined and powerful force, not some ragtag alliance of 'barbarian' tribes, as one might have expected. A cohort of well-armed and disciplined Sarmatian cataphracts would perfectly fit the bill.

Much of the account could be applied to Artorius and his Sarmatians with the simple substitution of names, and the possibility is that Riothamus was based on recollections of a commander of Sarmatian cavalry in Burgundy in the second century AD.

The existence of an extensive Roman fort, Camp Cora, which overlooks the confluence of two rivers, the Cure and the Cousin, suggests another scenario. Coinage and other remains found at the site, dating from the first century to the fourth, suggest that it was built sometime in the reign of Nero. Its position overlooking the Via Agrippa, a major highway that runs from Sens (Agedincum) to Autun (Augustodunum) in Belgic Secunda – take us a step further.

The presence of the camp is a clear sign of the importance of the area, and though its prime function was to guard the road, it also protected two important foundations: an extensive set of

Plate 28. Nineteenth-century illustration of the remains of Camp Cora. (Authors' collection)

Plate 29. The Via Agrippa today. (Jane May)

iron smelting works, dating back as far as 3,000 BC, and a nearby group of springs known as the Fontaines de Salées. The iron foundries were developed by the Celts in the area, who operated a mint producing coins stamped ABALLO, and saw to it that there were good roads and water supplied to the site. The Romans reorganized, extended, and regulated this during the reign of the Emperor Hadrian.

Swords and Fountains

A little way to the north of Avallon, and still close to the Via Agrippa, lies a small village named Sermizelles, known in the twelfth century as Sarmisoliae. This name is believed to be derived from the name of the 'Sarmates' (Sarmatians) who had garrisoned the fort of Cora from the second century and who, according to local archaeological records, were present in the area well into the third century or even later. Much of the area had in fact been occupied by the Sarmatians in the first century AD, so that any who came there later would quite possibly have encountered relations in the immediate area. The number of place-names of Sarmatian origin found throughout Burgundy tells us unequivocally that they were there for a long period. [25] Could the specific garrison at Camp Cora be the remaining troop of the original 8,000 Sarmatians who were not sent to Britannia with Artorius? We cannot know for certain, and it's possible that the original Sarmatian warriors sent west by Marcus Aurelius may have been split up among several of the legions throughout the Empire. There is a group of Sarmatians who settled on the island of Sardinia in the late second century; yet there is at least a strong possibility, given the dates and situation of the fort, that they were part of the original group.

It is unclear which of the legions were based at Cora, though it appears to have been the VIII Augusta. In any case, the existence of a settlement named for the Sarmatians suggests long-term occupation, and the large flat plains adjacent to the area, similar to the Fylde next to Bremetenacum, make this an ideal site for raising horses, which, as we have seen, was a central occupation of the tribes from the steppes. It's also possible that the large force of cataphracts mentioned in Dio's account of the battle at Lugdunum between Severus and Albinus would have included horsemen from this area, perhaps reuniting some of the original force of 8,000 Sarmatian warriors from the time of Marcus Aurelius.

The foundations of a large third-century villa were discovered close to the centre of the widely scattered smelting pits, possibly the residence of a Roman supervisor of the mines. A forum is also known to have existed there, and a bronze statue of the god Mercury was unearthed there. The ruins of a temple dedicated to Mars can still be seen on the hillside overlooking the Via Agrippa and close to the fort of Cora. The Sarmatians who were stationed there worshipped a nameless god whom the Greeks and Romans identified as Mars, and, as we have seen, he was the only god to whom the Sarmatians built a fixed temple.

The presence of metal-smelting in the area cannot help but recall the tribe closely related to the Sarmatians, known as the Kalybes, who specialized in the production of armour and weapons – a name that offers a possible root for the name of Arthur's magical sword, Caliburnus, later renamed Excalibur. Another curious

Plate 30. The remains of Camp Cora today. (Jane May)

connection arises from a reference in a twelfth-century poem, *Le Chanson de Girart de Roussillon*, noted by Marilyn Floyde, which describes the hero's father, Drogon, obtaining 'a marvellous coat of mail from the forge d'Espandragon' shortly before fighting a battle at Vaubeton – believed by Floyde and Paul Meyer, who edited the poem, as having taken place in the area not far from the forges. The name Espendragon immediately recalls that of Arthur's farther, Uther Pendragon, while Drogon is said to be of Burgundian origin. Could this be another reference to the famous draco banner?

Interestingly, Robert de Boron, who was the first to write of the sword in the stone in connection with Arthur, was also a

Plate 31. *L'Estoire du Merlin*, featuring Merlin carrying a dragon banner. (Bibliothèque Nationale)

Burgundian. In the MS of his twelfth-century poem *L'Estoire du Merlin*, we see an illustration of Arthur fighting under a windsock-style banner of the type used by the Sarmatians and later adopted by the legions. (see Plate 31) In addition, Floyde points out, during the Third Crusade in 1190, Richard the Lionheart gave a gift to Tancred of Sicily – the sword Caliburn, which had formally belonged to King Arthur. He did so in the town of Vézelay, which may well have kept the sword in the

Plate 32. The Foundation of the Wells. (C. Matthews)

treasury of its cathedral, which lies only a short distance from Avallon.

Could this have been a sword created at the forges of Espendragon? If so, the very name of the place could have associated it with Arthur; and if Artorius himself had been in the areas several hundred years earlier, the connection would have been even stronger.

The second important foundation, Les Fontaine de Salées, were said to be tended and protected by a group of women (possibly priestesses) famed for their healing skills. These bear a strong resemblance to Geoffrey of Monmouth's description of the nine sisters of Avalon, and to the equally magical 'Maidens of the Wells' described in the thirteenth-century poem *L'Elucidation*,[26] who were seen as guardians of the Grail. The name of the Fontaines de Salées, which actually derives from the name for 'willows', may also stem from the name of the Celtic god of metal workers, Sucellus, most often shown with a mallet or a hammer in his hand, perhaps linking him with the nearby smelting works.

The fountains were extended and built upon by the Romans in the second century, turning them into a widely frequented spa with helium-infused waters, and Artorius could have been familiar with the place. The nearby resort of Morvan was a well-known summer destination for well-to-do Roman families, who came to bathe in the sacred waters of Le Fontaines Salées, and it's quite likely that members of the Artorii family – even Castus himself – may have come there.

When all of these details are gathered together, we have a series of parallels which, rather than the shadowy figure of Riothamus, place both Artorius and the Sarmatian warriors he had once commanded in the area of the final conflict between Severus and Albinus. Add to this the fact that the Emperor's march towards Lugdunum led him through this area, and we have a scenario suggesting that this could be the setting for Artorius' final adventure. We may also remember that in the battle against Albinus on Gaulish soil, some of the Sarmatians switched allegiance, enabling them to be on the winning side and to return to Britannia after the expedition into Gaulish lands. It may well be no coincidence that another battle, fought in the area of the Avallonnaise at Lugdunum, though attributed to Riothamus, also ended with part of his army changing sides.

If, as we believe, the battle in which Artorius was either killed or severely wounded took place not far from Avallon, then it's possible that this may mark the beginning of the final journey of this remarkable soldier, perhaps by boat, either along the Cure or the Cousin to Avallon itself, where he may have rested or died, and which could have been the first point on a journey which led back to Liburnia, perhaps from Marseilles to Spalato (Split), courtesy of his former fleet, the classis Misenatium.

If he were, like Arthur, suffering from a head wound and still alive, there is still another possibility. He could have been taken toward Abellinum (modern Avellino in Campania, Italy, the province where Artorius was born) east of Nola where Augustus Caesar died, to an area which, according to local tradition, was also famous for women associated with water, healing, and magic, much as Geoffrey's Arthurian story says. In fact, enough of Nero's partially completed canals were still functioning well enough that a boat could have carried an injured man as far as Nola without resorting to the hazards of travel over land. Anyone who accompanied him that far, perhaps some of his loyal Sarmatians, would have returned to Britannia with news that they had either left Artorius alive at Avellinum or that he'd died there. From that site his ashes or body could have been transported back to Liburnia via Barium (modern Bari), taking a final journey by ship.

Burial in Dalmatia

Artorius was buried in the tomb he had prepared on the seashore not far from the Adriatic Highway. As described earlier, a small plaque, carved with the posts he considered most important, his time *as primus pilus* of the V Macedonica and his time as praefect of the VI Victrix, was placed either beneath the urn containing his ashes or on the sarcophagus containing his mortal remains. And as we noted, the Romans believed that as long as someone remembered their story their soul would survive in the Afterlife. The name 'Lucius Artorius' survived in the family through that of Lucius Artorius Pius Maximus during Diocletian's reign, which proves that the line continued after Artorius' death and that his remarkable life was remembered.[27] If we are right and Artorius is the historical figure behind the legends of King Arthur, when it came to his name and story, it far outlived his mortal form.

10

KING

Throughout this book we have traced echoes of the life and deeds of Lucius Artorius Castus in the historical record and found many that relate to the figure of Arthur. It is time to look at the legends and literature that have surrounded this figure from at least the fifth century and very probably earlier, to some degree partly obscuring his character from us. Do we find echoes here of an older, Roman figure? The answer is that we do, to the extent that it is almost impossible to dismiss the parallels between the life of Artorius and the semi-mythical Arthur. The first place we need to look is at the surviving references to Arthur from the fifth century onwards.

Remembering Artorius

As we have seen, a brief mention is made in a ninth-century epic poem known as *Y Gododdin*, where a warrior is described as being a mighty fighter 'though he was no Arthur'[1] and which interestingly mentioned a 'wall'. The kingdom of Gododdin, where the battle described in the poem took place, lay north of Hadrian's Wall along the major Roman road of Dere Street, which is precisely the area in which Artorius was active.

The next are two brief mentions in the *Annales Cambriae* (Annals of Wales), a list of significant events covering the years AD 447-594, which describe Arthur as fighting at the Battle of Badon in 515 and dying in a later battle of 537 with Medraut, identified with the later character of Mordred. This is believed to have been complied in the mid-tenth century, although the oldest surviving copy is 12th century. The next source is the *Historia Brittonum*, attributed to the monk Nennius, which dates from the ninth century. This gives us a good deal more about Arthur:

> Then Arthur along with the kings of Britain fought against them in those days, but Arthur himself was the military commander ['dux bellorum'].[2]

The text then goes on to list the twelve battles fought and won by Arthur, which, as we saw in Chapter 6, fits well alongside those fought by Artorius and the Sarmatians around the area of Hadrian's Wall.

We may note immediately that Arthur was chosen as the commander of the Britons multiple times – just as Artorius served as *praefectus* twice and *dux* (Equestrian governor) according to the mausoleum inscription, for several years. It has been noted numerous times that Nennius' text clearly indicates that Arthur was not one of the kings of the Britons, though he fought alongside them, which again fits well with an Equestrian commander and governor of Britannia.

Other poems, such as the eleventh-century poem *'Pa Gur?'* from the *Black Book of Carmarthen*, claim that someone named Arthur fought battles either near or north of Hadrian's Wall in Roman times.[3] Gerald of Wales (Giraldus Cambrensis, c. A.D. 1195) designates the Picts and Scots as Arthur's opponents in his book *De Principis Instructione* and includes the interesting detail that, according to Gildas, the Roman auxiliaries and legions were 'worthless' against the Picts and Scots.[4] Again, this is exactly what we see when Artorius fought against their ancestors, the Caledoni. Only the Sarmatian cavalry were effective.

Although Gildas does not mention Arthur by name, Gerald assumed that the military commander mentioned by him was Arthur.[5] Several of the battles associated with Arthur's defence of Britannia, mentioned by Gildas and other authors, have been identified as locations in Scotland or near the Scottish border.

Sigmund Eisner, in his study of the Arthurian Tristan legend, drew attention to the proliferation of nomenclature originating in the north – not only in the Tristan legend, but also in other Arthurian stories – adding significantly to the idea that the Arthur legends emerged from the northern part of the country.[6]

Regardless of whom Arthur fought, he consolidated Britannia, which suffered from infighting among various groups following the death of a previous leader, usually said to be Ambrosius Aurelianus, Aurelius Ambrosius (probably the same person) or Arthur's father, Uther Pendragon.

The next significant reference comes from a much later text, *The Book of Taliesin*, written down in the fourteenth century but attributed to a much older figure, the eponymous bard of that name, who lived in the sixth century. Not all of these poems were written by the man to whom they are attributed – the figure of Taliesin acquired a semi-mystical persona, which accounted for almost any older work, usually anonymous and containing mysterious or oblique references, to be added to the list of his works.[7]

It has been pointed out that this text is quite late, at least in its present form, but authorities such as J. T. Koch and Kenneth Jackson[8] have studied the original texts, as we have, and demonstrated that it is possible to see traces of much older versions embedded within the medieval books in which these poems are assembled. Indeed, it is difficult without this understanding to make sense of many of the works contained in what are generally known as *The Four Ancient Books of Wales*: namely *The Black Book of Caermarthen*, *The White Book of Rhydderch*, *The Red Book of Hergest* and *The Book of Taliesin*. A careful reading of these works can tell us a great deal about the way in which memories of far earlier times were preserved, initially orally and only later in written form. While the poems in *The Book of Taliesin* appear to be late and may even be seen to contain contemporary references to current events, as well as invocations to Christ inserted by the pious monks who wrote them down, it's still possible to see beyond these to a far earlier time. Additionally, many of the texts transcribed in the medieval era were themselves copies of much earlier works, now lost.

The great Arthurian scholar William A Neitz, who also believed that Artorius was a most promising contender for the original Arthur, wrote 'That the shift occurred which made him in Nennius the British Champion, not only against the Picts and Scots but also against the Saxons, is part of the epic process'[9]. This process is a recognised pattern in both folklore and literature, in which heroes are augmented and their lives expanded by the addition of materials from other heroic events. This is very much the case with the Arthurs of history and legend, the 'epic process' continued throughout the Middle Ages, and almost certainly looked back to the deeds of his Roman namesake.

One of the most intriguing and enlightening accounts of Arthur from this source came to light in 2004. At the time, Caitlín Matthews was working on new translations of poems attributed to Taliesin. A full translation of this poem *Areith Awdyl Eglur* ('The Sovereign's Chair') is included in Appendix 2. For the purposes of our current argument, we need to focus on specific lines.

Declare the clear *awdl*   [epic poem]
In *awen's* own metre.   [inspiration]
A man sprung of two authors,
Of the steel cavalry wing,
With his clear wisdom,
With his royal rule,
With his kingly lordship,
With his honour of scripture,
With his red lorica,
With his assault over the wall,
With his poet-praised seat,
Among the defenders of the wall.
He led from the enclosed wall
Pale saddled horses...

Arthur the blessed,
In harmonious song,
In the forefront of battle,
Trampling down nine...

Those pierced and lost,
Like such an array,
From the slaughter of the chieftain,
From the radiant ranks,
From loricated *Lleon*,   [City of the legions/York?]
Will arise a king
For the fierce border.

Strange accents flow,
Eloquent assaults
Of seafarers.
From the children of *Saraphin*.   ['the snake-armoured ones']

Here, then, we have an epic poem concerning a hero sprung of 'two authors', by which we can assume two cultures or races, of 'a steel cavalry wing', who defends from the wall and leads from a walled enclosure – probably a fort. He is Arthur the blessed, who leads from the front in battle, from loricated Lleon – probably a reference to the City of Legions. There are voices heard with strange accents, from the snake-armoured ones.

It is hard not to see here a clear reference to a Roman cavalry officer, leading his men into battle from the Wall (we offer the capitalization here for emphasis; this isn't the case in the manuscript but very clearly in the context of the poem refers to Hadrian's Wall). Here strange accents are heard and the children of Saraphin, which also translates (literally) as 'snake-armoured ones', are either allies or enemies of men from the City of the legions. There have been a number of alternative suggestions for the identity of this site (*urbs legionis*), including Chester and Caerleon-upon-Usk, but Malory scholar P. J. C. Field makes a good argument for its identity as York. This would fit well with the locale of Artorius' campaign against the Caledoni.[10]

It is hard not to see this as a reference to Artorius and the Sarmatian cavalry wing, whose scaled armour caused them to be seen as lizard-like (Chapter 4). The text is late of course, but there is no mistaking the references to earlier times, while the language itself is laced with words and end rhymes from the older

Brythonic language spoken in Britannia around the time of the Roman occupation. It's easy to see how the monks who were recording these poems might have misunderstood them, or even more likely, tried to update them, rather as if a modern writer tried to modernise the language of Shakespeare.

Another work, also from *The Book of Taliesin*, recently translated as *The Short Poem of Lludd's Conversation*, includes the following lines:

Albion's ruler will be shaken
By a Roman leader – splendid his terror.
He's not bold, nor a wily king of fluent speech –
Who'd see those foreigners as I see them.[11]

The implication here is that a Roman leader is able to see and recognize the threat offered by an incoming force – perhaps, in this context, the Saxons of Arthur's time. But the reference to a Roman leader suggests an earlier contender: Artorius. We note also that he is not a bold or wily king – perhaps not a king at all, but as Nennius says, a leader who fought alongside the British kings. Such words, written long after the time of Artorius, when placed alongside the other references we have surveyed, appear full of meaning.

It is our contention that the period of time between the original texts on which so much of the Welsh poetry was based and the period when Lucius Artorius Castus fought on and around Hadrian's Wall, simply goes to show how deep and lasting was the memory of events that were vital to the survival of the Britons of the second century. And in the sixth, they faced the Saxons with a man named Arthur at their head, as their ancestors had faced the Caledoni with the help of a man named Artorius.

Echoes from the Steppes

When we look at the mythic traditions of the Sarmatians who served under Artorius we find remarkable echoes of the legends of Arthur and his knights, some of which we have seen already.

One particular group is the Narts, heroic and sometimes godlike figures who feature in an extensive cycle of epics, sagas, and folktales springing from the traditions and beliefs of the Alano-Sarmatians. It was from these people, whose homeland is in the area generally known as the Caucasus, including the South Russian Steppes, that the ranks of the warriors later commanded by Artorius, were drawn. They brought with them an early form of the Nart sagas and legends, chronicling the lives and adventures of this heroic, quarrelsome, warlike band. Although these were not seriously collected until the 19th century, we believe that the tales, which are 'extremely archaic',[12] became embedded in the fledgling tales of 'King' Arthur already being composed and retold in the halls of Celtic and Roman-British settlements as early as the sixth century AD.

A major story concerning the Narts describes how they numbered among their possessions an object known as the Amonga, or Nartamonga, the cup of the Narts. This was a type of cup or cauldron that would only feed heroes of significant stature, and in one tale, centring on their leader, we can see more than one echo of later Arthurian legends, both the Welsh tales of the sacred, wonderworking cauldron of Pen Annwn, from which only heroes can be fed, and which may even bring back the dead to life, or the Cauldron of Diwrnach, 'which will not boil the food of a coward' and the later mediaeval accounts of the Quest of the Round Table knights for the Christian Grail.

The story of the Amonga can be summarised as follows. The Narts were quarrelling among themselves over who should keep the Amonga, the sacred cup that would only serve the most perfect hero, and for which they had sought for a long time. First, Urzymag said that without him they would not have succeeded in their quest for the cup, so he should have it. Then Soslan and Sosryko, who were also famous warriors, claimed to be the greatest hero. In each case Batraz, who was the leader of the Narts, refuted their claims, instancing times when they had failed to live up to the highest standards of heroism, where he had not. Finally, Batraz challenged any man there to find one time when he personally had failed them. No one could do so, and he therefore kept the Amonga.

The nature of the Amonga, its ability to enhance heroic abilities and bring inspiration to the one who owns it, leaves little room for doubt that the Nart Sagas represent an important link in the chain that would lead in time to the Grail Quest of later Arthurian legend.[13] Its ability to serve as a truth-telling object ties it firmly to both Irish tradition – in the case of the Four-Sided Cup of Truth, from the 13th-century *Adventures of Cormac in the Land of Promise,* which breaks apart when a lie is uttered and reassembles when a truth is told – and to the Cauldrons of Annwn and the goddess Ceridwen, which offer different kinds of truth and vision according to the nature of the story. The Amonga is sometimes known as the *Uiciamonga* or 'revelatory vessel' of the Narts.[14]

Batraz himself has a number of parallels with Arthur, one of the most startling being the story of his death.[15] As Batraz lies wounded on the field of battle, he asks twenty of his men – because that's how many it takes to lift his sword, Dzus-Quara – to throw this magical weapon into the sea. The men originally fail to do so, carrying out their master's wishes on the second or third attempt. Then multiple miracles happen: the sea becomes turbulent and turns blood-red. Finally, a storm rises and carries off the dead Batraz. This is so remarkably like the later stories in which Bedivere, Arthur's lieutenant, is asked by the wounded king to do exactly the same with Excalibur, followed by the miracle of the Lady of the Lake (the Queen of the Sea in the 12th-century romance, *Lanzalet*) catching it, waving it three times and drawing it under the water, after which Arthur dies, that one has to consider these stories as either following each other or both drawing upon the same or similar sources.

The story appears nowhere else in this form other than in the Arthurian legends. In addition, it should be noted that the battle which ends in Batraz's death is also an internecine one, as was Arthur's battle against his son/nephew Mordred, and that at the time of his birth Batraz is described as 'tempered like steel in a forge', which makes him invulnerable. Arthur, in the poem quoted above, is described as born of 'the cavalry's steel wing', the ala or mounted cavalry unit, wearing armour. Later, as long as he carries the magical Excalibur and the sheath in which it is held, he cannot be hurt, as is the case with the Sarmatian hero.

These parallels are striking and suggest long-standing links between the two cultures. Nor is it necessary to believe that the Sarmatians posted to Britannia in the second century was the only means by which these stories could have cross-fertilized each other, influencing the later Arthurian saga. T. Sulimirski, the great expert on Sarmatian history, points out that there were a number of opportunities for contact between the Sarmatians and the Celts during the sixth to first centuries BC. During this period the Celts migrated across Europe and Asia Minor into the area of the Danube and across the plains of Central Europe, to what is still today Southern Russia. Sulimirski adds that by the first century AD the Iazyges occupied the plains of Northern Hungary and had 'partly displaced, but mostly subdued, the Celto-Dacian occupants' of this area.[16] Nor should we forget the presence of Sarmatian peoples in and around the area of Gaul now known as Burgundy, as we saw in the previous chapter.

Even earlier evidence for a Celtic influence on the Sarmatians is evidenced by the discovery of Celtic-style helmets and weapons found at Sarmatian sites in the Ukraine and Crimea. There was, in effect, sufficient contact between the two cultures for a particular type of Sarmatian brooch to have evolved from a Celtic original, making it more than likely that a transmission of stories and traditions also flowed between the two peoples at this early date. The Sarmatians who found themselves in Britannia in the second century may well have recognized elements of story and myth among the natives with whom they were suddenly associated.

The fourth century writer Ammianus Marcellinus says of the Alans (a tribe related to the Sarmatians) that their only idea of religion was

...to plunge a naked sword into the earth with barbaric ceremonies, and they worship that with great respect, as Mars, the presiding deity of the regions over which they wander.

Elsewhere, the fifth-century Greek historian Herodotus gives a lengthy description of Scythian practices in which a kind of wooden pyramid was constructed, flat on top with an altar into which an ancient iron sword was stuck to represent the war-god, Ares. Prisoners were lined up in front of the altar. Their right arms were severed and thrown into the air and left on the ground wherever they fell. The blood from the prisoners was collected in a golden cup and poured over the iron sword. Animal sacrifices were also offered to this god, their meat boiled with other ingredients in their stomachs, creating a dish not unlike haggis or blood pudding, which the worshippers then feasted on. The Scythians were cousins to the Alans, Iazyges, and other Sarmatian tribes, and it's more than likely that they shared such ceremonies.

With this in mind we may be forgiven for suggesting that this practice, carried by the Sarmatians to Britannia, influenced the later Arthurian legends in which Arthur draws a sword from a stone to prove his right to the kingship of Britain. We have seen, too, how even the name of this magical weapon, Caliburnus, white steel – from *chalybus* (steel) and *eburnus* (white) – echoes the name of the Sarmatian smiths known as the Kalybes. The very name of Arthur's sword may have originated with the warriors from the steppes. The presence of the Sarmatians in the area of Burgundy famed for the production of weapons and armour, and close to a place called Avallon, can only reinforce this conclusion.

The Stories People Tell

This may all seem a long way in time and space from the more usual setting for the Arthurian period in the late fifth to early sixth centuries, never mind the later medieval romances. Yet oral memory can extend over much greater lengths of time and old stories have a way of re-surfacing and affecting those that come after. As we can see from the subsequent medieval development of the Arthurian legends, Arthur is himself a construct of all that went before, with each new version of the story (begged for at the tables of the nobles, who listened eagerly to the Arthurian sagas as today we enjoy the next instalment of the latest soap or movie franchise) adding to what was remembered. This same process was almost certainly at work as the defence of Britain fell to successive leaders.

A recently coined term 'Arthurianism' addresses this by examining the way in which history has been 'used' – reconstructed even – by succeeding generations for political or cultural gain. The idea that medieval kings modelled themselves on Arthur has been recently explored,[17] making it clear that a later warleader could well have chosen to call himself Arthur in recollection of a memory, however distant, of a Roman commander who found himself facing similar opposition and acted accordingly. We cannot know this with any certainty, but we must at least allow the possibility of such an event.

As we have seen, following the Sarmatians' arrival in AD 175, the base for the conscripts for at least two, or maybe three, centuries was at Bremetennacum. The stability provided by such a long stay gave an unparalleled opportunity for Sarmatian stories, myths, and legends – as well as tales of their one-time commander, Lucius Artorius Castus – to pass into the lore of the surrounding tribes, particularly the Brigantes, on whose land the fort stood, and the Cornovii, a tribe living at this time in the area that would become North Wales. The same may be said of the Sarmatians based in Burgundy, which we have shown to bring a likely contribution to the myths of Arthur's final battle and his subsequent fate.

Legends are told as if they are factual accounts, whether or not the events recounted actually happened. As part of the verisimilitude, they become attached to places or people familiar to the audience.[18] The importance of this familiarity is underscored by the fact that legends do not transmit easily beyond the region of their creation.[19] So we would expect to find stories of Artorius in the region where his deeds took place, in this case northern Britannia, and this is indeed what we have.

The Arthurian legends follow a developmental pattern that is well known to scholars of British legend.

1. The presence of an historical figure who did something that struck a chord with his contemporaries and caused some of them to transmit his story

2. The use of the hero's name by members of the transmitting culture after a gap in time during which the name is not used, and

3. The attraction of other bodies of folklore to the existing cycle to create a new form of the legend.

The first two of the three points are easily discernible. The third is shown by the burgeoning number and variation of Arthurian texts in the twelfth and thirteenth centuries. Many of these tales were attracted to the Arthurian cycle after having had an independent existence elsewhere.

When studying the primary Arthurian texts, great care is called for. As the anthropologist Carl von Sydow pointed out, the earliest known variants of a traditional story are seldom either the most complete or the best.[20] Tales may be far older than the manuscripts in which they appear, as we saw with the poems attributed to Taliesin. Legends, in the early stages of their transmission, are generally interjected into discussions to emphasize a detail[21] ('We may remember how such and such a hero fought a great battle in this place').

The important point is that what emerged in the twelfth and thirteenth centuries and that continued to grow until the end of the fifteenth was a full-blown tradition, complete with historical elements and folktales incorporated from a variety of sources. The sheer number of parallels between details in Arthur's fictional biography and details from Lucius Artorius Castus' reconstructed biography become a compelling argument for an account of his career serving as the seed for the later Arthur's life and military exploits.

Drawing connections from names alone is a risky prospect at best, but names backed by story parallels are another matter. When story parallels are present, the similarity of names becomes an important detail, often pointing to the source of the legends. When the parallels match the biography of the figure whose name precedes the gap in usage, that predecessor usually turns out to be the catalyst for the formation of the cycle of legends.

The Brothers Grimm believed that historical legends that were tied to individuals died out faster than those that were tied to places.[22] The two great cycles of Britain, the legends of Arthur and the legends of Robin Hood, prove to be major exceptions to this notion. The origins of the Robin Hood figure can be traced back to the ancient archetype of the Green Man,[23] while the development of the Robin Hood cycle paralleled the development of the Arthurian legends in the medieval period.[24] Thus many different historical figures contributed to the figure of the outlaw of Sherwood, while the first historical figure known as Robin Hood had his name recorded in AD 1225.[25] By AD 1261-2, the legend had developed sufficiently for the surname Robinhood to appear in British documents and for a clerk to change an outlaw's name from 'William son of Robert' to 'William Robehod'.[26]

The legend continued to develop, with bits of history from different events over the centuries being added to the tales, until the fifteenth century. In the 1400s a major fusion occurred that combined the existing Robin Hood tales with independent cycles of Maid Marion, Little John, and Friar Tuck.[27] What also stuck were the place names of Nottingham and Sherwood Forest, which may have helped stabilize the legend. In any case, the result was the Robin Hood legends as we know them today. This is almost certainly what happened to Arthur, as his stories became tied to places throughout Britain, and indeed to other areas where the Sarmatians are known to have stayed.

The Beheading Game

These are not the only close parallels between the Arthurian legends and the Nart Sagas. One of the most interesting is the apparent influence of the latter on the great Middle English poem *Sir Gawain and the Green Knight*. This justly famous story begins with a version of the Beheading Game, where a terrifying figure, a giant warrior, green from head to toe and riding a green horse, appears at Arthur's court during a midwinter feast, and challenges his knights to a supreme test of courage: to exchange blows, using the knight's own mighty axe.

The only one to accept is Gawain, Arthur's nephew and one of the foremost knights of the Round Table. With a single blow Gawain beheads the Green Knight, only to see the grizzly head picked up by the headless body and hear from its mouth that he must seek out the Green Chapel one year from that day to accept a return blow. When Gawain sets forth in search of the Green Knight's Chapel, he stops overnight with an ebullient knight named Bercilak, whose wife offers herself three times to Gawain while her husband is out hunting, an offer which Gawain restricts to kisses only. Finally, the lady gives him a green sash which will protect him from death.

Gawain proceeds to the Green Chapel and faces his opponent, finally admitting to the green sash after two unsuccessful blows. The Green Knight then reveals himself as Bercilak and spares his opponent for having passed the test of his wife's attempted seduction. He reveals that he has been under the spell of Morgan le Fey (here, uniquely, described as a goddess) who is pretending to be Lady Bercilak's servant. Gawain is shamed and returns to Arthur wearing the green sash as a badge of his failure.

The sources of this powerful tale have been attributed to the early Irish text, *Bricriu's Feast*,[28] and to the influence of several Continental stories, including the 13th-century *Romance of Hunbaut*, The Middle High German *Diu Crône* and the Grail story as re-told in the text known as *Perlesvaus*. Yet there are some very close parallels in the Nart Sagas also, in particular 'Nart Batradz and the Giant with a Coloured Beard'. This begins with a feast, during which Batradz is commissioned to defeat a terrible enemy. A beheading game follows with the multi-coloured giant, following which the hero takes the head and carries it away on a stake as a war trophy to the land of the Narts.

This recalls the *Hunbaut* variant of Gawain's story, where he prevents the challenger from reattaching his head, while in most variants, including the Gawain poem, the challenger carries away his own head, sometimes in his hands and sometimes by reattaching it. Note that the challenger in this case is a giant with unnatural colours, signifying that he is not of Batraz's world, even though the Narts are themselves sometimes shown as giants.

In the second story from the sagas the parallels are more systemic and can be found not only in the Beheading Game but also in the attempted seduction that follows. In 'Nart Soslan and

Tar's Sons' there is a huge horse-rider, a contest to test the famous heroes, a beheading game with a sharp-edged axe, an attempt at a voluntary decapitation with the victim's own weapon and a woman exercising her charms on a man three times in order to alter the outcome of the beheading game – all of which are elements we find in the Gawain story.

Here, the setting is not a feast, but there is the same abrupt change of atmosphere from joyfulness to fear and danger experienced by the feasting leader and his subordinates at the sight of the Green Knight. The Nart hero Soslan is singing with joy when he manages to find grazing grounds for his cattle. But soon he sees a cloud whirling at him, which turns out to be Mukara, the savage owner of these lands, who is furious at somebody trespassing on his property. Like the Green Knight, who 'stood towering before [Arthur], higher than any in the house, by his head and more', Mukara is a horse rider, and he is huge: 'his horse is the size of a mountain', while he is 'the size of a haystack'.

It is to be noted, that in both cases the protagonists are ethnically different. The Knight's otherworldly nature is highlighted by his unusual attire, unnatural and overall greenness, and physical immensity. Yet this strange alien half-giant, an '*aghlich mayster*', is a man.

The ethnicity of the Knight is not identifiable, but giants in all traditions are of exogenous origin. Yet they are not total strangers, as both the Green Knight and Mukara had heard about those they challenged. Mukara learns from Soslan, whom he takes for a shepherd, that the Narts have dared to occupy his fields, and he gives way to his curiosity and envy of the fame of Soslan, the most renowned Nart of his time. The Green Knight, in his turn, challenges the Knights of the Round Table, since they are the worthiest opponents:

'I am come because the fame of thy knights is so highly praised, and thy burgesses and thy town are held to be the best in the world, and the strongest riders on horses in steel armour, and the bravest and the worthiest of all mankind, and proof in playing in all joustings; and here, too, courtesy is well known, as I have heard say; and it is for these reasons that I am come hither at this time.'

Mukara, who had heard about the mighty Nart, and the Green Knight, informed about the excellence of Arthur's noble men, both have this vocational hazard: both are eager to outperform their opponents and rival their fame. And here the motif of the game appears. The Green Knight himself suggests the terms of his game, while Mukara becomes curious of Nart Soslan's favorite pastimes and will readily engage in the most extreme of his games. Soslan grasps at this chance to slay the dangerous adversary and schemes to kill him in combat.

Mukara is not in the least surprised by the dangerous nature of the game, since Soslan is reputed as a daring contender, audacious adventure-seeker, and self-assured challenger. To Soslan's disappointment, this strategy does not bring him the outcome he desired: he strikes Mukara's neck with all his might, after the giant voluntarily puts his head on the block, but the Nart fails to hurt him. Soslan at last succeeds in beheading his enemy by using Mukara's own weapon.

While there are some differences between Soslan's story and that of *Sir Gawain and the Green Knight*, the parallels are highly significant. Gawain takes one blow to behead the Green Knight, and Soslan takes several tries to sever Mukara's head. But notice that Arthur claims the Green Knight's axe and gives it to Gawain, who uses it to cut off the Green Knight's head. Soslan takes Mukara's axe and uses it to cut off his adversary's head. We have, then, two renowned warriors beheading two supernatural giants with their own axes.

Having defeated Mukara, Soslan has to confront his even mightier brother, Bibyts. This encounter eventually leads to a seduction game is which a female relative, in this case the challenger's mother, Shatana (Satana) offers herself to Soslan while her son is off hunting, just as Lady Bercilak, the Green Knight's wife, offers to help Gawain outsmart her husband while he is hunting. Each lady hosts the competitor on her own premises. Shatana three times tries to learn the secret of Bibyts' immortality, eventually finding three objects: a pillar of the house at his Yellow Fortress, a stone from its hearth, and an iron box beneath the stone where three doves (his soul, his strength, and his hope) were kept. To defeat Bibyts, Soslan beheads the three doves.

Similarly, with the agreement that Gawain and Bercilak will exchange gifts at the end of the day, Lady Bercilak tries to seduce their guest. On the first day, while Bercilak hunts and beheads a barren doe, Gawain and the lady talk of honour before the lady kisses him. From the first kiss, exchanged for the spoils of the day, the story moves to the second day. This time Bercilak hunts and beheads a boar while the lady and Gawain talk of valour and she kisses him twice. Gawain gives Bercilak a kiss on each cheek in return for the carcass of the boar. On the third day the lady kisses Gawain three times and gives him the girdle that will prevent the Green Knight from cutting off his head, while Bercilak hunts a fox, which he skins but does not behead. At dinner Gawain kisses Bercilak three times and Bercilak gives Gawain the pelt of the fox that was not beheaded. Soul, valour and hope, the topics Gawain talks about with the lady and the three doves that Soslan beheads after his encounter with Satana offer a striking parallel. The Green Knight feigns two blows at Gawain and slightly cuts him on the neck with the third for holding back the girdle Lady Bercilak had given him, so essentially Gawain defeats the Green Knight by keeping his head attached to his shoulders. Likewise, Soslan defeats Bibyts.

The Faeries of Avalon

We saw in the previous chapter how the medieval accounts of the Island of Avalon can be seen to echo those concerning the town of Avallon in Burgundy, as well as Avellinum in Italy and Avella in Northern Britain. The etymology of all three names derives from Celtic and proto-Celtic sources: *Aballū, Aballon*, etc. Each of these refers to the apple, a fruit sacred to the Celts and with its own lore and to a place associated with a goddess or a group of otherworldly women, much as the Greeks told a story of the Isle of the Hesperides where nine nymphs guarded trees that bore golden apples. We saw also how a group of women healers guarded and serviced Les Fontaines Salées and are paralleled in the Arthurian legends by the nine sisters of Avalon, while at Avellinum there are still stories of magical women associated with water and healing. A less familiar text, dating from the thirteenth century and generally known by the name *L'Elucidation*, tells a different story of wells protected by faery women.

> ....by them great things were served
> That no-one who wandered the by-ways,
> Be it in evening or morning,
> Whether to drink or to eat
> Would need to change his route,
> Save he who turned towards the wells.
> He could request nothing
> By way of fine food that pleased him
> That would not be given to him,
> Provided he asked reasonably.
> Then would arise, as I understand,
> A maiden from out of the well...[29]

The fact that this story focuses on a series of wells, guarded and serviced by women, points at once both to Les Fontaines Salées and to the Avalonian sisters who offer healing to Arthur. Given that the Sarmatian Lady Satana, the mother of the heroes in the Nart sagas, was also associated with healing springs and that she belongs to a number of goddess-like figures whose blood, on her death, produces such a spring, if the Sarmatians learned a local legend of healing fountains while they were stationed in Britannia, they could very easily have transferred it to the story of the wounded king taken to Avallo(n) to be healed by the women of the wells. Equally, if those stationed at Camp Cora in Burgundy visited the sacred Fontaines Salées, they could have added to the story of the wounded officer who was known to them or their brothers as a famous warrior.[30]

Roger Sherman Loomis suggested in his 1938 book *Arthurian Tradition and Chrétien de Troyes*, that the original name for the Wounded King of the Grail romance was Margon, Mangon or

Amangon.[31] Scott Littleton followed this up by drawing attention to the similarity between these names and the Amonga, the sacred cup belonging to the Narts. Intriguingly, the *Elucidation*, as quoted above, features an evil king named Amangons, who steals a sacred cup belonging to one of the 'maidens of the wells' causing the land later ruled over by King Arthur to become wasted. This story has been clearly identified as a prototype of the Grail story as written by Chrétien de Troyes, to which the *Elucidation* is described as a prelude – though in fact it is more of an independent version of the myth. When aligned, these elements add up to a set of links between the Grail and the Amonga, with the striking parallel in nomenclature and the focus on the fountains or wells in both the story of the *Elucidation* and the physical setting of Les Fontaines Salées, in an area with a long-standing Sarmatian presence.

The Round Table of the Narts

The specific parallels between the myths and traditions of the Sarmatians, Ossetians, Alans, and their kin have already been explored in some depth in the published work of Littleton and Malcor[32] and don't require rehearsing again here. There are several themes, however, that have come to light recently, which seem to us to indicate a lasting connection between the stories of one ethnic group and another.

Since our main aim is to show how much the stories and legends of Arthur echo those of the Roman officer Lucius Artorius Castus, we should turn our view outwards to see what other characteristics exist. Several leap into focus immediately. As well as the character of Batraz, who was born from a lump on the back of the Nart Khæmyc and raised by Satana, the Mother of the Narts, we note several parallels between the latter and a variety of female figures in the Arthurian legends: notably the Lady of the Lake and possibly Morgan le Fey – always presented as ambivalent in nature.

Satana is a significant figure in the Nart sagas. John Colarusso wonderfully describes her as 'a figure of beauty, eternal youth, passion, and lust, devotion and treachery ... the embodiment of profound wisdom and intelligence, while also being a sorceress and seeress'.[33] This description seems to combine the lofty power of the Lady of the Lake and the wily, seductive, and dangerous Morgan. Satana is also known as Lady Tree and in at least one myth[34] she explains the nature of a world tree, with its branches in the heavens and its roots deep below the earth, in terms that would be equally recognized in both Celtic and Norse traditions. As we saw above, her blood is also said to have created a magical fountain with healing properties.

Satana is also, like Guenevere, abducted more than once by sinister adversaries, just as Arthur's queen is described as stolen away by a dark otherworldly figure named Melwas in the *Life of Gildas*, written by the Welsh cleric and author Caradoc of Llancarfan, c 1130.[35] Guenevere is held prisoner at a stronghold often identified with Glastonbury in Somerset and the story says that Arthur spent a year searching for her and assembling an army to storm Melwas' fort, while Gildas negotiated a peaceful resolution. The episode could be related to the old Irish abduction motif called the *aithed*, in which a mysterious stranger kidnaps a married woman and takes her to his home, from whom the husband rescues her.

This is important, since the earliest Arthurian story to appear out of the early Middle Ages, is exactly the story of Guenevere's abduction. It appears carved into the stone archivolt of Modena Cathedral in Italy. This was begun in 1099 and finished sometime before 1126. [36] It depicts a woman named Winlogee in a tower along with two men named Mardoc and Burmaltus. The tower is besieged by Artus de Bretania and Isdernus, while another knight, identified as Carrado, is battling three knights named Galvaginus, Galvariun, and Che. These have been identified as follows: Artus is Arthur, Winlogee is Guenevere; Che is Kay, Galvaginus is Gawain, and Carrado is Caradoc, another famous knight of the Round Table. The story clearly shows Arthur and his men rescuing Guinevere, and as the carving is older than any of the written texts, it is probable that, among all the fragments that make up the Arthurian legend, this is one of the oldest, which bears witness to the existence of both older oral traditions and written tales that have since vanished.

The Arthurian traditions relation to the Lady of the Lake, who is always described as otherworldly or one of the faery folk, usually do not name her, but use her title only in at least one source, a Middle English poem compiled by the English priest Layamon (c 1190); she is named Argante.[37] This name is significant, because its etymological root is *argent*, silver or white (still used in heraldic language to this day). Lucy L. Paton in her book *Studies in Fairy Mythology in Arthurian Romance* noted a number of women wearing white in the Arthurian legends, generally showing them to be of faery origin.[38]

In the Merlin section of the *Lancelot-Grail* cycle, the Lady of the Lake is specified as not only wearing white herself, but insisting that her protégé, Lancelot, wear the same colour when he is knighted by King Arthur. Later in the same text she awards him white armour, a white sword and spear, and a white horse – details that were later passed to his son Galahad. [39] Even the name of Guinevere, Arthur's queen and Lancelot's lover, means 'White Shadow', and although she is generally represented as a mortal woman, in Welsh tradition she is the daughter of Avalach, who rules over an island not dissimilar to Avalon (after which he is perhaps named) and is most definitely of otherworldly origin.

Satana raises Batraz in the Otherworld as the Lady of the Lake raises Lancelot. They prepare their sons for a place among the Nart heroes or those of the Round Table. The Narts themselves are described as dancing on the edge of a great round table, with displays of skill with weapons, horsemanship, and bravery very similar to the tournaments arranged by Arthur for the entertainment, and testing, of his knights.[40] Among the adversaries they encounter are several giant warrior herdsmen, recalling vividly those encountered by Arthur's knights in the 'Story of Culhwch and Olwen', or again in 'The Lady of the Fountain', where the hero encounters a one-eyed giant who could easily have stepped from the pages of any one of the Nart sagas.[41]

The hero Batraz acquires his mighty sword with help from Satana, as Arthur is aided by the Lady of the Lake to get his. When Batraz is seeking vengeance on a man who has killed his father, Satana tells him where to find the man and instructs him to ask to see his sword because he seeks to make a copy of it. At first reluctant, the killer is persuaded to hold the sword out to Batraz hilt foremost, at which point the young hero seizes it, kills his enemy and claims the sword for himself.

Batraz's fellow Nart, Sosruquo, also possessed a magical sword, which, similarly to the first sword owned by Arthur, was made on an anvil that the hero drew from nine layers of earth. In the Arthurian legend Arthur draws his magical blade (which later breaks and is replaced by Excalibur, the gift of the Lady of the Lake) from an anvil which sits atop a stone; Satana requests that a sword be made for her other son by the smith Tlepshw, as later Arthurian legends describe the similarly named Trebuchet as forging Excalibur. Before it's even begun the brothers are arguing over it, and the smith offers to make more than one. When the boys insist that he makes only one sword, so that only the strongest and bravest among them get to keep it, the smith challenges them by saying that he will do as they ask, but only for the one who can lift the anvil from beneath the ground, under which he has placed the blade of a scythe from which the sword will be forged. Needless to say, Sosruquo, who practised pulling the anvil out of the ground just as Arthur had to repeatedly pull the sword out of the anvil, succeeds and has the sword made for him.

In another related story from the Irish recension of the *Quest del Saint Graal*, Galahad arrives at a graveyard and finds a grave that is on fire. As soon as he lays his hand upon it, the fire dies away, and a dead knight speaks to him from within the tomb. Though this may refer to the idea that the soul of the knight is in Hell, it reminds one irresistibly of the Scythian and Sarmatian practice of building a fire on top of a grave.[42]

The Narts remind us of the Round Table knights in many ways; though they are rougher and, in some ways, more like the Red Branch heroes of ancient Ireland. They have a code by which they live that reminds us of Arthur's declared wish for his knights

> ...never to do outrageousity nor murder, and always to flee treason; also, by no means to be cruel, but to give mercy unto him that asketh mercy, upon pain of forfeiture of their

worship and lordship of King Arthur for evermore; and always to do ladies, damosels, and gentlewomen succor upon pain of death. Also, that no man take no battles in a wrongful quarrel for no law, ne for no world's goods. Unto this were all the knights sworn of the Table Round, both old and young.[43]

When the gods ask the Narts if they would prefer long lives but no fame, they declare:

If our lives are to be short,
Then let our fame be great!
Let us not depart from truth!
Let fairness be our path!
Let us not know grief!
Let us live in freedom![44]

Echoes of this kind are everywhere in the Nart sagas, leading us to the inevitable conclusion that the stories must have been known by the British bards and storytellers who composed the first tales

Plate 33. The Nart deity Westygy, Protector of Men and Travellers. (Elmira Gutieva)

of Arthur and his warriors. Despite the length of time between the two, this in no way precludes the transfer of hero sagas from one culture to another, and from one period to a later one. We are convinced that the stories told by the Sarmatians during their extended stay in Britannia became part of the repertoire of native British stories, and that these, when mingled with memories of their leader, Lucius Artorius Castus, flowed into the creation and development of the Arthur tradition and forward into the fully fledged romances of the twelfth to the fifteenth centuries.

It is from these ancient tales, we believe, that the roots of the Arthurian legends grew, retaining aspects of the Sarmatian sagas and the deeds of their Roman commander and establishing one of the greatest cycles of epic stories ever told.

Appendix 1

THE SOVEREIGN'S CHAIR

We give here the full text of this poem, in a new translation by Caitlín Matthews, since it offers evidence for a continuing memory of Artorius through the centuries.

The Sovereign's Chair (Areith Awdyl Eglur)
from the *Llyfr Taliesin (Book of Taliesin)*
Early 14th century

Declare the clear *awdl*	[epic poem]
In *awen's* own metre.	[inspiration]
A man sprung of two authors,	
Of the steel cavalry wing,	
With his clear wisdom,	
With his royal rule,	
With his kingly lordship,	
With his honour of scripture,	
With his red lorica,	
With his assault over the Wall,	
With his poet-praised seat,	
Among the defenders of the Wall.	
He led from the enclosed Wall	
Pale saddled horses.	

The venerable lord,
The nurturing cup-bearer,

One of three wise ones
To bless Arthur.
Arthur the blessed,
In harmonious song,
In the forefront of battle,
Trampling down nine.

Who are the three stewards
Who guarded the land?
Who are the three storytellers
Who kept the portent?
Who will come eagerly
To welcome their lord?

Noble is the virtuous embankment,
Noble is the tall, tree-like man,
Noble the horn that's passed round,
Noble the cattle in their midday resting,
Noble is truth when it shines forth,
Nobler still when it is spoken,
Noble when came from the cauldron
The three spears of awen.   [The three drops of inspiration]

I have been a torquated lord,
With horn in hand.
Unworthy of the chair,
Is he who spurns my word.
Bright is the contested chair!
Eloquence of awen's excellence!

What are the names of the three *Caers*   [fortresses]
Between flood and ebb?
No-one knows nor importunes
The nature of their stewards.
There are four Caers
In Britain's regions;
Tumultuous nobles.
From nothing can nothing be,
Nothing can come from nothing.

Fleets will come.
The wave covers the shingle,
Dylan's country, the sea, is inevitable.   [Dylan, god of the sea]
There will be neither shelter nor refuge,
Neither hill nor dale,
Nor any refuge from the storm
From the wind when it rages.

The sovereign's chair:
Skilful the leader who preserves it,
Let the candidate be sought,
Let his generosity be sought.

Those pierced and lost,
Like such an array,
From the slaughter of the chieftain,
From the radiant ranks,
From loricated *Lleon*,   [City of the legions/Carlisle?]
Will arise a king
For the fierce border.

The *braggart*'s froth shall disperse–   [drink of ale and honey]
– Fragile by nature –
Noisy for a while,
At the disputed border.

Strange accents flow,
Eloquent assaults,
Of seafarers.
From the children of *Saraphin*,   [the snake-armoured ones]
The cursed folk of the wicked world,
Let us release *Elphin*.   [Taliesin's patron, who was imprisoned]

Appendix 2

THE LIFELINE OF LUCIUS ARTORIUS CASTUS

(Dates are approximate, based on the Castus inscription)

141 Born.
159 Entered army as a centurion of the III Gallica.
163 Transferred to the IV Ferrata as a centurion.
167 Transferred to the II Adiutrix as a centurion.
171 Transferred to the V Macedonica as a centurion.
175 *Primus Pilus* of the V Macedonica.
176 Escorts Sarmatians to Britannia.
177 Transfers to classis Misenatium as *praepositus*.
181 *Praefectus* of the VI Victrix twice.
187 Becomes *Dux* of the three legions of Britannia
191 *Procurator Centenarius* of Liburnia.
197 Dies at or following the Battle of Lyon.

Appendix 3

GLOSSARY

Aediles	Magistrates in charge of public buildings.
Ala	Wing. E.G., cavalry unit, hallway in a house.
Armatos	Armed men.
Auxilia	Foreign, non-citizen troops, supporting legions using Roman fighting styles.
Cataphracti	Heavy armoured cavalry.
Centurion	Commander of a century.
Century	Basic unit of a legion.
Cognomen	Nickname or middle name.
Cohort	Six centuries, one tenth of a legion.
Consul	One of the chief magistrates of the Roman State, the highest level of the *Cursus Honorum*.
Cursus Honorum	An ascending sequence of public offices to which politicians aspired.

Deva	Chester
Duovirum	Highest two judges in a city.
Dux	Officer in command of two or more legions; officer leading troops outside his normal area of operation.
Eboracum	York
Equestrian	Member of the second rank of Roman nobles, Knights of Rome.
Gens	Family, Clan
Gensnomen	Family name
Hyparkontes	Sub-governors
Jus gladii	'Power of the Sword', right to issue death sentences.
Kontari	Heavy armoured cavalry fighting with a long, lance-like spear.
Kontos	'barge pole'; long, lance-like weapon.
Lacerna	Military cloak.
Legatus augustus juridicus	Lawyer
Legatus augustus pro praetore	Governor of some imperial provinces of the Roman Empire.
Legatus legionis	an ex-praetor in command of one of Rome's elite legions.
legion	Basic unit of the Roman army.
Londinium	London
Numerus	Foreign, non-citizen troops supporting a legion but maintaining their own style of fighting.

Pater familias	Head of a *gens* or family unit.
Pilum	Spear
Praefectus	Commander
Praefectus alae	Officer in command of a cavalry wing.
Praefectus castrorum	Commander of the camp of a legion.
Praefectus classis	Commander of a Fleet.
Praefectus cohortis	Commander of a unit of six centuries.
Praefectus equitatus/equitum	Commander of the cavalry.
Praefectus fabrum	Officer in charge of artisans, engineers, etc.
Praefectus laetorum	Officer in command of Germanic people.
Praefectus legionis	Equestrian legionary commander.
Praefectus legionis agens vice legati	Acting Equestrian (as in the rank) in command of a legion.
Praefectus orae maritimae	Officer in command of an important part of the coast.
Praefectus Sarmatarum gentilium	Officer in command of Sarmatians.
Praefectus socium/ sociorum	Officer in command of an *ala* from a tribe or city-state in Italy.
Praenomen	First name

Praepositus	Officer in temporary command of a special unit.
Praepositus reliquaionis classis	Officer serving as accountant to the Fleet.
Praetor	Commander of a field army or a magistrate.
Praetorian Guard	Bodyguards for the emperor.
Primus Pilus	First Spear, most senior centurion. Ninth in command of a legion.
Procurator	Governor of a small province.
Procurator Centenarius	Procurator making 100,000 sesterces per year.
Rex	King
Senator	First rank of Roman nobles.
Straegos	General, governor or praetor.
Tamga	Personal mark, similar to a cattle brand or heraldic device.
Tres militae	Three offices, Equestrian version of the Senatorial *cursus honorem*.
Tribunus legionis	Second in command of a legion.
Vexillation	Detached unit.
Villa rustica	Fortified inland farm.
Villa maritime	Fortified seaside villa.

Appendix 4

A NOTE ON SOURCES

Our quest for the historical figure behind the Arthurian tradition has taken us through a variety of sources, from ancient and modern texts to Roman and Greek inscriptions and even to statuary and the decorations surrounding inscriptions. We have wandered through the fields of history, archaeology, literature, art history, folklore, mythology, and anthropology. We have tackled modern and ancient manuscripts in numerous languages. Given this diversity in our sources, it is only appropriate that we spend a little time sorting them out.

The Inscriptions. The primary sources for Roman inscription used in this work are the *Corpus Inscriptionem Latinarum* (CIL), compiled by Theodor Mommsen, and *The Roman Inscriptions of Britain,* edited by Collingwood and Wright. Greek inscriptions are from the *Corpus Inscriptiones Graecarum,* edited by August Böckh. In addition to these major resources, several journals, and smaller, more recent collections have been used, such as that compiled by Hermannus Desau. The work on the large Artorius inscription is original field research, including the reconstruction by Linda A. Malcor, Antonio Trinchese and Alessandro Faggiani, and that on the smaller inscription is courtesy of Professor Cambi of the University of Split, Croatia. A third Artorius inscription is housed in the Louvre and a possible fourth in the British Museum.

The Archaeology. The projects undertaken at the site of Artorius' villa have been under the auspices of the Archaeological Museum of Split and the Department of Archaeology of the Faculty of Humanities and Social Sciences at the University of Zagreb. Those in Britain have been detailed by Collingwood and Wright with additional material collected at the Ribchester site by the University of Central Lancashire, in conjunction with project partners Ribchester Roman Museum, the Australian National University, and the Institute for Field Research. Archaeology performed regarding the Early, Middle and Late Sarmatian culture is from the summaries provided by Sulimirski (1970). Primary sources in Rome include Trajan's Column, the Arch of Titus, the Column of Marcus Aurelius, and the Coliseum. Linda A. Malcor examined additional material at Pompeii, Nola, Avalinum, Capua, Pozzuoli (Puteoli), Baia, Misenum, and Naples. John Matthews conducted further research research at Camp Cora in Burgundy, Vindolanda in the UK, Hadrian's Wall, and Bremetenacum Fort, Ribchester.

Giuseppe Nicolini researched a variety of museums in Northern Britain for archaeological evidence of the Sarmatian presence in Britain.

Graeco-Roman Sources. Book Four of Herodotus' *History* provides the oldest written evidence for the Northeast Iranian sources. Known as the father of both Anthropology and History, Herodotus travelled the ancient world, interviewing people and recording what he learned. Some material he saw for himself. For the Sarmatians and related cultures he relied on first-hand witnesses. Other Greek and Roman historians who mention the Sarmatians and Alans include Dio Cassius, Herodian, Jordanes, Paulinus Pallaeus, and Ammianus Marcellinus.

The Nart Sagas. The main collections on the Nart sagas are those by the late Georges Dumézil, who collected many of the Ossetian Nart sagas, and our colleague John Colarusso (see Foreword) who has written essential books and papers on the Circassian, Ossetians and other Nart sagas. Much of our material on the tales comes through communication with him.

The Arthurian Tradition. The bulk of the Arthurian tradition makes it impossible to cover everything here. Important sources for this work include that written by Gildas in the sixth century AD, which mentions the battle of Badon but not Arthur. The ninth-century compiler Nennius collected many early mentions of Arthur, as did the medieval author Geoffrey of Monmouth, whose work scrambles actual history with folktales and must be treated with caution. Other sources include the thirteenth century *Lancelot-Grail* cycle from the Continent and the works of Chrétien de Troyes.

In addition to the written sources, we have also relied on illuminations in the manuscripts, which sometimes record stories that have nothing to do with the text they accompany. They show that the tales were passed by word of mouth as well as being written down for posterity. Some of the oldest Arthurian stories are shown in a variety of artistic sources, such as the story of the Abduction of Guinevere from the archivolt of Modena Cathedral and the image of Arthur in the mosaics at the Cathedral of Otranto, both in Italy.

There is a chronocentric tendency among those alive today to think of those who lived in the past as less sophisticated. The people of the Middle Ages not only had access to many of the Greco-Roman sources that we do today, but also drew upon them – sometimes updating them – in the creation of their own works. They didn't have iPhones or aircraft, but they were just as sophisticated at transmitting information that was important to them. The main way they did this was through the stories that they told, and one of the greatest cycles they ever produced has the tale not of a medieval king or warlord but of a Roman soldier at its base.

NOTES

Introduction: In Search of Arthur
1. Zimmer 1890:488-528.
2. Oman 1910: 211
3. Nos. 1919 and 12791.
4. Malone 1925: 367-374.
5. Nickel 1975: 1-18.,
6. E.g., Littleton 1978: 512-527, 1979: 326-333, 1981: 269-280, 1983: 67-82.
7. Littleton and Malcor, 2000.
8. Loomis, Celtic *Mythology and Arthurian Romance*.
9. Skene, 1868:50-51.

1 *The Artorius Mystery*
1. In 'Artus Ring? The Finding of the Golden Ring of the Gens Artoria in Ancient Britannia', Linda, Malcor, Giuseppe Nicolini, Alessandro Faggiani, Antonio Trinchese, Feb 2021 accessed at Academia.edu.

2 *The Artorii*
1. Corpus Inscriptionum Latinarum III 14195.27.
2. E.g., the inscriptions raised by Augustus to his physician Marcus Artorius Asclepiades; *Corpus Inscriptionem Graecarum*, ii 4116, iii 570.
3. Livy 23.5.
4. *Satire 3*. Translated by A. S. Kline, 2011

5. Zimmer 1890: 785 ff.
6. Green 2009:25.
7. The Artorii were no cleverer when it came to naming their slaves, since they tended to number them or give them names of famous people, like Cleopatra.
8. Badian 1967:181-182.
9. Bertram, 2011, Plutarch, Lives… vol 2. See also: Moles, J. L., "Plutarch's Vita Brut Ch 41. A Commentary on Plutarch's Brutus" *Histos*, Newcastle, 2017
10. Green, Caitlin R. "But Arthur's Grave is Nowhere to be Seen" www.arthuriana.co.uk (accessed 7.4.22)
11. Jones 2006.
12. Tacitus *Annales* xiv, 1-9.
13. D'Arms 1970: 304n., 317.
14. Faggiani, A. https://www.academia.edu/37679155/ Gens Artoria La Gens vicina agli Imperatori Romani (Italian Edition)
15. Cf. Ban (leader). The "b"/" v" shift can be seen in the medieval spellings of Abelinum, Abella/Avella. Cf Chapter 9.
16. Dumézil 1970, 1:270. Varro (ll. 5.74) claimed that Flora was one of the deities introduced to Rome by Titus Tatius; Dumézil 1970, 1:169-170.
17. This sanctuary, between the Palatine and Aventine hills (Rose 1948:73-74), was founded in 238 B.C. (Adkins and Adkins 1994:261; Lindemans 1995-2000, s.v. "Flora."). Tacitus (*Ann.* 2.49) gives Tiberius credit for building (more likely rebuilding) this temple (Spaeth 1996:82). The original temple near the Circus Maximus was erected c. 238 BC and the Floralia grew out of its dedication ceremony (Rose 1948:73-74).
18. Flora overlapped functions with Robigus and Pomona as well as with Feronia. Flora was associated with cereals by Augustine, *Ciu. D.* 4.8; Dumézil 1970, 1:270; Aldington and Ames 1968:211. In addition to being honored by the military, Flora was the patroness of courtesans, a role she shared with Isis (Turcan 1996:89).
19. Zophyrus of Capua may have been named after him.
20. Iazyges as well as Thracians lived in Thrace, and it is possible that the Thracians themselves were a tribe of Sarmatians. They were also in Dacia.

21. Thorns were added in a later myth when Cupid's arrows missed their mark.

22. Ovid, Fasti, v. 25-258; 43 BC; Malcor,2004; Aldington and Ames 1968:217.

23. According to a rationalized version of this story, the rose celebrated Flora's gift of a monetary fortune she earned as a courtesan and that she bequeathed to Rome upon her death.

24. Five petals, which are frequently featured in Roman iconography, are more common than four. Think of the four-petal rose as a variant of the four-leaf clover. Today the flower is known as the Rosa Gallica and is native to, among other places, the Caucasus Mountains.

25. Ovid Fasti 5, 193 ff. A. Boyle, tr. Roman Poetry: first century BC to first century AD

26. Ogilvie 1969:82-83; Rose 1948:73-74. Flora is mentioned on the Tablet of Agnone (c. 250 B.C) as a deity associated with Ceres, Fluusaí Kerríiaí (Spaeth 1996:2). Cicero identified Flora as a Mother Goddess and stated that the purpose of the Floralia was to reconcile the Roman people to her; Cicero, *Verr.* 2.5.36; Spaeth 1996:89.

27. Bunson 1991:159. This was a minor flamen of plebeian rank (Spaeth 1996:90), whose clerical garments included a white conical hat (Adkins and Adkins 1994:254).

28. Aldington and Ames 1969:210; Adkins and Adkins 1994:283. These dates are traceable to Augustus' time (Ogilivie 1969:82-83). The Floralia was discontinued at some point during the fourth century AD; Lindemans 1995-2000, s.v. "Flora"

29. Ogilvie 1969:82-83. Starting in 173 B.C, the Ludi Florales, lasted six days and included a parade, banquet and the snaring of goats and hares. Bunson 1991:246; Adkins and Adkins 1994:283; Carcopino 1968:204, 207; Ogilvie 1969:82-83; Lyttelton and Forman 1985:47. Flora was the patroness of the Greens faction of chariot racing (Dumézil 1970, 1:270). The plays performed during the Floralia were mimes and had the distinction of being the only time that actresses were permitted to appear entirely in the nude (Carcopino 1968:230). Details of the festivities, including the eating of vetch, beans and lupines, are recounted by Horace (*Satires* 2.3.182) and Valerius Maximus (2.10.8; Briscoe 1998, 1:149). See Ogilvie 1969:82-83 and Lyttelton and Forman 1985:47 for more information.

30. Aldington and Ames 1969:210; Adkins and Adkins 1994:261, 285. It is possible that there were actually three festivals associated with Flora. Pliny (18.284) associates the Robigalia (August 25th) and Vinalia (August 19th) with the Floralia (Dumézil 1970, 1:184).

31. J. Ferguson (1970:24-25) saw the death connection in the Floralia as well. Flora shared the second festival with Feronia, whose cult was tied to that of Feronia was a goddess of both the Latins and the Sabines who overlapped Flora's functions, particularly spring flowers and vegetation. Feronia was closely associated with wolves, whereas Flora's connection was mainly with the rose and, by extension, with Mars. Soranus was a solar god who had his origin as a Sabine deity, and the cult center was at Mount Soracte. The Hirpini were a fire-walking Roman family that was closely associated with the cult. For more information see Aldington and Ames 1969:210.

32. Walker 1983:316; Dumézil 1970, 1:270; cf. Brelich 1949:37. A statue of Flora graced the baths of Caracalla (Carcopino 1968:262).

33. Walker 1983:455-456.

34. Ferguson 1970:25-26, 239; Walker 1983: 455-456.

35. Ogilvie 1969:82-83. The customs surrounding Flora's spring rituals led Lactantius Firmianus (ca. AD 250-330) to decry the goddess as a "Lady of Pleasure."

36. Mary took over the symbolism of Venus' rose at the same time. Cf. Moldenke 1953.

37. Moldenke 1953.

38. Moldenke 1953. The rosary, Catholic prayer beads used in connection with supplications to the Virgin, can be traced back to the third century AD and is so called because it represents a crown of roses, something that can be seen to follow on from the worship of Flora.

39. Moldenke 1953.

40. Moldenke 1953.

41. Laing 1963:95-96.

42. Adkins and Adkins 1994:261, 285.

43. Malcor 2004.

44. The golden rose symbolized ultimate achievement (Cirlot 1962: 275). From the time of Pope Gregory, I (r. 590-604), the golden rosette was a symbol of "special papal benediction" (G. Ferguson 1961:38).

45. It is perhaps a profound irony that, years later, the pieces of that tomb were used to construct part of a Christian chapel's graveyard wall.
46. Some of the men in the family have the cognomen "Rufus." Contrary to popular belief, this cognomen does not mean "Bloody" but rather that someone had red hair.
47. Malcor, field collection 2004.
48. Nagel 1979:354.

3 *The Centurion*

1. Parker 1971:200-201, 204.
2. Parker 1971:163. The future Roman emperor served in Syria as his first post, but since he was roughly 14 years older than Artorius, they did not cross paths at that time. Grant 1985: 103.
3. Grant 1985:86.
4. Burnham and Wacher 1990:34-35; Harper 1928:117-121.
5. Goldsworthy 1996:102,229.
6. Parker 1971:163
7. The Jews fought battles against the Seleucids there as well as against the Romans.
8. Parker 1971:202
9. Wilkes 1969:328-329, Parker 1971:166.
10. Wilkes 1969:328-329
11. This is the same group of Quadi that would later cross the frozen Rhine with the Alans in AD 406 and who would go on to found a kingdom along with the Alans in Iberia.
12. The I Italica was stationed at Regensburg in 171.
13. Dio 71.3, Cary 132:11; cf. Grant 1985:103; Connolly 1991:14.
14. Wilkes 1969:328-329; Parker 1971:167-168
15. Grant 1971:90.
16. Parker 1971:165
17. Cary 1932:23-25; Dio, 72.7-13
18. Goldsworthy 1996:102, 229
19. Dio, 72.7.1-5; Cary 1932:22-25.

4 *Rising through the Ranks*

1. Parker 1971:204
2. Parker 1971:204

3. Parker 1971: 204

4. We know that Artorius served time in the V Macedonica before becoming *primus pilus* because his inscription says that he was at first a centurion of the V Macedonica before becoming "*primus pilus* of the same."

5. Cary 1932:37; Dio, 72.16

6. For more details about the fort of Bremetennacum, see Bruce 1923: 228-229.

7. Connolly 1991:26.

8. Richmond 1945, p23

9. Collingwood and Wright 1965: 194-195, no. 583, 196-199 and 587.

10. Burnham and Wacher 1990:34, Salway 1965:29; Richmond 19:15ff.)

11. Parker 1971:213.

12. Parker 1971:214.

13. Parker 1971:214.

14. Salway 1965:29.

15. Collingwood and Wright 1965:174, no. 522.

16. Collingwood and Wright 1965:409, no. 1242.

17. Parker 1971:214.

18. Collingwood and Wright 1965:469, no. 1453. ·

19. Collingwood and Wright 1965: 470, no. 1459, 476-477, no. 1481. For names of Sarmatians being M. Aurelius, see Malcor 1999.

20. For the possibility of 'naked' horsemen representing Sarmatians in scale mail, see Richmond (1945:17). For the steppe practice of wrapping the horse's tail, see Sulimirski (1970: 253, plate 3).

21. Sulimirski 1970:253-254, plate 10; Hyland 1990:6.

22. Collingwood and Wright 1965:464, no. 1435.

23. Collingwood and Wright 1965:413-414, no. 1255.

24. Frere, Roxan and Tomin 1997:19-21, no. 2401.8)

25. Parker 1971:242.

26. Starting with Antoninus Pius, the grants were limited to the soldier and one wife. Frere, Roxan and Tomlin 1997: 23-27, nos. 2401.9, 2401.10, 2301.12 and 2401.13. Journal of Roman Studies 28, 1938: 177-178. See also Collingwood and Wright 1965:361, no. 1083; Salway 1991:207-208.

27. The basis of the place name may derive from the Celtic word *nemeton*, meaning a sacred place.

28. National Trust: The Roman Fort at Ribchester. London, n.d.
29. ibid
30. ibid
31. Goodburn and Waugh 1983.
32. E.g., Marcus Aurelius Victor, Collingwood and Wright 1965:477-478.

5 *Praepositus*

1. Malcor, 2014.
2. The soldiers who played them were called *buccinators*.
3. The Coliseum was first, and the Capuan arena, where Spartacus fought, was second.
4. Malcor, Trinchese and Faggiani 2019.
5. Another provenance for these inscriptions is Pannonia, but Salona makes more sense because of its proximity to Artorius' family tomb.

6 *The Battle for Britannia*

1. Parker 1971:189.
2. Collingwood and Wright 1965:472, no. 1463; Frere 1978:187; Shotter 1996:98.
3. Dio 72.16 and 73.2 73; Cary 1932:73.
4. Leach, John. (1962) "The Smith God in Roman Britain". *Archaeologia Aeliana* 40. Pp 40-42
5. Nickel 'Last Days of Roman in Britain and the Origin of the Arthurian Legends'
6. Shotter 1996:94.
7. Littleton and Malcor 1994:26
8. Collingwood and Wright 1965:48, no. 152.
9. *L'Année Epigraphique* 1927:no. 6; Collingwood and Wright 1965:194-197, nos. 583 and 587.
10. Malcor 1999a.
11. Ovid's *Poetry of Exile*, trans. by David R Slavitt, Baltimore & London, Johns Hopkins, 1990.
12. E.g., Collingwood and Wright 1965:200, no. 595 and Routledge 1854:238.
13. Higham, N. King Arthur: the Making of the Legend, Yale U. P. 2018 p68 et seq
14. Nicolini, G. 'New Archaeological Findings about Sarmatians in Britannia in English museums, especially, beads, necklaces and

bracelets of Sarmatian Origin." September 2020 (sourced on Academia.edu

15. John Colarusso, personal communication.
16. Sulimirski 1970: plate 46.
17. Routledge 1854:238; this item may be identical with the stele found at Chester.
18. Nickel in Lacy et al. 1996:13; Dixon and Southern 1992:60-61, fig. 29, plate 10.
19. Dixon and Southern 1992:60-61.
20. Littleton and Malcor 2000:101.
21. Malcor 2000:1.
22. The XX Valeria Victrix may have been helping them with the region south of the Antonine Wall.
23. Salway 1993:157.
24. Dio 72.16 and 73.2 73
25. Routledge 1844:234, 238.
26. Also spelled Aballava and Avallava. For more details about the fort, see Frere et al. 1987:13. For the Roman roads in Britannia, see Margary 1957.
27. Collingwood and Wright 1965:576.
28. Collingwood and Wright 1965:606, no. 1978. For more details about the fort, see Collingwood 1978:228-229.
29. Collingwood and Wright 1965:314-315, no. 946; Rostovtzeff 1923:96.
30. Margary 1957: map.
31. The principle manuscript itself dates to the twelfth century and is found in British Library (B.L.) MS Harley 3859, where the text appears along with a copy of the *Annales Cambriae* (c. AD 960-80). Although the attribution to Nennius is now thought to be in question, we have chosen to use his name throughout the rest of this book for simplicity's sake.
32. Jackson 1945:44.
33. Malone 1925:373.
34. Nennius 56; Morris 1980:55.
35. Field 1999.
36. Jackson 1945:55-56.
37. Jackson 1945:44-57 and 1949-1950: 48-49.
38. Jackson 1945:46; Giles 1986:30.

39. Ekwall 1928:129-33.
40. Jackson 1945:47.
41. Jackson 1945:48; cf. Giles 1986:30.
42. Jackson 1945:48; Giles 1986:30.
43. Jackson 1945:49; Giles 1986:30. Jackson (1945:49) holds that the etymological connection to Binchester/Vinovia to be impossible. Anscombe (1904:110), Farrell (1929:142), Lot (1934:69, 195), Johnstone (1934:381), and Crawford (1935:287) all agree with the identification as Binchester, and Jackson (1945:49) admits that some manuscripts do attest the form Vinovia, which could possibly render Guinnion in Old Welsh.
44. Jackson 1945:50; Field 1999. Nennius glosses the entry for the "City of the legions" as 'Caer Lion' (Caerleon), which Giles (1986:30) in turn glosses as Exeter. York remains the most likely identification.
45. Jackson 1945:52. Giles (1986:31) suggests either the Brue in Somersetshire or the Ribble in Lancaster. The Ribble is most probably the correct identification.
46. Jackson 1949-1950:49. Jackson takes Mount Agned for an indecipherable corruption, preferring the reading 'Breguoin.' Geoffrey of Monmouth (2.7) equates Mount Agned with Maidens' Castle. There is a Maiden Castle near the border between Cumbria and Durham along a road that may have seen some fighting during the Caledonian invasion.
47. Morris 1980:5; cf. Field 1999.
48. Jackson 1948-49:48-49.
49. E.g., Collingwood and Wright 1965:196-197, no. 587.
50. Salway 1993:157.
51. Frere et al. 1987.
52. Collingwood and Wright 1965:650, no. 2117.
53. Frere et al. 1987.
54. Collingwood and Wright 1965:420-424, nos. 1272, 1277, and 1279-1282.
55. Collingwood and Wright 1965:406-407, no. 1234.
56. 73.6; Cary 1932:89.
57. Frere et al. 1987.
58. Collingwood and Wright 1965:471-472, no. 1462, 1465.
59. Collingwood and Wright 1965:472, no. 1463, 1464.

60. In the late second century, VI legion Victrix garrisoned this legionary fort (Frere et al. 1987).

61. Standard wisdom is that the person killed was the current governor of Britannia, since Rome suddenly sent a replacement for him rather than for the *legatus* of the legion VI Victrix, but we think Dio got the identification correct.

62. Salway 1993:157.

63. Chap. 30; Morris 1980:24.

64. 73.2; Cary 1932:87.

65. Chap. 23; Morris 1980:24.

66. Salway 1993:156-157.

67. Salway 1981:211 and 1993:157.

68. Salway 1981:210.

69. Sulimirski 1970:176.

70. Collingwood and Wright 1965:259, no. 767.

71. Giles (1986:31) and others have suggested Edinburgh as the site.

72. For the inscription detailing the restoration, see Collingwood and Wright 1965:214, no. 637.

73. Jackson 1949-1950

74. Wacher 1978:127; see also Richmond 1945.

75. Salway 1993:155.

76. Collingwood and Wright 1965:652, nos. 2121-2122.

77. Jackson 1945:51.

78. Jackson 1945:52

79. Shotter 1997:39.

80. Jackson 1945:47-48, 57.

81. Thorpe 1966:213.

82. Field 1999.

83. Field 1999.

84. Thorpe 1966:212-213.

85. Collingwood and Wright 1992, 2 [Fascicule 4]:207, no. 2479. Frere, S.S. and Tomlin, R.S.O. (eds) The Roman Inscriptions of Britain Volume II Instrumentum Domesticum Fascicule 3 No. 2479.

86. See Jarrett 1994:43.

87. Ashe in Lacy et al. 1996:203.

88. E.g., Crawford 1935:287.

89. Ferris and Jones 1980:233-54.

90. Crawford 1935:285.
91. Jackson 1945:48.
92. Collingwood and Wright 1965:475, 481, nos. 1473 and 1501 (Cilurnum-Chesters), 1589 Housteads; honors a consul of AD 258), 2115 (Birrens; probably second-century).
93. Collingwood and Wright 1965:254, no. 754.
94. Collingwood and Wright 1965:108-109, no. 317.
95. Barber and Barber
96. Reno
97. Dumville in Lapidge and Dumville 1984:63-64.
98. Salway 1993:157.
99. Malcor 1999.
100. Dio 73.2a-10, Cary 1932:89-91; Herodian I.9.5-8, Whittaker 1969, 1:56-57; Frere 1967:150. Herodian mentions this event and the Armorican uprising under a figure named Maternus (Herodian I.9-I.10, Whittaker 1969, 1:53-67. In spite of protestations that the two events should not be linked, there is no evidence that they shouldn't be (Todd 1981:162-163).
101. Herodian I.9.5-8, Whittaker 19969, 1:56-57.

7 *Dux Artorius*

1. Cassius Dio 73.9.2a. The soldiers in Britain chose Priscus, a lieutenant, emperor; but he declined, saying: 'I am no more an emperor than you are soldiers.' Cary 1932:89.
2. Le Bohec 1989.
3. Giles 1986:30.
4. Cf. CIL 06, 41127 '[praep]osito vexill(ationum) [leg(ionum) III(?)] / [Brita]nnicar(um?)'
5. Cf. CIL 3.3228: 'G]ermaniciana[r(um)] / [e]t Brit{t}an(n)icin(arum).' Like Germanicianarum, we can see *Britanicimiarum* as a variant of *Britannicianarum*, whose nominative *Britannicianus* means 'serving in Britannia'.
6. The technical expansion is ' legions serving in the lands of the Britons.'
7. Mommsen's expansion of '*cohortium alarum*' will not fit the space, so it cannot be correct.
8. Migliorati 2011:247.

9. 73:8; Cary 1927:85.

10. Stevenson 1838.

11. Stevenson 1838: xxviii.

12. Gildas, chap. 6; Stevenson 1838:xxviii.

13. Nennius 56; Chambers:1927.

14. Stevenson 1838:14.

15. Higham 1994:152.

16. Stevenson1838:14.

17. Littleton and Malcor 1994:63, 72-73.

18. Collingwood and Wright, RIB 12, p. 6.

19. Collingwood and Wright, RIB 8, p. 4.

20. Collingwood and Wright, RIB 662-663, pp. 222-223.

21. Collingwood and Myers, Roman Britain and the English Settlements. OUP, 1949.

22. Malone, *Modern Philology* vol. 22, May 1925: 367-374

23. Migliorati 2011:428.

24. Di Martino 2003.

25. Di Martino 2003.

8 *Liburnia*

1. Grant 1985:104.

2. Cf. Tacitus, Histories, 3.68; Barrett 1957:247; Rives 1996: n. 9; Pflaum 1960, 1:537.

3. Matthews and Cambi, 2006 p96

4. Littleton and Malcor 2000 pp 256-263.

5. Littleton and Malcor 1996: 233-280.

6. 13 Cambi & Matthews 2014, pp8-9

7. Mommsen 1873: no. 5336. There are two inscriptions, one spells the name Sellius, the other Gellius.

8. The name may also indicate a family connection with the city of Florence.

9. Felicissimus' inscription was found in a building in Siljek, but his dates are also in question; Mommsen 1873:297, no. 1846.

10. Scarre 1995:122. See also Dio 49.36.4, Cary 1917:415)

11. Grant 1985:104.

12. Kirigin and Marin 1989:143.

13. See Chapter 9.

14. Arthur holds a standard in his right hand and a sword in his left. See Loomis and Loomis, Plate 15, 1938.

9 *Civil War*

1. Grant 1985:112.
2. Grant 1985:111.
3. *Morien: A Metrical Romance Rendered into English prose from the Medieval Dutch* by Jessie L. Weston. David Nutt, 1901.
4. Dio 76; Cary 1932:203-215; Grant 1985:109. Coincidentally, it was near Châlons that a contingent of the Sarmatians cousins, the Alans, helped defeat the Huns some two-and-a-half centuries later (Littleton and Malcor 1994:37).
5. Frere 1978:187.
6. Grant 1971:57.
7. Cary 1932:207.
8. Salway 1991:220.
9. Grant 1985:338; Parker 1971:163.
10. Frere 1978:185-186.
11. Grant 1985:109; Parker 1971:168.
12. Grant 1985:336.
13. (Grant 1985:339
14. Frere 1978:221.
15. Dio 76.6-7, Cary 1932:209-211.
16. Ashe, 1960, passim.
17. Ashe, *The Discovery of King Arthur*, passim.
18. Ibid.
19. Historia, Trans. Thorpe. P224.
20. Vita Merlini, Trans. Clarke, p101
21. Vita Merlini, Clarke, p102
22. Vita Merlini, Clarke, p103
23. Matasovic, Ranko, *Etymological Dictionary of Proto-Celtic*, Brill, 2009, p. 23; Delamarre, Xavier , *Dictionnaire de la langue gauloise. Une approche linguistique du vieux-celtique continental*, Paris, éditions Errance, 2003) p. 29. cf. Old Irish *aball*, Welsh *afall*, Old Breton *aball(en)*, apple tree.
24. Euric may actually have been the Alan Goeric, king of the Alans who were allied with the Visigoths and who were close relatives to the Sarmatians.
25. Including: *Sarmaha, Castrum Sarmatii, Sarmacia, Sarmasia, Sarmatiense Castrum, Sarmatiaca, Saimasia, Samaise, Salmacia, Saulmaise, Sarmazes, Sermaise Sermaisos, Sermaize, Sermasse, Sermoise, Sharmasse,* etc

26. Matthews, *The Lost Book of the Grail*, passim.

27. Mommsen 1973: no. 14195.27.

10 King

1. 'Y Goddoddin,' Stanza 99, Jarman, p 64
2. https://d.lib.rochester.edu/camelot/text/nennius-history-of-the-britons (Accessed 1.4.2019)
3. Bromwich et al 1991: 33-71
4. Stevenson, 1838: xiii. (Chap. 20)
5. Stevenson 1838: xiv-xv.
6. Eisner, 1969 pp 75-85
7. Matthews: *Taliesin*, 2000, passim
8. Koch, *The Celtic Heroic Age: Literary Sources for Ancient Celtic Europe and Early Ireland and Wales,* 2003 et al; Jackson, *Language and History in Early Britain*, Edinburgh Univ. Press, 1953.
9. Neitz, 1949 p595
10. Field, "Gildas and the City of the legions". *The Heroic Age*, issue 1, Spring/Summer, 1999) www.heroicage.org/issues/1/hagcl.htm
11. Lewis and Williams, *The Book of Taliesin*, Penguin books, 2019 p153
12. Colarusso, 2016, p xiii
13. Littleton & Thomas, 1978
14. Littleton, 1979 pp 326-333
15. Colarusso, 2016, pp 418-421
16. Sulimirski, 1970, p120, 128, 130, 133, 171
17. Berard, Arthurianism pp1-11 et seq.
18. Ward 1981, 1:1, 2:374.
19. Ward 1981, 1:1.
20. Dundes 1965:233.
21. Ward 1981, 2:373.
22. Ward 1981, 2:372.
23. Matthews, 2017, ibid.
24. Holt 1989.
25. Holt 1989:190, 196.
26. Holt 1989:187-189.
27. Holt 1989:192.
28. Gantz, 1981 pp 219-55
29. Matthews, 2019. Translated by Gareth Knight and Caitlín Matthews.

30. All these accounts are taken from the masterly collections edited by John Colarusso. (See references cited.)

31. Loomis, 1939, pp 242-3

32. Littleton and Malcor, 2000, passim.

33. Colarusso: "The Woman of the Myths: the Satana Cycle," http:// circassianworld.com (accessed 3.4.2019)

34. Colarusso,1989 'Myths from the Forests of Circassia', http:// circassianworld.com/colarusso-3.html (Accessed 3.4.2019)

35. Hugh Williams, trans., *Two Lives of Gildas by a monk of Ruys and Caradoc of Llancarfan*, first published in Cymmrodorion Record Series, 1899. Facsimile reprint by Llanerch Publishers, Felinfach, 1990

36. Lacy, Norris J. *The New Arthurian Encyclopaedia.* New York: Garland, 1991; Loomis, Roger Sherman, *Celtic Myth and Arthurian Romance.* Columbia University Press.1971

37. Lawman [Layamon] *Brut,* trans Rosamund Allen l. 14278.

38. Paton, Lucy L. *Studies in the Fairy Mythology of Arthurian Romance* New York Burt Franklin, 1970

39. Lacy, N, Ed. *The Lancelot-Grail: The Old French Arthurian Vulgate and Post-Vulgate in Translation.* D. S. Brewer, 2010

40. Colarusso, p181.

41. These are both from the collection of medieval Welsh tales grouped under the title of the *Mabinogion.*

42. In the Perilous Cemetery there are twelve graves.

43. *Le Morte d'Arthur*, Book III, Chapter XV.

44. Colarusso and Salbiev p11.

BIBLIOGRAPHY

Adkins, Lesley, and Roy A. Adkins. 1994. *Handbook to Life in Ancient Rome*. Oxford and New York: Oxford University Press.

'Adventures of Cormac in the Land of Promise'. 1994. In: *The Encyclopaedia of Celtic Wisdom* Ed. John and Caitlín Matthews. Element Books.

Aldington, Richard, and Delano Ames, trans. 1987. *New Larousse Encyclopaedia of Mythology*. Edited by Félix Guirand. New York, New York: Putnam.

Allen, Rosamund, trans. 1992. Layamon, *Brut Lawman (Everyman's Library* Middlesex: The Echo Library.

Annales Cambriae. 2007. tr. Paul Martin Remfry. *Annales Cambriae: A Translation of Harleian 3859; PRO E.164/1; Cottonian Domitian, A 1; Exeter Cathedral Library MS. 3514 and MS Exchequer DB Neath*. SCS Publishing.

Anscombe, A. 1904. 'Local Names in the 'Arthuriana' in the Historia Brittonum.' *Zeitschrif für Celtishe Philologie* 5:103-23.

Ashe, Geoffrey 'A Certain Very Ancient Book' *Speculum* 56 1981 pp301-23

Ashe, Geoffrey. 1960. *From Caesar to Arthur*. Cork, Ireland: Collins.

___. 1985. *The Discovery of King Arthur*. New York: Doubleday.

Badian, E. 1967. *Roman Imperialism in the Late Republic*. Ithaca, New York: Cornell University Press.

Ball, Warwick. 2015. *The Gates of Asia: The Eurasian Steppe and the Limits of Europe*, London, East and West Publishing

Barrett, Charles Kingsley. 1957. *A Commentary on the Epistle to the Romans*. Peabody, Massachusetts: Hendrickson Publishers.

Barber, Elizabeth Wayland and Paul Barber. 2004. *When They Severed Earth From Sky: How the Human Mind Shapes Myth*. Princeton and Oxford: Princeton University Press.

Berard, Christopher Michael. 2019. *Arthurianism in Early Plantagenet England: From Henry II to Edward I*, Woodbridge, Boydell and Brewer.

Bishop, M. C. 2014. *Vt Milites Dicvntvr: A Dictionary of Roman Military Terms and Terminology* Wiltshire, Armatura Press.

Brengle, Richard L, ed. 1964. *Arthur, King of Britain*. Engle Cliffs, New Jersey: Prentice-Hall.

Böckh, August, and Röhl Hermann, eds., 1843. *Corpus Inscriptionem Graecarum*. Berlin: Officiana Academica.

Brelich. Angelo, 1949. *Die Geheimer Schutzgottheit von Rom*. (Albae Vigiliae N.F. 6). Zűrich: Rhein-Verlag.

Briscoe, John [ed] 1998. *Valerius Maximus: Bibliotheca Scriptorum Graecorum Et Romanorum Teubneriana*) De Gruyter.

Bromwich, Rachel, A.O.H. Jarman, and Brinley F. Roberts, eds. 1991. *The Arthur of the Welsh*. Cardiff: University of Wales.

Bruce, James Douglas. 1923. *The Evolution of Arthurian Romance from the Beginnings to the Year 1300*. Göttingen: Vandenhoeck and Ruprecht; Baltimore: Johns Hopkins Press. 2 vols.

Bryant, Nigel, trans. 1978. *Perlesvaus: The High Book of the Grail—A Translation of the Thirteenth Century Romance of* Perlesvaus. Ipswich: Brewer; Totowa: Rowman & Littlefield.

Bunson, Margaret R. 2012. *Encyclopaedia of Ancient Egypt*. Facts on File (Third Edition)

Burnham, Barry C., and John Wacher. 1990. *The Small Towns of Roman Britain*. Berkeley and Los Angeles: University of California Press.

Cambi, Nenad. and John Matthews, eds. 2014. *Lucius Artorius Castus and the King Arthur Legend*. Književni Krug Split

Carcopino. Jérôme. 1968. *Daily Life in Ancient Rome*. New Haven and London: Yale University Press.

Cary, Earnest, trans. 1917. Cassius Dio Coccianus, *Dio's Roman History*, Vol. 5. London: Heinemann; New York: Putnam.

___. 1925. Cassius Dio Coccianus, *Dio's Roman History*, Vol. 8. London: Heinemann; New York: Putnam.

___. 1932. Cassius Dio Coccianus, *Dio's Roman History*, Vol. 9. London: Heinemann; New York: Putnam.

Chambers, E. K., 1927. *Arthur of Britain*. London: Sidgwick and Jackson.

Cirlot, J.E. 1983. *A Dictionary of Symbols*. Translated by Jack Sage. second ed. New York: Philosophical Library.

Colarusso, John. 1989. 'Myths from the Forests of Circassia.' https://circassianworld.com/circassians/mythology/1191-forest-of-circassia (Accessed 7.7.2019.)

Colarusso, John. 1989. 'The Woman of the Myths: The Satana Cycle,' Annual Meeting of the Society for the Study of Caucasia. 3:3-11.

Colarusso, John. 2002. *Nart Sagas: Ancient Myths and Legends of the Circassians and Abkhazians*. Princeton and Oxford, Princeton University Press.

Colarusso, John, and Tamirlan Salbiev. 2016. *Tales of the Narts: Ancient Myths and Legends of the Ossetians*. Walter May, trans. Princeton and Oxford: Princeton University Press.

Collingwood, R.G. 2011. *A Guide to the Roman Wall*. Read Books Ltd.

Collingwood, R.G., and R.P. Wright. 1965. *The Roman Inscriptions of Britain*. Oxford: Clarendon. 2 vols.

Connolly, Peter. 1991. *The Roman Fort*. Oxford: Oxford University Press.

Cowan, Janet, ed. 1969. Sir Thomas Malory, *Le Morte d'Arthur*. Harmondsworth and Hew York: Penguin. 2 vols.

Crawford, O.G.S., 1935. 'Arthur and His Battles.' *Antiquity* 9:277-291.

D'Arms, John H., 1970. *Romans on the Bay of Naples and Other Essays on Roman Campania*. Bari: Edipuglia.

Dando-Collins, Stephen. 2010. *legions of Rome*. London, Quercus

Davies, Norman. 2011. *Vanished Kingdoms: The History of Half-Forgotten Europe*. London, Allan Lane.

Delamarre, Xavier. 2003. *Dictionary de la langue anolia. Une approache lainguistique du vieux-celtique continental*. Pars éditions. Paris: Errance.

De Sélincourt, trans. 1972. Herodotus, *The Histories*. New York and London: Penguin.

Dessau, Hermann. 1892-1916. *Inscriptiones latinae selectae*. 3 vols. Berlin: Weidmannos.

Di Martino, Vittorio. 2003. *Roman Ireland*. Cork, Ireland: Collins.

Dixon, Karen R. and Pat Southern. 1992. *The Roman Cavalry*. London and New York: Routledge.

Dumézil, Georges. 1970. *Archaic Roman Religion, With an Appendix on the Religion of the Etruscans.* University of Chicago Press

Dundes, Alan, ed. 1965. *The Study of Folklore.* Englewood Cliffs, New Jersey: Prentice-Hall, Inc.

Edwards, B. J. N. 2000. *The Romans at Ribchester: Discovery and Excavation.* Centre for North-West Regional Studies. University of Lancaster.

Eisner, Sigmund. 1969. *The Tristan Legend: A Study in Sources,* Evanston: Northwestern University Press.

Ekwall, Eilert. 1928. *English River-names.* Oxford: Clarendon.

Faggiani, Alessandro. 2021. Gens Artoria La Gens vicina agli Imperatori Romani. https://www.academia.edu/37679155/Gens_Artoria_La_Gens_vicina_agli_Imperatori_Romani Accessed March 30, 2021.

Farral, Edmond., ed. 1929. Geoffrey of Monmouth, *Historia Regum Britanniae.* In *La légende arthurienne,* Vol. 3. Paris: Librairie ancienne Honoré Champion.

Ferguson, George. 1961. *Signs and Symbols in Christian Art.* London: Oxford University Press.

Ferris, I.M., and R.F.J. Jones (with contributions by S.J. Dockerill). 1980. 'Excavation at Binchester 1976-9.' In *Roman Frontier Studies 1979: Papers presented to the 12th International Congress of Roman Frontier Studies.* Vol. 1. Edited by W.G. Hanson and L.J.K. Keppie. Oxford: B.A.R.

Ferguson, J. 1970. Livy, *Res Gestae Divi Augusti.* Harvard: University Press.

Field, Peter. 1999. 'Gildas and the City of the legions.' In: *The Heroic Age,* Issue 1. (http://www.heroicage.org/issues/1/hagcl.htm. Accessed 7.7.2019).

Fluriot, Léon, 1980. *Les Origines de la Bretagne,* Paris: Payot

Floyde, Marilyn. 2009. *King Arthur's French Odyssey: Avallon in Burgundy.* New York, NY: Vanguard.

Ford, Patrick K. 1977. *The Mabinogi and Other Medieval Welsh Tales.* Los Angeles and Berkeley: University of California Press.

Frere, Sheppard S. 1967. *Britannia: A History of Roman Britain.* Cambridge, Massachusetts: Harvard University Press.

Frere, Sheppard S., et al. 1987. *Tabula Imperii Romani—Britannia Septentrionalis.* London: Oxford University Press.

Frere, Sheppard S., Margaret Roxan and R.S.O. Tomin 1997. 'Military Diplomata'. In: *The Roman Inscriptions of Britain.* Vol. 2. Gloucester: A. Sutton.

Gantz, Jeffrey. 1981. Tr. *Early Irish Myths and Sagas*. New York, Penguin Books, 1981.

Geoffrey of Monmouth, *Vita Merlini*, 1925 Tr. Parry J. J. University of Illinois Studies in Language and Literature, Urbana.

Giles, J.A., trans. 1986. Nennius, *The History of the Britons*. Willits, California: British American Books.

Giraldus Cambrensis (Gerald of Wales) 2018. Ed. Robert Bartlett, *De Principis Instructione*. (Oxford Medieval Texts). Oxford University Press.

Giraldus Cambrensis (Gerald of Wales) 1978. Tr. Thorpe, L., Ed. Betty Radice. *The Journey Through Wales and the Description of Wales*. Harmondsworth, MIDX., Penguin Books.

Glavičič, Miroslav. 2012. 'Artorii u Rimskoj Provinciji Dalmachiji.' In *Lucius Artorius Castus and the King Arthur Legend; Proceedings of the International Scholarly Conference from 30th March to second of April 2012*, pp. 59-70. Podstrana: Ogranak Matice Hrvatske.

Goldsworthy, Adrian Keith. 1996. *The Roman Army at War, 100 BC–AD 200*. Oxford and New York: Clarendon.

Goodburn, Roger, and Hellen Waugh. 1983. *Epigraphic Indexes*. Vol. 1: Inscriptions on Stone. Gloucester: Alan Sutton. Index to R.G. Collingwood and R.P. Wright's *The Roman Inscriptions of Britain* (See above for full citation).

Grant, Michael, trans., 1971. Tacitus, *The Annals of Imperial Rome*. New York and London: Penguin.

___. 1985. *The Roman Emperors: A Biographical Guide to the Rulers of Imperial Rome, 31 BC – AD 476*. New York: Charles Scribner's Sons.

Gregory of Tours, 1974 Tr. Lewis Thorpe. *History of the Franks*. Penguin Classics.

Green, Caitlin R. 2009. *Arthuriana: Early Arthurian Tradition and the Origins of the Legend*. Lindes Press.

Green, Thomas. 2009. 'The Historicity and Historicization of Arthur.' In *Arthuriana: Early Arthurian Tradition and the Origins of the Legend*, pp. 3-46. Lindes Press.

Hamilton, Walter, trans. 1986. Ammianus Marcellinus, *The Later Roman Empire (AD 354-378)* New York and London: Penguin.

Harper, G. M. 1928. 'Village Administration in the Roman Province of Syria.' *Yale Classical Studies* 1: 117-121.

Higham, N. J. 1994. *The English Conquest: Gildas and Britain in the Fifth Century.* Manchester and New York: Manchester University Press.

Holt, J. C. 1989. *Robin Hood.* Revised and enlarged edition. New York: Thames and Hudson.

Hyland, Ann. 1990. *Equus: The Horse in the Roman World.* New Haven and London: Yale University Press.

Jackson, Kenneth. 1945-1946. 'Once Again Arthur's Battles.' *Modern Philology* 43: 44-57.

___. 1949-1950. 'Arthur's Battle of Breguion.' *Antiquity* 23: 23-24: 48-49.

___. 1953. *Language and History in Early Britain.* Edinburgh: Edinburgh University Press.

Jarman, A. O. H. (ed.) *Y Gododdin. Britain's Oldest Heroic Poem.* The Welsh Classics vol. 3. Gomer, 1988.

Jarrett, Michael G. 1994. 'Non- legionary Troops in Roman Britain: Part One, the Units.' *Britannia* 25: 35-72.

Johnstone, P.K. 1934. 'The Victories of Arthur.' *Notes and Queries* 166: 381-82..

Jones, David. 2006. The Bankers of Puteoli: Finance, trade and Industry in the Roman World. Gloucestershire: Tempus.

Kline, A.S., trans. 2005. Horace, *The Satires.* https://www.poetryintranslation.com/PITBR/Latin/HoraceSatiresBkISatII.php (Accessed 7/13/2019.)

-----. 2011. Juvenal, *Satires.* https://www.poetryintranslation.com/PITBR/Latin/JuvenalSatires3.php (Accessed 7/13/2019)

Knight, David J. 2008. *King Lucius of Britain.* Stroud, Tempus.

Koch, John T. 2003. *The Celtic Heroic Age: Literary Sources for Ancient Celtic Europe and Early Ireland and Wales* Aberystwyth, Wales: Celtic Studies Publications.

Kirigin, Branko, and Emilio Marin. 1989. *The Archaeological Guide to Central Dalmatia.* Split: Logos.

Lacey, Norris J., et al., ed. 1991. *The New Arthurian Encyclopaedia.* New York and London: Garland.

___, ed. 2010. *Quest del Saint Graal.* 2010. Ed. Norris J. Lacey, et. al. *The Old French Arthurian Vulgate and Post-Vulgate in Translation.* D. S. Brewer.

___, ed., 2010 *The Old French Arthurian Vulgate and Post-Vulgate in Translation*. D. S. Brewer

'Lady of the Fountain' 2008 in *The Mabinogion*. Tr. Sionad Davies Oxford. Oxford Wold Classics.

Laing, Gordon Jennings. 1963. *Survivals of Roman Religion*. Lanham, Maryland: Cooper Square Publishers.

Leach, John. (1962) 'The Smith God in Roman Britain'. *Archaeologia Aeliana* 40. Pp 40-42, *L'Année Epigraphique*. 1927: no. 6

Le Bohec, Yann. 1989. *The Imperial Roman Army*. Routledge: London and New York.

Lewis, Gwyneth and Rowan Williams, trans. 2019. *The Book of Taliesin*. London and New York: Penguin Books.

Lindemans, M. F. 1995-2000. The Encyclopaedia Mythica, http://www.pantheon.org/mythica. (Accessed 7/13/2019)

Littleton, C. Scott. 1979. 'The Holy Grail, the Cauldron of Annwn, and the Nartyamonga: A Further Note on the Sarmatian Connection.' *Journal of American Folklore*. 92: 326-333.

___. 1981. 'Susa-nö-wo versus Yamata nö Woröti: An Indo-European Theme in Japanese Mythology.' *History of Religions* 20: 269-280.

___. 1983. "Some Possible Arthurian Themes in Japanese Mythology and Folklore.'

Littleton, C. Scott, and Anne C. Thomas. 1978. 'The Sarmatian Connection: New Light on the Origin of the Arthurian and Holy Grail Legends.' *Journal of American Folklore* 91:512-527.

Littleton, C. Scott, and Linda A. Malcor. 1994. *From Scythia to Camelot: A Radical Reassessment of the Legends of King Arthur, the Knights of the Round Table and the Holy Grail*. First Edition. New York and London: Garland.

___. 2000. *From Scythia to Camelot: A Radical Reassessment of the Legends of King Arthur, the Knights of the Round Table and the Holy Grail. First Edition*. Second Edition. New York, New York and Routledge. Milton Park, Abingdon, Oxford,

Loomis, Roger Sherman. 1927. *Celtic Myth and Arthurian Romance*. New York: Columbia University Press.

___. 1939. *Introduction to Medieval Literature, chiefly in England*. New York, Columbia University Press.

___. 1949. *Arthurian Tradition and Chretien de Troyes*, New York: Columbia University Press.

___. and Laura Hibbard Loomis. 1938. *Arthurian Legends in Medieval Art*. London: Oxford University Press; New York: Modern Language Association of America.

Loriot, Xavier. 1997.,'Un mythe historiographiue: l'espédition d'Artorius Castus contre les Armoricains.' *Bulletin de la Société nationale des antiquaries de France*, pp. 85-87.

Lot, Ferdinand. 1934. *Nennius et L'Historia Brittonum*. Paris; Librairie ancienne Honoré Champion.

Lyttelton, Margaret, and Werner Forman. 1985. *The Romans: Their Gods and Their Beliefs (Echoes of the Ancient World)*. New York, NY: HarperCollins.

Malcor, Joseph V. 2014., 'Republic to Empire: The Tomb of Marcus 'Artorius Gemnius.' In *Lucius Artorius Castus and the King Arthur Legend*. Pp. 1979-185. Proceedings of the International Scholarly Conference from 30th of the March to Second of April 2012. Edited by Nenad Cambi and John Matthews. Split: Književni Krug Split, Ogranak Matice Hrvatske Podstrana.

Malcor, Linda A. 1999a. 'Lucius Artorius Castus, Part 1: An Officer and an Equestrian.' *The Heroic Age, Issue 1*. https://www.heroicage.org/issues/1/halac.htm. Accessed 27.3.2019.

___. 1999. 'Lucius Artorius Castus, Part II: The Historical King Arthur.' *The Heroic Age, Issue 2*. https://www.heroicage.org/issues/2/ha2lac.htm. Accessed 27.3.2019.

___. 2000. 'Merlin and the Pendragon: King Arthur's *Draconarius*.' In *Arthuriana* 10/1:3-13.

___. 2004. 'The Campanians of the Round Table: The Artorii, Flora and the Holy Grail' in *King Arthur: Tra storia e leggenda: Da Cimitile a Camelot*. Edited by Mario de Matteise e Antonio Trinchese, Oberhausen: Athena.

___. 2014. 'Artorius: By Land and By Sea' In *Lucius Artorius Castus and the King Arthur Legend*. Pp. 11-27. Proceedings of the International Scholarly Conference from 30th of March to Second of April 2012. Edited by Nenad Cambi and John Matthews. Split: Književni Krug Split, Ogranak Matice Hrvatske Podstrana.

Malcor, Linda A., Antonio Trinchese, and Alessandro Faggiani. 2019. 'Missing Pieces'. *Journal of Indo-European Studies*. Vol 4. No 3. Pp 415-437.

Malcor, L., Nicolini, G., Faggiani, A., Trinchese, A., 'Arthur's Ring? Finding of the Golden Ring of the Gens Artoria in Ancient

Britannia', 2021. https://www.academia.edu/46789053/Arthurs_Ring_ Finding_of_the_Golden_Ring_of_the_Gens_Artoria_in_ancient_Brita nnia?fbclid=IwARoudfTEhFQy9bJ4slPjBx2ql9UXBlDjrSZcsig X4pQ4ojhyHFUvBnMzvvk (Accessed 4/7/22).

Malone, Kemp. 1924-1925. 'The Historicity of Arthur.' *Journal of English and Germanic Philology* 23:463:491.

___. 1925. 'Artorius.' *Modern Philology* 22:367-377.

Margary, Ivan D. 1957. *Roman Roads in Britain.* Vol. 2: *North of the Foss Way, Bristol Channel (including Wales and Scotland).* London: Phoenix House.

Matasovic, Rank. 2009. *Etymological Dictionary of Proto-Celtic.* Brill.

Matthews, Caitlin, trans. 2008. 'Pa Gur?' In *King Arthur's Raid on the Otherworld: The Oldest Grail Quest.* Glastonbury: Gothic Image Books Ltd.

Matthews, Caitlín, and John. 2019. *The Lost Book of the Grail.* Inner Traditions.

Matthews, John. 2000. *Taliesin: The Last Celtic Shaman.* Inner Traditions.

Matthews, John & Caitlin. 2017. *The Complete King Arthur.* Inner Traditions.

Migliorati, Guido. 2011. *Inscrizioni per la Ricostruzione Storica Dell'Impero Romano da Marco Aurelio a Commodo.* Milano: EDUCatt.

Migliorati, Guido. 2021. 'Artorius Castus in the Period of Commodus' Accessed via Academia.edu.

Moldenke, Harold N. 1953. 'Flowers of the Madonna.' http://www. ewtn.com/library/MARY/MEDFLOWR.HTM (Accessed 7/13/2019.)

Moles, J. L. 2017. 'Plutarch's Vita Brut Ch. 41. A Commentary on Plutarch's Brutus' *Histos,* Newcastle.

Mommsen, Teodor, ed. 1873. *Corpus Inscriptionum Latinarum: Inscriptiones Asia Provinciarum Europae Graecarum Illyrici Latinae.* Vol. 3/1. Berlin Reimer.

Morris, John, ed. and trans. 1980. Nennius, *British History and the Welsh Annals.* In *History from the Sources,* Vol. 8. Chichester: Phillimore.

Murphy, Trevor. 2004. Pliny, *Pliny the Elder's Natural History: The Empire in the Encyclopaedia.* Oxford: University Press

Nagel, D. Brendan. 1979. *The Ancient World: A Social and Cultural History.* New Jersey: Prentice-Hall.

National Trust: *The Roman Fort at Ribchester.* Country Life Ltd, n.d.

Nickel, Helmut. 1975. 'Wer waren König Artus' Ritter? Über die geschichtliche Grundlage der Artussagen,' *Zeitschrift der historisch Waffen- und Kostümkunde.* 1:1-18.

___. 2014. 'The Last Days of Roman Britain and the Origin of the Arthurian Legends.' In *Lucius Artorius Castus and the King Arthur Legend.* Pp. 259-270. Proceedings of the International Scholarly Conference from 30th of March to Second of April 2012. Edited by Nenad Cambi and John Matthews. Split: Književni Krug Split, Ogranak Matice Hrvatske Podstrana.

Ogilvie, R.M., 1969. *The Romans and Their Gods in the Age of Augustus.* New York: Norton.

Oman, Charles. 1910. *England Before the Norman Conquest, Being a History of the Celtic, Roman and Anglo-Saxon Periods down to the Year AD 1066.* London, Methuen.

Ovid, *Fasti.* 2000. Boyle, A and R. Woodard. Ed and trans. Penguin Books.

Paton, Lucy Allen. 1903. *Studies in the Fairy Mythology in Arthurian Romance.* Boston: Ginn.

Parker, H.M.D. 1971. *The Roman legions.* Cambridge: H. Heffer & Sons, Ltd; New York: Barnes & Noble, Inc.

Perrin, Bernadotte, trans. 1998. Plutarch, *Lives.* Cambridge, Massachusetts and London, England: Harvard University Press.

Pflaum, H.-G. 1960. *Les carrières procuratoriennes équestres sous le haut-empire romain* 3 vols. Paris: Librairie Orientaliste Paul Geuthner.

Pollard, Nigel, and Joanne Berry. 2012. *The Complete Roman legions.* London, Thames & Hudson.

Puhvel, Jaan. 1987. Comparative Mythology. London & Baltimore. The John Hopkins University Press

Reno, Frank. D. 1996. *The Historic King Arthur: Authenticating the Celtic Hero of Post-Roman Britain.* Jefferson, North Carolina and London: MacFarland and Company.

Rhŷs, John. 1891. *Studies in the Arthurian Legend.* Oxford: Oxford University Press.

Richmond, I.A. 1945. 'The Sarmatae, Bremetennacum Veteranorum, and the Region Bremetennacensis.' *Journal of Roman Studies.* 35:15-29.

Rives, James. 1996. 'The Piety of a Persecutor'. *Journal of Early Christian Studies* 4/1: 1-25.

Robert de Boron, 2001 tr. Bryant, N. *Merlin and the Grail: Joseph of Arimathea, Merlin, Perceval: the trilogy of Arthurian Romances attributed to Robert de Borron*. Woodbridge: Boydell and Brewer.

Rose, H.J. 1959. *A Handbook of Greek Mythology*. New York: Dutton.

Rostovtzef, M. 1923. *Iranians and Greeks in South Russia*. Oxford: Oxford University Press.

Routledge, George. 1854. *The Pictorial History of the County of Lancaster, with One Hundred and Seventy Illustrations and a Map*. London: Manning and Mason.

Salway, Peter. 1965. *The Frontier People of Roman Britain*. Cambridge; University Press.

___. 1993.*The Oxford Illustrated History of Roman Britain*. Oxford and New York: Oxford University Press.

Scarre, Christopher. 1995. *Chronicle of the Roman Emperors: The Reign-By-Reign Record of the Rulers of Imperial Rome*. London and New York: Thames and Hudson.

Shannon, William D. 2007. *Murus ille famosus (that famous wall)*. Cumberland and Westmorland Antiquities and Archaeological Society, Tract Series Vol. XXII

Sherley-Price, Leo, trans. 1968. Bede, *A History of the English Church and People*. New York: Dorset.

Shotter, David. 1996. *The Roman Frontier in Britain*. Preston: Carnegie.

___. 1997. *Romans and Britons in North-West England*. Second edition. Lancaster Centre for North-West Regional Studies, University of Lancaster.

Sire, Paul. 2014. *King Arthur's European Realm* Jefferson, North Carolina, McFarland & Co. Inc.

Slavit, David. Tr. 1990. *Ovid's Petry of Exile,* Baltimore and London: Johns Hopkins.

Skene, W.F. 1868. *The Four Ancient Books of Wales*. Edinburgh.

Spaeth, Barbette Stanley. 1996. *The Roman Goddess Ceres*. Austin, Texas: University of Texas Press.

Stevenson, Joseph. 1838. Gildas, *De Excidio Britanniae*. London: Sumptibus Societatis.

Strabo. 1989. Ed. H. L. Jones. *Geography: v. 1*. Loeb Classical Library.

Sulimirski Tadeusz. 1970. *The Sarmatians*. New York: McGraw-Hill.

Thomas, J.W. Tr. Heinrich von dem Türlin *The Crown* [Diü Cröne] Lincoln & London University of Nebraska Press.

Thorpe, Lewis, ed. and trans. 1966. Geoffrey of Monmouth, *The History of the Kings of Britain*. Middlesex and New York: Penguin.

Todd, Malcolm, ed. 1989. *Research on Roman Britain, 1960-89. Britannia Monograph Series* no. 11. London: Society for the Promotion of Roman Studies.

Von Sydow, Carl. 1965. In *The Study of Folklore*. Edited by Alan Dundes. Berkeley and Los Angeles: University of California Press.

Wacher, John. 1978. *Roman Britain*. London: Dent.

Walker, Barbara G. 1983. *The Woman's Encyclopaedia of Myths and Secrets*. San Francisco: Harper and Row.

Ward, Donald J., ed. and trans. 1981. *The German Legends of the Brothers Grimm*. Philadelphia: Institute for the Study of Human Issues. 2 vols.

Whittaker, C. R., trans. 1969. *Herodian*. 2 Vols. London and Cambridge: Harvard University Press.

Wilkes, J. J. 1969. *Dalmatia*. Cambridge, Massachusetts: Harvard University Press.

Williamson, G. A., trans. 1969. Josephus, *The Jewish War*. New York: Dorset.

Winters, M. 1984. *The Romance of Hunbaut: An Arthurian Poem of the Thirteenth Century*. (David Mediaeval Texts & Studies) Brill.

Wright, Neil, ed.1984. *The Historia Regum Britanniae of Geoffrey of Monmouth*. Vol. 1: Bern. Burgerbbliothek, MS 568. Cambridge: D.S. Brewer.

Zimmer, Heinrich. 1890. 'Review of Gaston Paris' *Histoire littéraire de la France,* Tome XXX', Göttingische gelehret Anzeigen.

INDEX

Also available from Amberley Publishing

'A remarkable book ... an inspiration from the heart of the Shire'
ROBERT PLANT

THE MAGICAL HISTORY OF BRITAIN

MARTIN WALL

Also available from Amberley Publishing

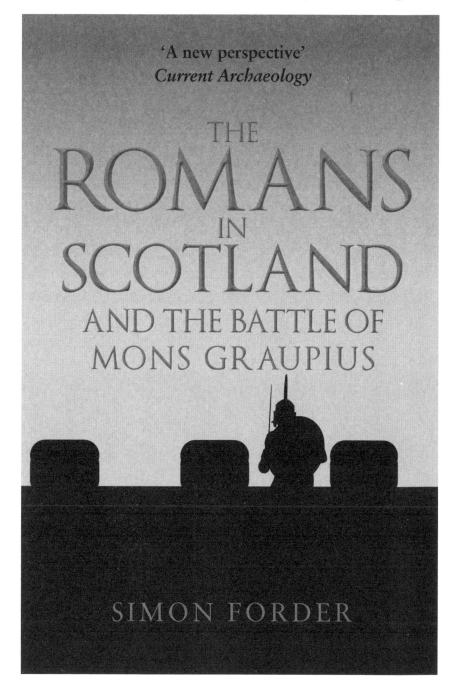

'A new perspective'
Current Archaeology

THE
ROMANS
IN
SCOTLAND
AND THE BATTLE OF
MONS GRAUPIUS

SIMON FORDER

Available from all good bookshops or to order direct
Please call **01453–847–800**
www.amberley-books.com